CRITICAL ACCLAIM FOR *HOW TO USE YOUR COMPUTER*

The tone of the book is gentle but not patronizing, and the coverage is comprehensive.

...this book is a great resource for rounding out your computer knowledge.

—**Mindy Basser,** *COMPUTER SHOPPER*

...the book to read before you go keyboard crazy.

—**Pam Kane,** *HOMEPC*

How to Use Your Computer

Bestseller Edition

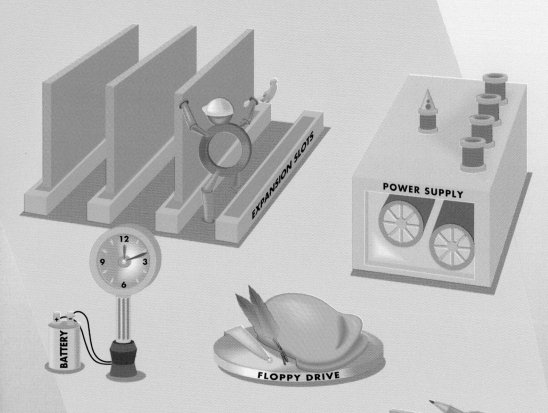

EXPANSION SLOTS

POWER SUPPLY

12
9   3
6

BATTERY

FLOPPY DRIVE

HARD DRIVE

RAM

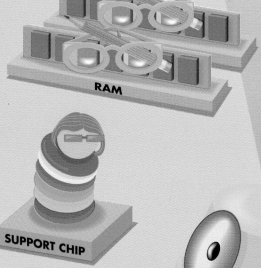

SUPPORT CHIP

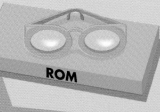

ROM

CPU

How to Use Your Computer
Bestseller Edition

LISA BIOW

With illustrations by
PAMELA DRURY WATTENMAKER

ZIFF-DAVIS
ZD
PRESS

ZIFF DAVIS PRESS
EMERYVILLE, CALIFORNIA

Development Editor	Valerie Haynes Perry
Copy Editor	Deborah Craig and Margo R. Hill
Technical Reviewer	Richard Ozer
Project Coordinator	Madhu Prasher
Proofreader	Tim Loughman
Cover Illustration	Pamela Drury Wattenmaker
Cover Design	Carrie English and Kenneth Roberts
Book Design	Dennis Gallagher/Visual Strategies, San Francisco
Technical Illustration	Pamela Drury Wattenmaker, Sarah Ishida, and Mina Reimer
Word Processing	Howard Blechman
Page Layout	M. D. Barrera
Indexer	Deborah Craig

Ziff-Davis Press, ZD Press, and the Ziff-Davis Press logo are licensed to Macmillan Computer Publishing USA by Ziff-Davis Publishing Company, New York, New York.

Ziff-Davis Press imprint books are produced on a Macintosh computer system with the following applications: FrameMaker®, Microsoft® Word, QuarkXPress®, Adobe Illustrator®, Adobe Photoshop®, Adobe Streamline™, MacLink®*Plus*, Aldus® FreeHand™, Collage Plus™.

If you have comments or questions or would like to receive a free catalog, call or write:
Macmillan Computer Publishing USA
Ziff-Davis Press Line of Books
5903 Christie Avenue
Emeryville, CA 94608
800-688-0448

ISBN 1-56276-381-4

Manufactured in the United States of America
10 9 8 7 6 5 4 3 2

*To Kelly Lynn
Pecore, niece
extraordinaire*

TABLE OF CONTENTS

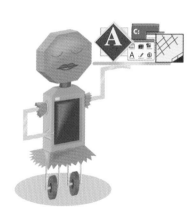

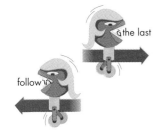

ACKNOWLEDGMENTS

Literally dozens of people helped make this book happen, both the first time around and in this second edition. In particular:

Pamela Wattenmaker created the whimsical and inspiring artwork that adorns most of these pages. She consistently transformed my often vague ideas into clear and evocative images, and was great fun to work with as well.

Deborah Craig, one of the world's finest editors as well as the world's greatest girlfriend, polished my drafts and soothed my soul during the two-month rewrite.

Friend and colleague Heidi Steele read the material on Windows and the Internet with her usual care and precision, providing large dollops of moral support along with her invaluable feedback.

Richard Ozer, technical editor, again went above and beyond the call of duty, researching questions for which I'd almost given up on finding answers.

Susan Adrian took me on a whirlwind tour of the Net and patiently answered weeks-worth of Net-101 questions.

Gerry Kaplan, one of my all-time favorite students and teachers, spent hours answering queries about the Macintosh operating system, multimedia, and Kodak CDs.

Richard Lesnick and the staff at RL & Associates answered numerous technical questions.

Adrienne Cool and Anne Simon let me borrow their Mac and made me a wonderful dinner during the harried last week of writing.

Madhu Prasher, project editor, kept me entertained on my trips to ZD Press and did a splendid job of tying all the loose ends together.

Margo Hill, copy editor, was unmitigatedly pleasant to work with and a pro to boot.

Lysa Lewallen, acquisitions editor, is better at getting things done than almost anyone I know. Her patience and efficiency made the rewrite practically painless.

M. D. Barrera did another wonderful job on the layout, as did Howard Blechman with his flawless and timely word processing.

And certainly not least, thanks to my friends Sue Scope, Greg Franke, and Jennifer Wriggins for helping me have fun even while writing a book, to Moki and Pogo for taking me on walks, and to Merle Yost for a happier second childhood.

INTRODUCTION

Over the last ten years, personal computers have moved from the hobbyist's basement to most of the offices, storefronts, factories, banks, supermarkets, farms, and classrooms in the United States. They've found their way into almost a quarter of the homes as well. Given this, the question has become not whether you'll have to deal with computers, but whether you'll understand them when you do.

In most cases, the difference between someone who likes computers and someone who doesn't is a matter of knowledge. If you see the computer as a tool that can assist you in work or play, and that you can use for your own ends, then you'll probably like it. On the other hand, if you see the computer as a mysterious contraption that you have to tolerate and/or appease in order to keep your job, you may need some time to warm up to it. This book is aimed at helping you turn the computers in your life from adversaries into willing helpmates.

I've written the book for four types of readers:

▶ *People who have recently been confronted with a computer, either at work or at home.*

▶ *People who don't have a computer, but are either thinking about getting one or simply wondering what the fuss is about.*

▶ *People who've been using a computer for a while (a week, a month, three years) without ever feeling comfortable with it.*

▶ *People who are fairly proficient with one particular program or one particular area of computer use, but who want to round out their knowledge.*

If you're totally new to computers, this book will tell you a little about everything you need to know. By the time you're through, you'll know what a computer is, what it's good for, and how it works in general. In short, you'll know the basic terms and concepts you'll need no matter how you plan to use your computer.

This book will also tell you enough about different ways of using computers to help you decide what areas you want to delve into further. When you're through, you may decide to learn all about spreadsheet programs so you can do your own financial projections. Or you may want to experiment with telecommunications so you can start working out of your home. In any case, you'll get enough of a background that you'll know where you want to head next. You'll also get the foundation you'll need for these further explorations. One of the hardest aspects of learning about computers is that most computer books and classes—even ones allegedly designed for beginners—assume that you already know the fundamentals (as if people were born knowing the term "random access memory"). By starting from the very beginning, this book gives you the knowledge you need to use other resources such as books, classes, computer users' groups, and technical support staff. It will even enable you to converse with and understand computer salespeople and repair technicians.

If you're already using a computer, you can use this book to fill in the gaps in your knowledge. If you've spent years throwing around terms like memory, bits, and bytes without ever quite knowing what you're talking about, this is the book that will finally explain them to you. It will provide you with the concepts and skills you need to use your computer with more confidence, to move from knowing what keys to press to knowing what those key presses are doing (and what to do when they don't work).

HOW THIS BOOK WORKS

The heart of this book is pictures. Not just pictures of what a particular computer program or piece of equipment looks like, but pictures that illustrate concepts like how the parts of a computer interact, or how information is organized inside a computer, or what you can do with a particular type of program.

Many of the figures (and much of the text) draw analogies between computer components and things that are more familiar to you. You'll find parts of the computer compared to a set of mailboxes in a post office, for example, or to a sports stadium. You'll also find various computer components and programs personified in some of the pictures—not because I really believe there are little people in there, but because such images can help you visualize and remember the events taking place inside your computer.

This book covers the two major types of personal computers—PCs (meaning IBM computers and "compatibles") and Macintoshes. (You'll learn more about these two types in Chapter 1.) Information that applies to only one of those two types of computers is represented by the following symbols: **PC**   **MAC**

ABOUT THE SIDEBARS

Throughout this book, technical information is presented not for its own sake but so you can understand what's going on when you use a computer effectively.

For those of you with a technical bent or a wealth of curiousity, there are also sidebars that look just like this one. These sidebars present additional technical information—extra details or related topics that will prove interesting to at least some of you but are not necessarily essential. Feel free to skim these or skip them altogether if you'd rather stick with the basics.

CHAPTER 1

THE BASICS

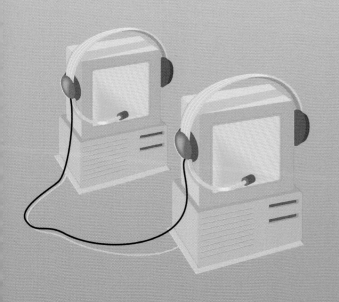

Learning to use computers is like learning a new language. Along with the new vocabulary and skills you will inevitably acquire some new ways of thinking about and interacting with the world. Even if all you learn to do is plug in the computer and compose letters, the computer may change the way you write, or at least change the process of writing, by making it so much easier to revise what you've written. Learning about computers will also give you access to new ways of obtaining and working with information. Once you know how to operate a computer, you can easily use it to chat with people across the country or the globe, about everything from the "new world order" to recipes for bouillabaisse to Chinese word processing programs. If you have an office job, computer literacy may even enable you to carry out some of your work from home—letting you communicate with the office computer using your own computer and a telephone. Finally, you may gain glimpses of what the future might be like, when computers are sure to be far more ubiquitous and capable than they are today.

In short, learning about computers will probably change your life, at least a little. Consider it an adventure.

COMPUTERS ARE NOT FRAGILE

Before you start using your computer, there is one critical thing you should know. Contrary to much popular opinion, computers are hard to break. There is no key or combination of keys that you can press that will damage the machine. Shy of dropping the computer on the ground or spilling soft drinks on it, there is little havoc you can wreak that is irreversible or even more than annoying. The one fragile part of the whole setup is your computer's disks, which do not take kindly to magnets, extreme heat, or spilled coffee. But for the most part, your computer is a sturdy object, without any auto-destruct sequence or ejector seat.

Computers are also very forgiving. Even if you blindly press every key in sight, the worst possible result is that you will delete some of the information you just entered. (Even this will take a little doing and, if you notice the mistake immediately, can often be corrected with a single command.) If you issue an instruction that doesn't make sense, the computer will usually let you know by displaying a message on the screen. As soon as you acknowledge the message (often by pressing another key), it disappears and the computer discards all knowledge of the misdeed. Worst comes to worst, you will inadvertently tell the computer to do something other than what you intended. Once you notice the problem, you can almost always find a way to undo what you just did and then try again.

NOTE *This is not to say that computers never break down. They do. But they break because of electronic or mechanical failure rather than because you pressed the wrong key at the wrong time.*

HOW TO LEARN ABOUT COMPUTERS

The prospect of learning about computers can be very intimidating for the following reasons:

▶ *People who already know about computers speak a dialect guaranteed to frighten off newcomers.*

▶ *It seems that everyone else, including all the five year olds on the block, already know how to use them.*

▶ *Maybe it's been a while since you've explored such thoroughly new terrain.*

For those of you who feel a little anxious or inadequate at the thought of "learning computers," here are some suggestions for approaching the learning process itself:

Tip 1: **Assume That You Have the Capacity to Do This.** Just about anyone can learn to use a computer. You don't need to be good at math. You don't need mechanical aptitude. And you don't need to be geared toward logical or linear thinking. You do, however, need some patience. And you need enough self-confidence and determination not to give up when something doesn't work the first (or even the second or third) time you try it.

Tip 2: **Acquire New Knowledge in Bite-sized Pieces.** Don't try to read about and absorb everything at once. Instead, learn only as much as you can comfortably assimilate in a single session, and then review and/or practice until you have mastered the material. Then go back and learn some more.

Tip 3: **Make It Concrete.** Whenever possible, try to put at least some of the information or skills you acquire to immediate use: Your new knowledge is much more likely to "stick" if you find some way to put it to work. When you read about computer equipment, see if you can locate the various components in your own computer system. Try to figure out exactly what type of equipment you have. When you read about a particular type of computer program, try to imagine how you might use such a program (or whether you'd have no use for it at all). Or at least imagine how other people or businesses you know might use the program.

COMPUTERS ARE NOT FRAGILE

Contrary to much popular opinion, computers are hard to break.

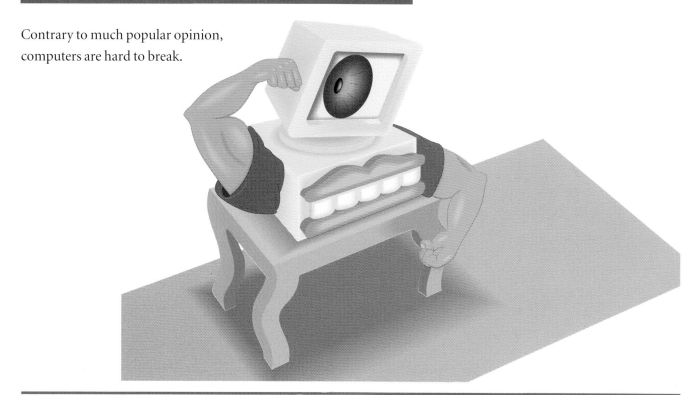

Tip 4: **Cultivate Curiosity.** The best way to get really good at computers is to experiment, to question, to wonder if you can do x or what would happen if you did y. Don't just passively accept what you read here or in computer manuals. Try to figure out at least some things on your own.

Tip 5: **Don't Try to Be Productive Immediately.** If at all possible, keep the learning process free of deadline pressure. (For example, don't decide to learn how to produce a newsletter the day before the newsletter needs to be finished.) Try to make learning about computers a task in itself rather than a means to an immediate end, scheduling plenty of time for the process and, if possible, working on something that interests or amuses you.

Tip 6: **When in Doubt, Don't Panic.** Your aim, in learning about computers, should not be to avoid mistakes, but to discover what to do when they happen. I'll give you lots of hints for what to consider when the thing is not behaving itself, and suggestions about where to go for more help.

Tip 7: **Avoid Bad Teachers.** Thousands of people have learned to hate computers at the hands of well-meaning friends, spouses, and coworkers—someone who tries to tell them everything they need to know about computers in fifteen minutes, or who forgets that there was ever a time they didn't know what a CD-ROM drive is. If you feel stupid every time a certain someone tries to teach you about your computer, you can probably assume that the problem lies in the teaching, not in you or in the subject matter itself. Tell them gently but firmly to leave you alone.

If you want someone to hold your hand while you learn computers, make sure it's someone you're not afraid to ask "stupid questions," someone you don't need to impress. For most of us, this means avoiding a teacher who's either a boss or an employee, and quite possibly a spouse or child as well.

Tip 8: **Remember: You Don't Need to Be a Computer Expert to Use a Computer.** The purpose of the computer is to help you do something. You shouldn't (and don't) need a Ph.D. in electrical engineering to get some work done. Although you can make a career or a permanent hobby out of learning about computers, it's fairly easy to do the easy things. If you just want to use your computer to compose and print simple letters, you can probably learn everything you need to know in an hour or two. If you want to learn to produce a professional-looking newsletter, expect to spend weeks. (If you want to learn to converse with computer salespeople, you may need months.) In any case, learning everything you want to know about computers may take a while, but you can fairly quickly learn enough to get some work done.

Tip 9: **Have Fun Whenever Possible!**

There's one last thing to know about computers before you start. As you may have already heard or experienced, computers are completely and often maddeningly literal. If you spell something wrong or accidentally press the wrong key, they don't even *try* to guess what you mean. There is, however, a positive side to this trait: Namely, when you do everything correctly, it works. In most cases, computers provide immediate and decisive feedback. When you press the right keys, you get the right results; when you don't, you don't. If you have a job (or a life) in which it's sometimes hard to tell how well you're doing, you may find such clarity refreshing.

WHAT IS A COMPUTER?

A computer is a general-purpose machine for storing and manipulating information. Beyond this, there are two very different schools of thought.

▶ *Computers are dumb but very fast machines equivalent to extremely powerful calculators.*

▶ *Computers are thinking machines capable of awe-inspiring, almost limitless feats of intelligence.*

Both of these things are true. In themselves, computers have a very limited set of skills. They can add numbers, compare numbers, and store numbers. This probably seems very strange. The computers we know or have heard about seem to do far more than this. They manipulate text, display graphic images, generate sounds, and do lots of other things that, to us, seem nonmathematical.

But internally, the computer handles all information as numbers, and everything it does involves storing and manipulating those numbers. In this sense, computers are like fancy adding machines. But assuming that you know how to "talk" to a computer in the language of numbers, as some programmers do, you can get it to do some amazing things. Any kind of information that can be represented numerically—and this includes everything from music to photographs to motion picture videos—can be manipulated via a computer, assuming someone knows how to provide the computer with the proper instructions.

This does not mean that you need to know how to learn to program computers (write your own instructions) in order to use them. Chances are you will simply buy and use programs that other people have created. Then you simply need to learn how to use those programs, a task that is far easier and less demanding than learning to write programs of your own.

PERSONAL COMPUTERS

Even if you have yet to encounter a computer at work or buy a computer for home, you probably deal with computers on a daily basis, whether you want to or not. Every time you use an automated teller machine, or watch the checker scan the bar code on your milk carton into an electronic cash register, or use a hand-held calculator, you are using a computer. Some of those computers—like the calculator, for example—are designed to do a very specific task, and the instructions for performing that task are built into the equipment itself.

The type of computer you will probably be dealing with at your home or office is more general purpose. It can do just about anything provided it is given appropriate instructions.

Computers come in a multitude of shapes, sizes, and types, ranging from those that fit in the palm of your hand or hide in the corner of your microwave or VCR to those that occupy entire rooms, from ones that are generally used by one person at a time to those that are simultaneously used by dozens or even hundreds of people. This book is about *personal computers*—that is, computers primarily designed for use by one person at a time.

Personal computers are newcomers to the computer scene. Although the first computers were built in the 1940s, the first personal computers were only introduced in the 1970s and were primarily the province of hobbyists, almost like new-fangled ham radios. In 1975, Apple produced the first Apple computer, followed by the Apple II in 1978. By 1980, there were a number of microcomputers on the market that could practicably be used in small businesses, but they were used only by people and companies that were either particularly adventurous or especially in need of automation. Then in the fall of 1981, IBM introduced the original IBM PC, whose instant popularity astounded everyone, including IBM. The success of the IBM PC was due to a combination of good timing (a lot of small to medium-sized businesses were itching for a financially feasible way to automate) and the IBM name, which lent new credibility to the whole notion of small desktop computing. The budding personal computer mania was further spurred by Apple's introduction, in 1984, of the original Macintosh computer: a type of computer specifically designed to be easy to learn, fun to use, and unintimidating for the nontechnical user. Meanwhile, the speed and capacity of the machines continued to increase almost as fast as their size and prices shrank, making them all the more practical and popular. (Today's personal computers are hundreds of times more powerful than those sold ten years ago, generally cost less, and can fit in packages the size of a notebook.) By the end of the decade, personal computers had gone from being the province of hobbyists and retired engineers, to being an almost ubiquitous fixture in the work world and a member (so to speak) of almost 20% of U.S. households.

NOTE *Just because personal computers are "personal" doesn't mean they can't talk to each other. Many businesses and other organizations have computer* networks—*groups of computers that are linked together so that they can share information, programs, and/or equipment such as printers. You'll learn more about networks in Chapter 8.*

Even if you have yet to encounter a computer at work or buy a computer for home, you probably deal with computers on a daily basis.

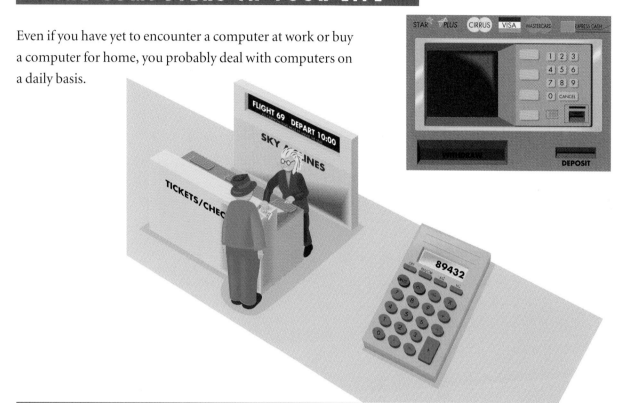

THE TWO PERSONAL COMPUTER CAMPS

The majority of personal computers currently used in business fall into two camps:

▶ *IBM PCs and compatibles*

▶ *Apple Macintosh computers (often referred to simply as "Macs")*

The terms *IBM clone* and *IBM compatible* mean a computer that uses similar components and a similar design to IBM-manufactured PCs, and therefore can use the same type of programs as IBM computers.

Macintosh clones are extremely rare, due to both certain technical complexities of the machine and Apple's very tightly held copyrights. In contrast, when it first created the PC, IBM decided to allow others to imitate its machines. The theory was that the more IBM imitations there were, the more likely it was the IBM would become the business standard. While this did probably enhance IBM's standing in the marketplace, it also spurred the development of literally thousands of brands of IBM "workalikes" (aka *clones*).

THE MACINTOSH CAMP AND THE PC CAMP

The majority of personal computers currently used in business fall into
two camps: the Macintosh camp and the PC camp.

Several other types of personal computers are also widely used at home (Ataris and
Commodores, for example), as school computers (Apple II's in particular), or in specific
types of work (Amigas, for instance, are popular among musicians because they have built-
in musical capabilities). While some of these machines sell well in Europe, they are less
widely used in the U.S., particularly within the business world. In offices, the standard is still
IBM and clones, followed by Macs.

NOTE   *Although the term PC was coined by IBM as the name for its first personal computer,
its meaning has expanded over the years. Some people use PC as shorthand for any personal
computer. Others, including myself, use it to mean IBM-type computers, including IBM compatibles. In this book, PC means any computer designed to work like IBM personal computers
and capable of running programs designed for those computers.*

Until recently, the main difference between PCs and Macs had to do with what is
known as their *user interface*—that is, the way they presented information on the screen and

solicited and responded to your input. In general, Macs had a more playful, less intimidating interface, centered around pictures and *menus* (lists of options) on the screen. The PC interface tended to be a bit more stark and more text oriented. In recent years, however, most PCs have started employing a graphical user interface, much like the Mac's.

If you are planning to buy a computer, one of the big decisions you'll need to make is whether to get a Mac or a PC. If possible, try playing with both types of computers and see whether you prefer one of the two. Investigate whether you can get any special deals on one type of computer through your school or job. And while you're making up your mind, consider the following:

▶ *If you use a computer at work and have any plans to bring work home, you might want to get the same type of computer you use at your job.*

▶ *If you have friends who are willing to help you learn about computers and ride to the rescue when something doesn't work, you may want to get the type of computer they know how to use.*

▶ *If you're planning on using your computer for a fairly specialized task—like editing video or managing an auto repair shop—start by picking the program you want to use, and then pick the computer that the program will run on. Most programs will run on a Mac but not a PC and vice versa. Even if you're doing something that's not all that specialized, you may want to find out what type of computer most people in your field are using. Most graphic designers use Macs, for example, and most tax and financial consultants use PCs. If you stick with the computer that most of your colleagues are using, you're more likely to find a wide range of applicable programs and to find people who know both your business and your computer, in case you need help. If, on the other hand, you're buying a computer to do word processing, you can base your decision solely on price and personal preference.*

PROGRAMS: THE WIZARD BEHIND THE CURTAIN

People who are new to computers sometimes think that computers come ready and willing to do anything they want them to do, like electronic Wizards of Oz. Although computers can theoretically do just about anything, by themselves they do nothing at all. They are like player pianos without a roll of music, or VCR machines without tapes. What allows your computer to actually do something are programs: that is, sets of instructions that tell the computer what to do and how to do it. Programs are like the man behind the curtain, turning the knobs and pulling the levers, making your computer perform or seem to perform magic.

Let's take an example. If you want to use your computer to compose and print letters, you use a word processing program. (As I'll discuss shortly, word processing is essentially electronic typing.) The word processing program contains instructions that tell the computer what colors, characters, and/or images to display on your screen, and how to respond to your actions (such as pressing various keys). When you run this program, you get a kind of interactive word processing movie. Your screen appears largely blank, resembling the electronic equivalent of a blank sheet of typing paper. You may see a list of options at the top of the screen that allow you to perform word processing tasks, like setting margins or underlining or adding footnotes.

If you want to do something else with your computer—keep track of customers, for example, or play a game of solitaire—you need to find a program designed for that purpose. The computer is not "set up" to do that task, or any other task, on its own.

In a sense, you could say that the basic function of a personal computer is to "play" different programs—just as VCRs are designed to play VCR tapes. In both cases, the machinery is the same, but the resulting "movies" will be very different.

A single computer can and usually does hold several programs at once. When you buy a computer, it sometimes comes with one or more programs already *installed*—that is, already on your computer and set up to work with your equipment. You can install new programs whenever you like, and once they are installed, they remain stored inside the computer, ready for you to use. The number of programs that you can store in a single computer is limited only by the amount of disk space that you have. You will learn about disks and disk space in the next chapter.

WHAT YOU CAN DO WITH A COMPUTER

There are dozens of types of programs that you can run on a personal computer, from ones that teach typing to ones that prepare your tax returns. For now, we'll just outline some of the major categories:

▶ *Word processing programs let you use your computer to compose and print letters, papers, reports, and other types of documents. They offer much more extensive editing*

"PLAYING" A PROGRAM

The basic function of a personal computer is to "play" different programs—just as VCRs are designed to play VCR tapes.

capabilities than typewriters—allowing you to insert new characters and delete existing ones, and to move blocks of text from one part of the document to another, all without retyping. Most also have features for handling page numbers and footnotes. They also generally include a feature, known as mail merge, that allows you to generate personalized form letters by "merging" a letter with a set of names and addresses.

▶ **Desktop publishing (DTP) programs** enable you to combine text, pictures, graphics, tables, lines, boxes, and other design elements in a single document. They let you perform the type of page layout operations required to produce documents such as newsletters, books, and flyers—the kind of operations otherwise performed in a typesetting shop.

▶ **Spreadsheet programs** are number crunchers. They let you perform almost any kind of mathematical calculations. Although they are most often used for financial calculations (budgeting, financial analysis, and forecasting), they can be used for scientific or *engineering calculations as well. They also often have built-in graphics capabilities, permitting you to transform a set of numbers into a bar graph or pie chart, for example.*

▶ *Database management programs let you store, retrieve, and manipulate large collections of information, such as mailing lists, inventories, student rosters, or library card catalogs. They enable you to keep your data up-to-date, sort it, generate statistics, print reports, and produce mailing labels. Database programs also let you extract portions of your data based on some kind of selection criteria, listing all your customers in Oregon with a credit limit of over $100, for example, or all the inventory items of which there are less than three items in stock.*

▶ *Accounting programs help you manage your money. They let you track and categorize income and expenses, reconcile your bank statements, and produce standard financial reports such as income statements and balance sheets. At one end of the spectrum are simple personal money management programs that let you balance your checkbook and track personal expenses. At the other end are sophisticated business accounting programs that generate extensive financial reports, produce invoices and statements to customers, handle accounts payable and receivable, print payroll checks and payroll reports, and track inventory.*

▶ *Graphics/presentation programs let you create pictures or designs either to display on screen or to print. This category includes painting and drawing programs that let you either combine and modify existing pictures or construct your own. It also encompasses presentation graphics programs, which let you create line graphs, pie graphs, organizational charts and other types of diagrams and, in many cases, to combine these images into slide shows. (As mentioned, some presentation graphics capabilities are often built into spreadsheet programs as well.) This category also includes programs that let you edit or enhance photographic images.*

▶ *Communications programs allow computers to "talk" to each other over phone lines, via a special piece of equipment known as a modem (see Chapter 10). You can use this capability to access electronic bulletin boards and information services like CompuServe, Prodigy, Internet, and Lexus. These services let you do everything from sending messages to other people via "electronic mail," to conversing with others about topics ranging from global warming to vacation hot spots, to shopping in "electronic malls" (kind of like a computerized catalog and order-taking system), to discovering which airlines are flying to Albuquerque tomorrow morning or how your stocks are doing on Wall Street.*

▶ *Game, entertainment, and educational programs let you do everything from playing backgammon to doing battle with computer-generated dragons. There are programs that let you step inside detective and science fiction novels, work on your golf swing, and attempt to save the world from ecological disasters. There are also dozens of games for children, many of them educational in intent. There are programs that "read" children's stories, for example, highlighting each word on the screen while pronouncing it through the computer's speakers.*

In Chapter 7 you will learn more about the major types of programs, and how to select the right one for you.

HARDWARE VERSUS SOFTWARE

Now that you know what a program is (a set of instructions), you are ready for your first two pieces of computer jargon. In computer terminology, all computer equipment is referred to as *hardware* and all computer programs are known as *software*. These two terms emphasize the fact that the equipment and program are two essential parts of a working computer system. Hardware is the machinery and its physical accoutrements, including the keyboard (the part that looks like a typewriter), the screen, and the printer. Software is the magic spell that brings the machinery to life.

Some people get a little confused about the difference between hardware and software. Part of this confusion has to do with the way software is packaged and sold. If you buy a new program, you get a box with one or more manuals explaining (hopefully) how the program works, plus one or more floppy disks on which the program is stored. When you get back to your home or office, you install the program by copying its instructions from the disks to your computer. As a result, many people think of disks as software. (If you've never encountered a *floppy disk*, they are round, flat wafers—kind of like small and flimsy records—that are encased in square plastic wrappers. They are used to store both programs and data. You'll learn all about disks in Chapters 2 and 3.) In fact, they are hardware. The basic rule of thumb for determining if something is hardware or software is whether you can touch it: And since disks can be touched, they're in the hardware camp. Software, on the other hand, is much more elusive. You can't touch, see, or taste it; you can only witness its results.

TYPES OF PROGRAMS

Word processing programs let you use your computer to compose and print letters, papers, reports, and other types of documents.

Desktop publishing (DTP) programs let you perform the type of page layout operations required to produce documents such as newsletters, books, and flyers.

Database management programs let you store, retrieve, and manipulate large collections of information, such as mailing lists, inventories, student rosters, or library card catalogs.

Spreadsheet programs are number crunchers. They let you perform almost any kind of mathematical calculation.

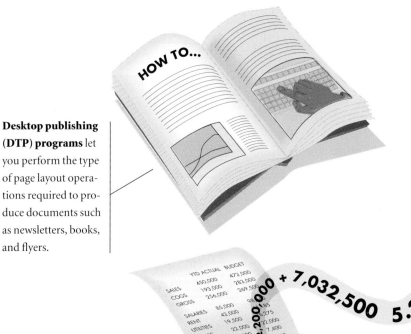

Note: Because spreadsheet programs are frequently used for financial calculations, many people have a hard time distinguishing them from accounting programs. Spreadsheets are completely open-ended: they can perform almost any calculation you can imagine, but only if you provide them with explicit instructions. Accounting programs, in contrast, already "know" how to handle accounting functions and generate standard accounting reports. All you need to do is type in your numbers.

Accounting programs help you manage your money. They let you track and categorize income and expenses, reconcile your bank statements, and produce standard financial reports such as income statements and balance sheets.

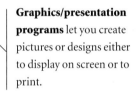

Graphics/presentation programs let you create pictures or designs either to display on screen or to print.

Game, entertainment, and educational programs let you do everything from playing backgammon to doing battle with computer-generated dragons.

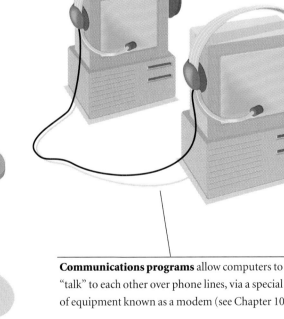

Communications programs allow computers to "talk" to each other over phone lines, via a special piece of equipment known as a modem (see Chapter 10).

N O T E   *From here on, I will be using the words* program *and* software *virtually interchangeably.*

When you buy a new program, then, the physical disks on which the program is stored are hardware. The program itself—the instructions stored on those disks—is software. The distinction here is a little subtle—like the distinction between the music and the records, magnetic tape, or compact disks on which that music is recorded. The music (which is analogous to software) is intangible; the part you can touch (the record, tape, or CD) is merely the medium on which the music is stored. Similarly, the disks you get when you buy a program are simply the medium on which the program is stored.

N O T E   *Recently, programs have also become available on CD-ROMs—special types of compact discs that are meant to be "played" on a computer. CD-ROMs fall under the rubric of hardware too, just like disks. You'll learn more about CD-ROMs in Chapter 3.*

THE TWO TYPES OF SOFTWARE

As mentioned, the native language of computers consists solely of numbers. Since very few of us are capable (or patient) enough to speak to a computer in this language, we almost never interact with the computer directly. We always "speak" to the computer through an intermediary, namely, a program whose function, among other things, is to translate our requests to the computer. And it is programs that enable the computer to "speak" back to us, by telling it how to display text or pictures on the screen, produce sounds, or print characters on paper.

There are actually two different types of software: applications software and operating systems. *Applications software* is the software that you use to actually perform your work. This includes all the types of programs previously described under "What You Can Do with a Computer."

N O T E   *The term* applications *is often used in computer circles to mean "things that you do with your computer." So if someone asks you what types of applications you intend to run, they are really asking you what you plan to do with your computer—that is, what types of programs you plan to use.*

In contrast, *operating systems* are programs that act as the intermediary between you and the hardware and, to some extent, between the hardware and the applications software. As you will learn in Chapters 5 and 6, operating systems serve several different functions.

HARDWARE VERSUS SOFTWARE

Hardware is the machinery and its physical accoutrements. It includes all parts of the computer system that you can touch.

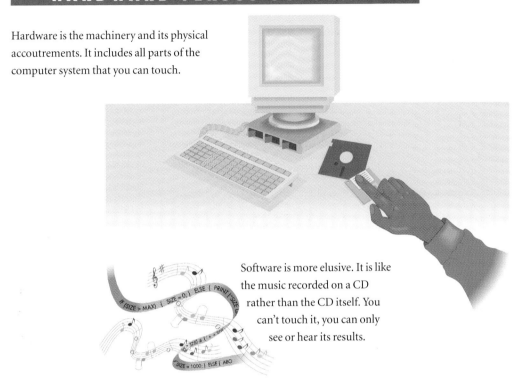

Software is more elusive. It is like the music recorded on a CD rather than the CD itself. You can't touch it, you can only see or hear its results.

For starters, the operating system controls various parts of the machine and allows them to talk to one another; in effect, it *operates* the hardware. The operating system also provides your basic working environment, the world you encounter when you first turn on the machine. Whether you see something like C:\> or a screen full of pictures when you power up your computer depends, in large part, on which operating system program you are using.

In addition, operating systems include various "housekeeping utilities" that allow you to find out what programs and data are stored on a disk, to copy programs and data to and from your computer, and to delete programs and data. And finally, it's the operating system that allows you to start up application programs. If you want to play chess on your computer, for example, you issue a command that tells the operating system "Go find the chess program and fire it up."

Different operating systems are designed for different types of computers. If you are running a PC, you will probably use an operating system named Windows 95, DOS, or, more rarely, one called OS/2. If you are running a Macintosh, you will use the Macintosh operating system, which you may have heard called System 7 or the Finder.

THE THREE STANDARD OPERATING ENVIRONMENTS

THE MACINTOSH
OPERATING SYSTEM

DOS

WINDOWS 95

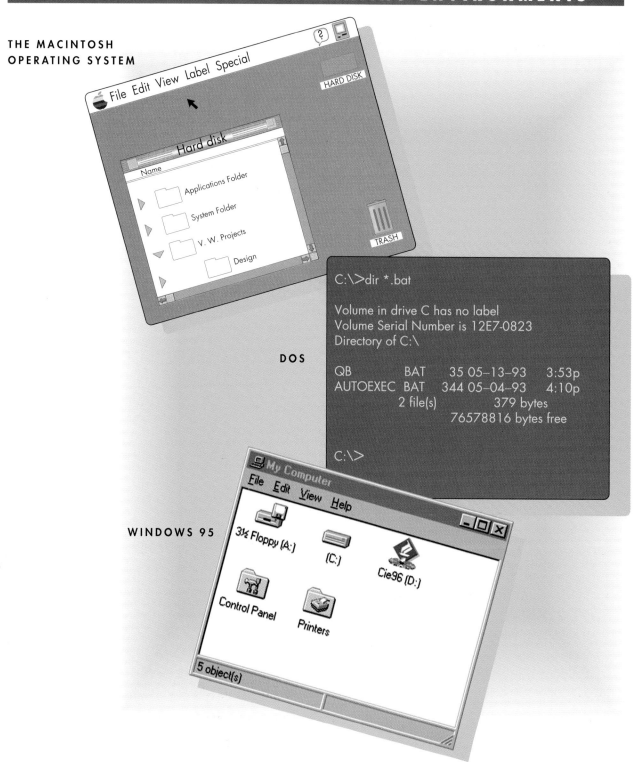

NOTE   *While Windows 95 is an operating system in itself, older versions of the Windows program worked hand-in-hand with the DOS operating system or, less frequently, the OS/2 operating system. You'll learn more about Windows and about the differences among its various versions in Chapter 5.*

Both Windows and the Mac operating system employ pictures and menus to help you manage your applications programs and data. In contrast, DOS, which prior to the advent of Windows 95 was the most common operating system on PCs, uses a command-driven interface—meaning that whenever you want the computer to do something you need to type in a command. And since there are no visual cues on the screen, you either need to memorize all the commands or look them up in a book as needed. Although DOS aficionados will insist that typing commands is a much more direct and efficient way to communicate with a computer, most beginners find the graphical, picture-oriented interfaces a lot easier to manage.

THE TASK AHEAD

Now that you know about the difference between hardware and software, and between application programs and operating systems, you can understand a little more what's involved in learning about computers. In a nutshell, there are three topics you need to know about:

▶ *Your Hardware. The type of machinery and accessories you will be using and how they work*

▶ *Your Operating System. The essential program that makes your computer "go"*

▶ *Application Programs. The individual application programs that let you accomplish whatever you intend to do with your computer—be it typing letters, producing newsletters, handling mailing lists, preparing your tax return, or playing Dungeons and Dragons*

In terms of hardware, you need to learn at least a little bit about what the different components are and how they work. At a minimum, you need to know something about how data and programs are stored inside your computer (so that you understand what happens when you "save" data, for example, or when it's safe to turn off the computer). You should probably also know enough to buy new equipment as needed, which unfortunately involves mastering a daunting number of buzzwords.

Learning about hardware has another purpose: It makes you feel more in control of your machine. While some people have made jokes about the necessity of sacrificing lambs to their computer, there's little fun in feeling subjugated to a capricious deity. The more you know about your computer's innards, the less likely you are to feel that there's an evil spirit in there, and the less fatalistic you're likely to be about hardware problems.

You also need to know some basics about the operating system that goes with your computer. At a minimum, you want to know how to use the operating system to start up various applications programs. You also want to know things like how to copy and erase programs and data.

Finally, you need to learn how to use particular application programs. If you want to use your computer to generate letters and other documents, for example, you need to pick out (if necessary) and then learn a particular word processing program. If you plan to crunch numbers, you'll need to find and master a spreadsheet program. Since there are literally thousands of application programs available, we can't explain how to use individual programs in this book. Instead, we'll discuss, in Chapter 7, how the major types of applications programs work, how to choose a program, and how to go about teaching yourself (including how to read computer manuals, locate good books, and obtain technical support).

CHAPTER

2

ANATOMY OF A COMPUTER

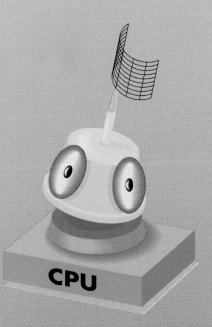

CPU

In this chapter, you will learn the fundamentals of computer hardware—what the essential parts are and how they interact with each other. I will start with the core elements of the computer—the parts that let you store and manipulate information, and allow you to communicate with your computer. Then at the end of the chapter I'll backtrack a bit and discuss the pieces that support and/or connect those core devices, turning the individual parts into a cohesive working system.

Probably the most important knowledge you will glean from this chapter relates to how your computer stores information. By the time you finish this chapter, you will know

▶ *What happens when you load a program*

▶ *Where the data you type into your computer goes*

▶ *What happens when you save data (where the computer puts it, and how you get it back again)*

Whenever possible, I'll use analogies to things you already know about and, for now, I'll give you just enough technical detail to get a feel for what's really going on inside your computer. You'll learn a bit more of the technical details in the next chapter and in Chapter 8.

THE BRAIN OF THE COMPUTER

At the core of every computer is a device roughly the size of a large postage stamp. This device, known as the *central processing unit*, or CPU for short, is the "brain" of the computer, the part that reads and executes program instructions, performs calculations, and makes decisions. The CPU is responsible for storing and retrieving information on disks and other storage media. It also handles moving information from one part of the computer to another. For this reason, some people compare it to a central switching station or control tower that directs the flow of traffic throughout the computer system.

In personal computers, the CPU (also known as the *microprocessor*) is comprised of a single integrated circuit. An *integrated circuit*, or IC, is a matrix of transistors and other electrical circuits embedded in a small slice of silicon. (*Transistors* are essentially microscopic electronic switches: tiny devices that can be turned on and off.) Like the dozens of other integrated circuits that inhabit your computer, from the outside, a CPU chip looks something like a square ceramic bug with little metal legs. These "legs" are designed to fasten the chip to a fiberglass circuit board which sits inside your computer, and to carry electrical impulses into and out of the chip. Inside the ceramic case is the chip itself, a slice of silicon about the size of a fingernail. At first glance, it's hard to imagine how this tiny device can run your entire computer. But under a microscope, the slice of silicon reveals an electronic maze so complex it resembles an aerial photograph of a city, complete with hundreds of intersecting streets and hundreds of thousands of minuscule houses. Most of the "houses" are transistors, and there are usually somewhere between one hundred thousand and three million of them on a single CPU chip.

The type of CPU that a computer contains determines its processing power—how fast it can execute various instructions. These days, most CPUs can execute on the order of millions of instructions per second. The type of CPU also determines the precise repertoire of instructions the computer understands and therefore which programs it can run.

THE SYSTEM UNIT

The CPU resides inside a box known as the system unit, along with various support devices and tools for storing information. (You will learn about these other residents of the system unit later in this chapter.) For now, just think of the system unit as a container for the CPU.

The system unit case—that is, the metal box itself—can either be wider than it is tall, in which case it usually sits on top of your desk, often underneath the screen, or it can be taller than it is wide, in which case it generally sits underneath your desk and is referred to as a *tower case.*

THE VARIOUS TYPES OF CPU CHIPS

In the PC world in particular, people often categorize computers by the model of CPU chip they contain, saying things like "I have a 386" or "My computer is a 486." The CPU chips currently used in PCs include the 8088 at the low end, 80286, 80386, 80486, and at the high end, the Pentium (the generation after the 486), and the P6. People usually omit the first two digits when referring to 80286, 80386, and 80486 chips. So if someone tells you that they have a 486 computer, they mean an IBM-type computer with an 80486 chip. (You can tell it's an IBM computer or clone because they're the only computers that use 80486 chips.) In the Macintosh world, people distinguish between models that contain the new Power PC chips and those that contain one of the 68000 series chips by Motorola.

The other parts of the computer system—that is, the parts outside the system unit—are primarily used as a means of communicating with the CPU—of sending in instructions and data and getting out information. Devices used to communicate with the CPU are

INSIDE THE CPU CHIP

When placed under a microscope, a CPU chip resembles an aerial photograph of a city.

STANDARD COMPUTER SYSTEMS

Standard system unit case

Tower case

Laptop computer

known, collectively, as *input and output devices*, or simply *I/O devices*. Input devices are all those things that allow you to "talk" to your computer—to pose questions and issue commands. Output devices are what allow the computer to talk back, providing you with answers, asking you for additional information, or, at worst, informing you that it has no idea what you are talking about.

NOTE *You may also hear the term* peripherals *applied to I/O devices. Technically the term peripheral means everything outside the CPU (including I/O devices).*

HOW FAST IS YOUR CPU?

Within each class of CPU, speed is measured in terms of the cycle time at which the computer was designed to operate. All computers have built-in clocks that help regulate the flow of information from one part of the computer to another, rather like a metronome. Each pulse of this clock is known as a cycle, and a CPU can perform, at maximum, one operation per cycle.

Every CPU is designed to work with a clock that "ticks" at a particular rate. A CPU may be designed to run at 16 megahertz (MHz) or 33 megahertz, for example, meaning 16 or 33 million cycles per second. Bear in mind, however, that this measurement is relative to the class of processor. In the PC world, a 25MHz 386 is faster than a 16MHz 386, for example, but a 25MHz 486 CPU runs much faster than a 25MHz 386 CPU.

In personal computers, the most common input device is the keyboard (the part that looks like a typewriter). The second most common input device is a mouse. The mouse is a handheld pointing device that allows you to point to words or objects on the computer screen. The mouse sits on your desktop or sometimes on a rubber pad, called a *mouse pad*, that allows it to move more easily than on the bare desktop. Moving the mouse forward and back, or left and right, causes an arrow on the screen (known as the *mouse pointer*) to move as well. And pressing the buttons on the mouse (called *pressing* or *clicking*, depending on how fast you do it) lets you make selections on your screen. You will learn more about using the mouse in Chapter 4. All Macintosh computer systems include a mouse, but the mouse is optional on PCs.

There are also lots of other input devices that you can use to communicate with your computers, including

▶ *A trackball, which is a pointing device that resembles a ball nestled in a square cradle, and serves as an alternative to a mouse.*

▶ *A scanner, which allows you to copy an image (such as a photograph, a drawing, or a page of text) into your computer, translating it into a form that the computer can store and manipulate.*

▶ *A joy stick, which lets you manipulate the various people, creatures, and machines that populate computer games.*

The most common output device is the display screen, which the computer uses to display instructions, ask questions, and present information. Computer screens go by many names, including monitor, VDT (video display terminal), and CRT (for cathode ray tube, the technology used in most desktop computer screens). (In laptop computers and their newer, smaller cousins the *notebooks*, both the screen and the keyboard are often built into the system unit itself.)

Almost all computer systems also include a printer for generating paper copies of your data. Like monitors, printers come in many shapes and sizes, and generate output ranging from the old grainy-looking computer printout to color printouts that rival the clarity of offset printing. (The main types of printers are discussed in Chapter 8.)

These days many computers also come equipped with a *sound board*—a device that resides inside the system unit and that allows your computer to generate sounds and music. Most computers that contain sound boards also have speakers, although it is also possible to listen to computer-generated sounds through headphones or through your stereo system's speakers. You'll learn about sound boards and speakers in Chapter 8.

Finally, there is one type of device—called a modem—that serves as both input and output device. A *modem* is a gadget that allows computers to communicate with each other over phone lines. You can use modems both to send data and messages to your friends and coworkers who have computers, to tap into electronic information services such as America Online and CompuServe. Many modems even have fax capabilities built-in, allowing you to send and receive faxes via your computer.

N O T E   *Some modems are separate devices that plug into the system unit. Others reside inside the system unit. You'll learn more about monitors and printers in Chapter 8 and about modems in Chapter 10.*

INPUT AND OUTPUT DEVICES

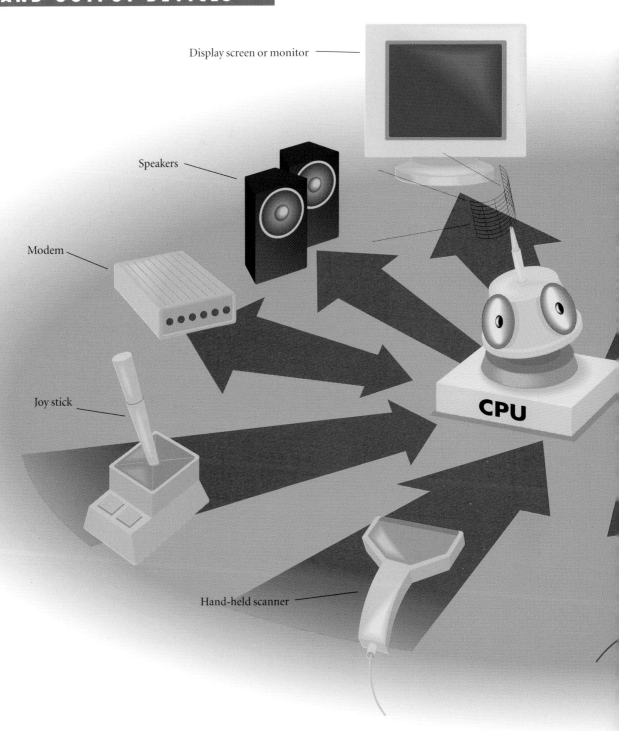

Display screen or monitor

Speakers

Modem

Joy stick

Hand-held scanner

CPU

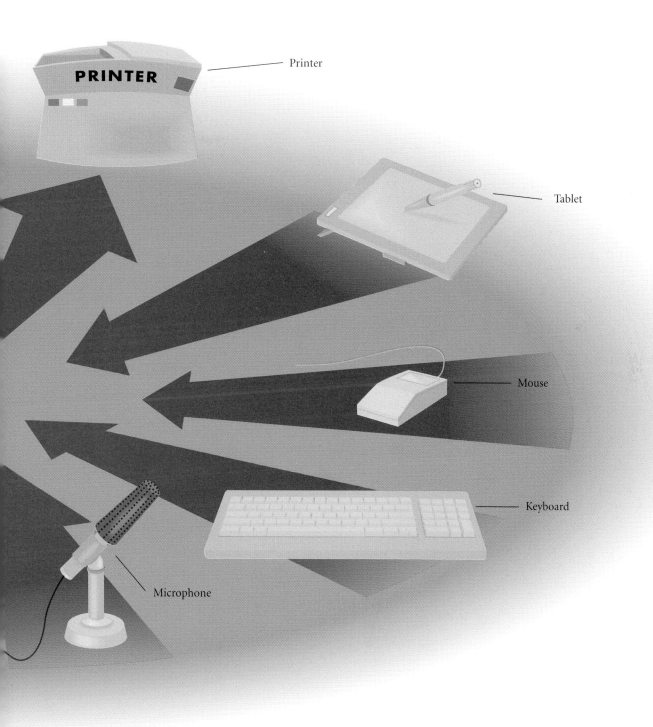

Printer

PRINTER

Tablet

Mouse

Keyboard

Microphone

STORING INFORMATION

Now you know a little about the CPU of the computer and the devices that you use to communicate with that "brain." There is still one very large gap in our image of a computer system, however. There is no storage space.

Although the CPU is terrific at manipulating data and following instructions, it has almost no capacity for storing information. (Think of it as a brilliant but extremely absent-minded professor.) In order to function, your computer therefore needs a place to store both programs (the instructions that tell the CPU what to do) and data. You need, in other words, the electronic equivalent of a closet or filing cabinet.

N O T E *In computerese, the term* data *refers to whatever type of information you are trying to manipulate. Data therefore includes far more than numbers; it includes any information that you type or otherwise input into the computer. You can also think of data as the raw material that is processed or manipulated by application programs. If you are using a word processing program,* data *means the document (letter, memo, poem, novel, legal brief, whatever) you are typing and/or editing. If you are working with a database program, it may be a set of names and addresses you are adding to your company mailing list.*

In most computers, the primary storage places are disks—flat, circular wafers that resemble undersized phonograph records. (You may be used to thinking of disks as square because they are always housed inside square plastic jackets. But the disks themselves are round.)

Like phonograph records or compact discs, they store information that can be "played" by devices specifically designed for that purpose. The device that "plays" computer disks is known as a *disk drive.* It is in several respects the equivalent of a turntable or CD player. Like turntables or CD players, disk drives have components designed to access the information on a specific area of the disk. These parts are called *read/write heads* and are equivalent to the phonograph needle on a turntable or laser in a CD player. Like turntables, disk drives turn around, thereby spinning the disk so that different parts of the surface pass underneath the read/write heads (just as records spin underneath the needle). Most disk drives have at least two read/write heads—one for each side.

Unlike record players or CD players, however, disk drives can record new information on disks as well as play existing information. (In this sense, they're more like cassette tapes

TYPES OF DATA

The term *data* refers to what-ever type of information you are trying to manipulate.

READ/WRITE HEAD

The read/write heads on a disk drive are like the phonograph needles on turntables or lasers in CD players, except that they can write (record) as well as read (play) information.

than records.) In computer terminology, the process of playing a disk is called *reading* and the process of recording onto a disk is called *writing*. (Hence the term read/write head.)

Computer disks come in two basic types: floppy and hard.

▶ *Floppy disks* *generally hold less information and are slower than hard disks. They can also be removed from their disk drives. In other words, you can "play" different floppy disks in the same drive by removing one and inserting another. The word floppy refers to the disk itself, which is a very thin, round piece of plastic on which information is magnetically recorded (much as music is recorded on the surface of plastic cassette tapes). This decidedly floppy disk is enclosed inside a sturdier, unfloppy plastic jacket to protect it from dust, scratches, liquid, and the oils on your fingers—all of which can erase or scramble the information recorded on the disk's surface. The disks used in personal computers are usually either 3½ or 5¼ inches in diameter.*

▶ *Hard disks* *hold more information and spin faster than floppies (about twenty times faster). They are also permanently enclosed within their disk drives. You can think of hard disks as records that are encased inside their record players so that the record and the record player function as a single unit. Contrary to what you may think, hard disks are not always larger than floppies; they're simply capable of packing information more tightly, and therefore can store more data in the same amount of space.*

DISK DRIVES

Computer disks and disk drives come in two basic types: floppy and hard.

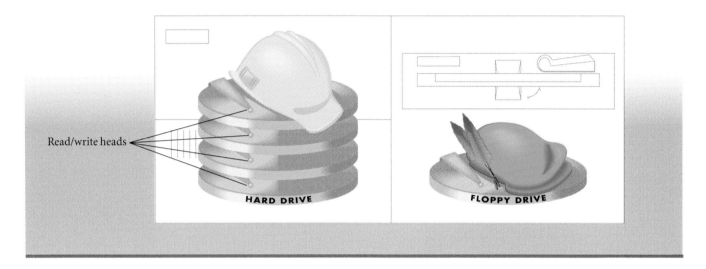

Read/write heads

HARD DRIVE

FLOPPY DRIVE

Most hard drives contain multiple disks, often called platters, *which are stacked vertically inside the drive. Typically, each disk has its own pair of read/write heads. Since you never remove hard disks, hard-disk drives do not contain doors or slots, as do their floppy counterparts. This means that the drive itself is completely invisible (and sometimes hard to locate) from outside the system unit. In most cases, the hard drive is adjacent to the floppy drive.*

These days, most personal computers have one hard-disk drive and either one or two floppy-disk drives. In general, you'll use hard disks as the primary repository of data and programs—the place you store the information that you work with day to day. You'll use floppy drives mainly as a means of getting information into and out of your computer, by transferring information to and from floppy disks. Floppy drives are, in this sense, like doors to the outside world. In particular, you use floppy-disk drives to:

▶ *Install new programs, by copying them from floppy disks to your hard disk.*

▶ *Make extra copies of programs or data for safekeeping by copying from the hard disk to floppies. This is known as* making backups. *If you are working on the great American novel, for example, you will keep your main working copy on the hard disk but keep an extra copy on a floppy disk, in case there is a mechanical problem with the hard-disk drive or you accidentally erase the original. If you want to be completely safe, you might even keep this duplicate copy in a safe deposit box or a fireproof safe.*

▶ *Archive data that you don't use regularly (and therefore don't want taking up space on your hard disk) but that you don't want to discard altogether.*

▶ *Transfer data from one computer to another, by copying information from one computer's hard disk to a set of floppies, taking the floppies over to the other computer, and copying from those floppies onto the hard disk.*

There are several things that you need to know to work with floppy disks, including how to determine which type will work in your disk drive, how to prepare them for use, how to insert and remove them, and how to take care of them. (You'll learn to do all of these in the next chapter.)

These days, many programs are stored on CD-ROMs instead of floppy disks. As mentioned, a CD-ROM is a type of compact disc that is meant to be "played" in a computer. CD-ROM stands for Compact Disc-Read Only Memory. You'll learn more about ROM (read only memory) soon. For now, you just need to know that "read only" means that while you can "read" (access) the programs or data that are stored on CD-ROMs, you cannot easily "write" (store) your own data or programs on them using most CD-ROM drives. (Recording information on a CD-ROM requires a special type of drive.) The reason that so many programs are now stored on CD-ROMs is that CD-ROMs can hold much more information than floppy disks: A single CD-ROM can hold more data than 300 floppies.

You can only use CD-ROMs if your computer has a CD-ROM drive. Most CD-ROM drives sit inside the system unit, and from the outside, look pretty similar to floppy-disk drives. These types of drives are known as internal CD-ROM drives. It's also possible to buy external CD-ROM drives. These drives work the same as the internal ones, but they come in their own little boxes which sit outside the system unit and are attached to the system unit via a cable. You'll learn more about CD-ROM drives in Chapter 8.

Although disk drives and CD-ROM drives are by far the most common means of storing data and programs, they are not the only ones. Other storage technologies include tape drives, magneto-optical drives, Syquest drives, and Bernoulli boxes. These storage devices are also discussed in Chapter 8.

THE MANY ROLES OF A FLOPPY-DISK DRIVE

You can use floppies to copy data from one computer to another, copying from hard disk to floppy on one computer and from floppy to hard disk on the other.

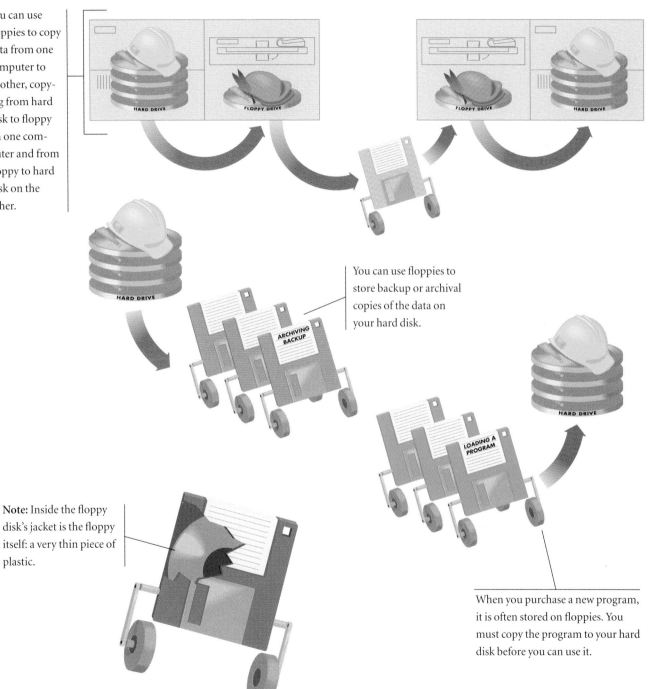

You can use floppies to store backup or archival copies of the data on your hard disk.

Note: Inside the floppy disk's jacket is the floppy itself: a very thin piece of plastic.

When you purchase a new program, it is often stored on floppies. You must copy the program to your hard disk before you can use it.

MEMORY: THE ELECTRONIC DESKTOP

Given what you've learned so far, you might assume that when you run a program, the CPU fetches instructions from the disk one at a time and executes them, returning to the disk drive every time it finishes a single step. If this were actually the way computers worked, they would be so slow as to be unusable.

Left to their own devices, most personal computer CPUs are capable of executing between one million and one hundred million instructions per second. But because the disk drive is mechanical—that is, composed of moving parts—it cannot deliver program instructions anywhere near that fast. Reading an instruction from the disk involves both rotating the disk so that the proper section is below one of the read/write heads and then moving the head closer to or farther from the center of the disk until it is positioned directly above the spot where the instruction is recorded. Even on a hard-disk drive, this process generally takes between 9 and 25 milliseconds (millionths of a second). CD-ROM drives are slower still.

Now if the CPU can execute millions of instructions per second and the disk drive can only deliver, say, one hundred thousand instructions per second, you have the equivalent of an assembly line in which one person on the line (the CPU) is moving somewhere between 10 and 100 times faster than the previous one (the disk drive). If this were really the way your computer worked, the speed of the CPU would be wasted while it waited for the disk drive to deliver the next instruction.

For the computer to function efficiently, it therefore needs some repository of information that is capable of keeping pace with the CPU. This extra piece is called *random access memory*, usually referred to as RAM or simply memory for short.

Physically, RAM consists of a set of separate integrated circuits (each of which looks something like a small CPU chip) which are often mounted on fiberglass boards; in practice, however, memory is treated as a single, contiguous set of storage bins. One useful way to envision memory is as a set of mailboxes, like those inside a post office. Each mailbox holds a single character, and the entire collection of boxes is numbered sequentially. (In computer jargon, the mailboxes are called *bytes* and their numbers are known as *memory addresses*.)

Like the CPU chip, memory chips store and transmit information electronically. Sending an instruction from memory to the CPU is therefore a simple matter of transmitting electrical impulses. There is no waiting for a disk to spin or a read/write head to move to the proper position.

CPU SPEED VERSUS DISK-DRIVE SPEED

It takes even a fast hard drive 10 to 100 times as long to deliver an instruction as it takes the CPU to execute one.

Because the CPU can move information in and out of memory so quickly, it uses memory as a kind of electronic desktop—the place it stores whatever it is working on this instant or plans to work with shortly. When you tell your computer that you want to use a particular program, for example, the first thing it does is find the program on your hard disk (or, less often a CD-ROM) and copy it into memory. This process is known as *loading* a program. This gets the comparatively slow process of reading instructions from disk over with at the start. Once the entire program has been loaded, the CPU can quickly read instructions from memory as needed.

Although you can compare placing a program in memory to moving it from a file cabinet (the disk) to your desktop (memory), there is also one important difference. Placing something on your desktop entails removing it from its usual storage place in the file cabinet. In contrast, when you place a program in memory, you do not remove it from anywhere. Instead, you make the equivalent of a photocopy of the program, and place the copy in memory. The original copy of the program stays on the disk, ready to load again whenever you need it.

STEPS INVOLVED IN LOADING A PROGRAM INTO MEMORY

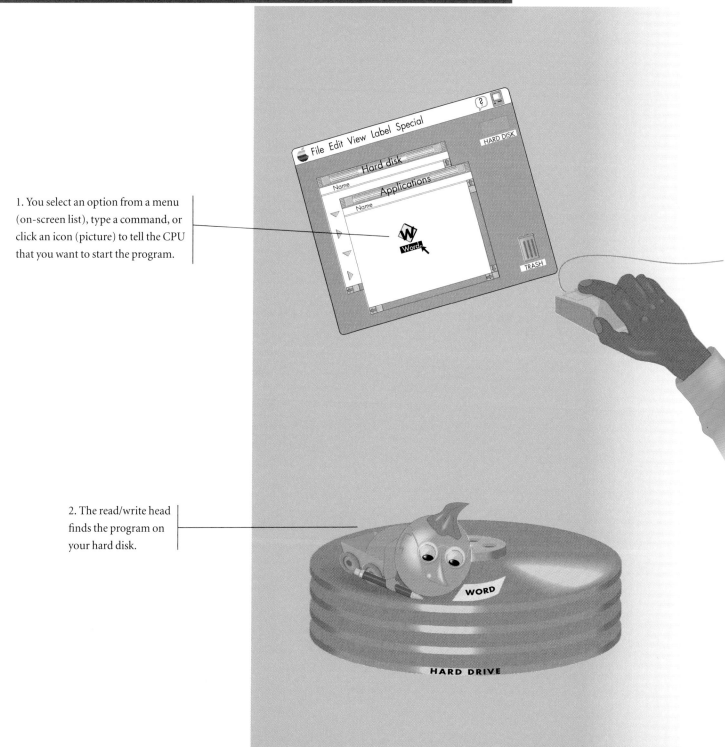

1. You select an option from a menu (on-screen list), type a command, or click an icon (picture) to tell the CPU that you want to start the program.

2. The read/write head finds the program on your hard disk.

3. Your computer copies
the program from disk
into memory.

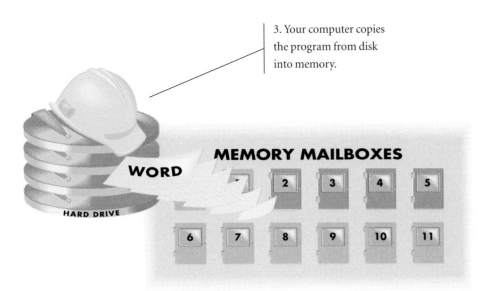

4. The program appears
on your screen and you
can start using it.

The first program that is loaded into memory in every work session is the operating system. In fact, just about the first thing your CPU does when you turn on your computer is hunt for and load the operating system program. This program then remains in memory until you turn off your computer. When you load application programs, they always share the electronic desktop with the operating system, and, in fact, application programs need to have an operating system around in order to function.

SAVING DATA

Programs are not the only thing that the CPU places in memory. It stores data there as well. As shown in the figure "Data Stored in Memory," each character that you enter, including any spaces, occupies a single "mailbox" of storage space.

There is one fundamental problem with housing data in memory, however: As soon as your computer is turned off, the contents of memory are erased. This means that if you accidentally kick your computer's power cord in the midst of typing a letter, for example, everything you have typed is lost. It also means that you cannot rely on memory if you want to return to a piece of work the next day or next week, since you will undoubtedly turn off your computer in between. Data is also erased from memory whenever you leave an application program, because the CPU assumes you'll need to use the space for the next task you choose to tackle. If you are using a spreadsheet program, for example, the CPU erases the spreadsheet you were using from memory as soon as you exit that program, just as you might clear your desk when you finish a particular project.

In order to protect your work and to store it for use in future work sessions, you need to copy it from memory to a more secure storage place: namely, a disk. This process is known as *saving* your data. Don't worry about how, exactly, you tell your computer to save data; the procedure may vary from one application program to another or, at minimum, from operating system to operating system. For now, just focus on when you need to save and why.

In general, you should save your data whenever:

▶ *You are done working with it and are ready to start on another project (if you finish typing one letter and want to start another one, for example)*

▶ *You are ready to leave an application program*

For your convenience, most programs automatically ask if you want to save when you give the command to exit or to close a document. You should also save to disk whenever you

DATA STORED IN MEMORY

Every character of data that you enter (including a space) occupies a single "mailbox" (byte) in memory.

MEMORY MAILBOXES

0	1	2	3	4	5
D	E	A	R		M
6	7	8	9	10	11
S	.		P	R	U
12	13	14	15	16	17
N	D	I	M	P	L
18	19	20	21	22	23
E	:		Y	O	U
24	25	26	27	28	29
	H	A	V	E	
30	31	32	33	34	35
W	O	N		T	E
36	37	38	39	40	41
N		T	R	I	L
42	43	44	45	46	47
L	I	O	N		D

have been working for a while and want to protect the work you have done so far. This protects your data against power failures, kicked power cords, or drastic mistakes.

How often you should save depends on what you are doing and how easy it would be to do over. A good rule of thumb is that you should save your work every time you'd be unhappy if you had to do it over again. For some people, this will be once an hour; for others, it will be every two minutes. Bear in mind that when you save something, you are not removing it from memory. You are simply making a copy and then storing that copy on disk. You can then continue modifying the original if you like.

NOTE *Occasionally, you will enter some data that you have no need or desire to save. For example, you may use a word processing program to type a short letter that you need to print but don't need to store for future reference. Or you may load your spreadsheet program to perform a few calculations and have no need to save the results. In such cases, simply leave the program without saving your data. (Most programs also have a command for throwing out the data in memory without leaving the program, in case you want to discard your work and start again.)*

Once something is stored on disk, you can always copy it back into memory when you want to use it again. This is known as *retrieving* data or as *opening* a document or file. (Again, don't worry about the exact command for doing this, since it may vary from one program to the next.) As soon as the data is copied back into memory, the data reappears on your screen and you can modify it if you like. In general, any data that appears on screen while you're using an application program is currently in memory, although not all the data in memory may fit on your screen at one time.

A QUICK REVIEW

So far, we have talked about three different types of information being stored in memory: the operating system, application programs, and data. Just to review:

▶ *When you first turn on your computer, the CPU automatically copies the operating system program from the disk into memory.*

▶ *When you tell your computer that you want to run an application program, the CPU copies that program from disk into memory (alongside the operating system).*

▶ *When you type in new data while working in an applications program or retrieve data from disk, the data is placed in memory as well, alongside the applications program and the operating system. The data remains in memory until you either issue a command to close the file (remove it from memory) or leave the application program. Whenever you leave an application program, both the program itself and any data that goes with it are removed from memory. The operating system stays put until you turn off your computer.*

You may find it helpful to think of these three different types of information as a set of layers, each of which depends on the one below. The operating system is at the bottom layer, followed by the applications program, followed by the data. If you unload any one layer, the layers above are erased as well. If you unload the operating system—for example, by turning off or restarting your system—memory is completely erased. If you unload an application program from memory, by issuing that program's exit or quit command, both the program and the data you were working on inside that program are erased. If you erase just the top layer—the data you are working with—the application/program and operating system remain loaded and ready to use.

PROGRAMS AND DATA IN MEMORY

When you are using an application program, there are three layers of information stored in memory.

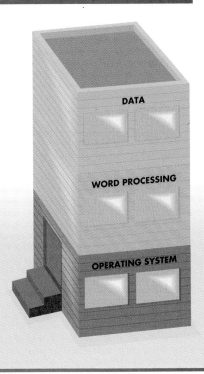

WHAT'S SO RANDOM ABOUT RAM?

As mentioned, the type of memory we have been discussing—that is, the memory used to temporarily house programs and data—is often referred to as *random access memory* or *RAM* for short. In order to understand where this name comes from, you need to know more about how information is stored in memory.

As mentioned, the CPU treats memory as a set of numbered storage bins, rather like a collection of mailboxes, each one of which holds a single character. In older computers, the CPU had to access the mailboxes (bytes) in numerical order, starting from the first mailbox and moving forward until it reached the one that actually contained the desired information. This is known as *sequential access*. With the development of random access memory, the CPU can go directly to whichever mailbox it is interested in.

You can conceptualize the difference between random access memory and this older type of sequential access memory by comparing records or CDs to cassette tapes. If you want to listen to the fifth song on a cassette tape (sequential access), you have to start at the beginning of the tape and move past the first four songs, even if you fast forward the tape. With a record or CD (random access), you can go directly to song five. Disks are random access devices, too. Rather than starting from the outside of the disk and reading inward, or the inside and reading outward, the read/write head can jump directly to the spot where the desired data is stored.

There is actually a second type of memory used in personal computers, in addition to RAM. This second type of memory is named *read-only memory*, or *ROM* (rhymes with Tom). Unlike RAM chips, ROM chips have software (program instructions) permanently etched into their circuitry. For this reason, ROM is often referred to as *firmware*—since it's kind of halfway in between hardware and software.

Unfortunately, the terminology here is a bit misleading, since both RAM and ROM allow random access. If the point is to distinguish RAM from ROM, then RAM would more properly be called read/write memory, meaning that you can not only retrieve (read) information from RAM; you can also record (write) information to it. In contrast, with read-only memory, instructions are frozen into the circuitry. The feature that sets RAM apart from ROM is its changeability: the fact that you can alter its contents at will.

The other difference between RAM and ROM is how long their memories last. RAM is short-term memory; it forgets everything it knows as soon as you turn off your computer. ROM is long-term memory; it remembers everything it has ever known as long as it lives. It's the elephant of the memory kingdom.

In personal computers, ROM is generally used to store some part of the operating system. In IBM-type computers, only a small part of the operating system is stored in ROM—just enough to get the hardware up and running and to tell the CPU how to locate and load the rest of the operating system from disk. In Macintosh computers, much more of the operating system is stored in ROM.

NOTE *Since ROM is not changeable, you will never have to deal with it yourself. It's just another part of your computer to know about, even if you never need to see it, touch it, or think about it much at all.*

RANDOM ACCESS VS. SEQUENTIAL ACCESS

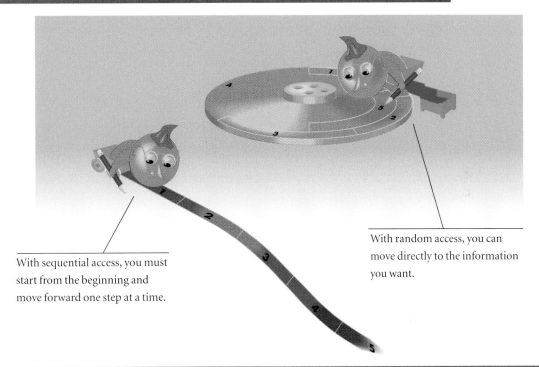

With sequential access, you must start from the beginning and move forward one step at a time.

With random access, you can move directly to the information you want.

READ-ONLY MEMORY (ROM) AND RANDOM-ACCESS MEMORY (RAM)

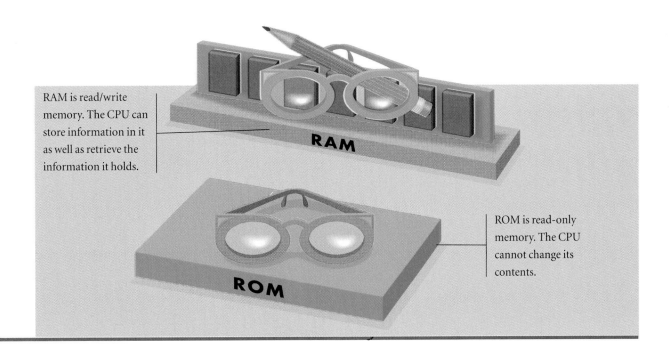

RAM is read/write memory. The CPU can store information in it as well as retrieve the information it holds.

ROM is read-only memory. The CPU cannot change its contents.

RAM

ROM

WHAT'S IN A BYTE: HOW MEMORY AND DISKS ARE MEASURED

As mentioned, the term *byte* means the amount of space required to represent a single character—a letter, a number, or even a space. (In our mailboxes analogy, it's a single mailbox.) This term is used regardless of whether you're talking about space in memory, on a disk, or on any other storage medium. Since many, many bytes are often required to accommodate an entire word processing document, spreadsheet, database, or program, computerese includes terms for several larger units of measurement.

▶ A kilobyte *(often abbreviated as simply K) is 1,024 bytes. To a computer's way of thinking, 1,024 is a nice round number. (Computers "think" in units of two, and 1,024 is 2 to the 10th power.) To us, however, it's a little unwieldy so most people think of a kilobyte as "around 1,000" bytes. So when someone tells you that they have a computer with 640K of RAM, they mean a computer that has 640 kilobytes or approximately 640,000 characters worth of random access memory. A floppy disk that holds 360K of data can accommodate a little more than 360,000 characters.*

▶ The term megabyte *(abbreviated as MB or simply M) means a kilobyte squared (1,024 times 1,024), or approximately one million bytes.*

▶ The term gigabyte *means a kilobyte to the third power (1,024 times 1,024 times 1,024), or approximately one billion bytes.*

While a few years ago, most computers had less than a megabyte of RAM, these days, many have as much as 8 or even 16MB. Hard disks typically hold between 40MB and 600MB, although there are some that store gigabytes. Just to give you a measuring stick, a typical printed page of text, using single spacing, contains 2,500 to 3,000 characters. Therefore, 1MB holds close to 400 pages of single-spaced text.

So why do you care how much memory and disk space your computer has? Because it determines what kinds of work you can do. The amount of memory in your computer dictates which programs you can run. (Many Windows programs, for example, run best with 8MB or more of memory, and you cannot run them at all on computers with less than four megabytes.) The size of your hard disk is important because it defines how many programs and how much data you can store on your computer at once. In general, you will want enough room on your hard disk to accommodate all the programs and data that you work with regularly. Otherwise, you'll waste time copying data or programs to and from floppies.

These days, each program you install requires from 1 to 25MB of disk space, not including room for data. The easiest way to find out if you have enough memory and/or disk space for a particular program is to read the program's packaging or user's manual.

You'll learn how to find out how much room you have in memory and on your disk when you learn about operating systems in Chapters 5 and 6.

NOTE   *Bear in mind that you can almost always add memory to your computer, by buying additional memory chips and having them installed. (If you are both brave and unintimidated by computer manuals, you may even be able to install them yourself.)*

INSIDE THE SYSTEM UNIT

Now that you know what the CPU, memory chips, and disk drives do, you're ready to learn about where they reside and how they're connected. In most computer systems, all three of these components are housed inside the system unit. (Some computer systems have an external disk drive instead of or in addition to the ones inside the system unit.)

The centerpiece of the system unit is a printed circuit board, known as the *motherboard*, which holds the CPU chip and its support circuitry. (You may also hear the motherboard referred to as the system board or a planar board.) The motherboard generally lies face up at the bottom of the system unit.

The motherboard contains several other types of chips, in addition to the CPU, that help the CPU perform its job. These support chips include:

▶ *The clock chip, which serves as the computer's metronome, setting the pace at which the various components function*

▶ *One or more ROM chips containing some part of the operating system software*

▶ *In some computers, a math coprocessor chip, which assists the CPU in performing specific types of mathematical operations*

Finally, the motherboard usually includes slots or sockets for memory chips. In most cases, memory comes in the form of small, plug-in boards call SIMMs (short for single in-line memory modules), each of which includes eight or nine memory chips.

Aside from the motherboard, the system unit includes disk drives (usually one or two floppy drives and one hard drive) and a power supply. The power supply brings in power from the wall socket and supplies it to the motherboard. It also contains your computer's

A TYPICAL PC MOTHERBOARD

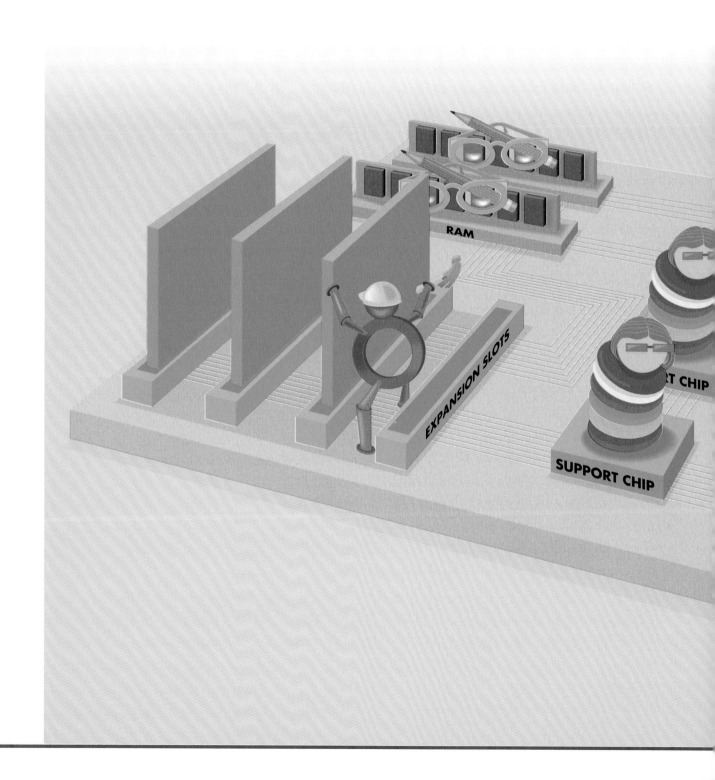

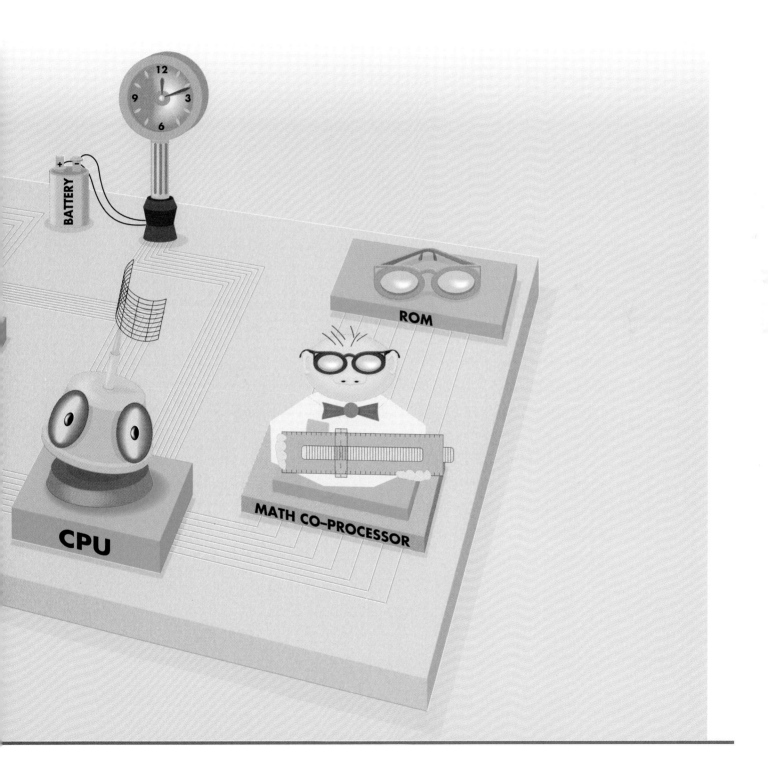

BATTERY

ROM

MATH CO-PROCESSOR

CPU

on/off switch and a place to attach the power cord that connects the system unit to a power outlet. The power supply unit usually contains a fan, to prevent the various chips from overheating. If your system includes a tape drive, it probably resides in the system unit as well.

Most computers also contain additional circuit boards, commonly known as *expansions boards*, which fit into slots on the motherboard. (The slots themselves are known as *expansion slots*; think of them as parking spaces for circuit boards.) Expansion boards sit at the back of the system unit at a right angle to the motherboard itself. The purpose of most expansion boards is to allow an I/O (input/output) device—like a display monitor or a scanner—to communicate with the CPU.

The advantage of this design—a motherboard containing all the standard circuitry of the computer and a set of expansion slots that allow you to plug in additional circuitry as needed—is that it allows you to customize your system. Two people can buy essentially the same computer but add on very different sets of peripherals. This design also allows you to easily add new parts to your computer as your needs change or as new forms of computer paraphernalia are invented.

Expansion boards that are designed to serve as intermediaries between the CPU and some device outside the system unit have *ports* on one end. Ports are sockets that protrude from the back of the system unit. You can think of them as places where you can "dock" various external devices, plugging them into a circuit board that, in turn, connects them to the CPU. (Expansion boards that are designed for components inside the system unit—such as disk drives—do not include ports.)

Finally, all motherboards contain a *bus*: a set of circuitry designed to carry data and instructions back and forth between various devices on the board itself. You might think of the bus as a collection of elaborate, high-speed conveyor belts. The bus not only carries data and instructions back and forth between the CPU and memory (both RAM and ROM), it also connects the CPU and memory to any expansion boards that are plugged into the motherboard.

INSIDE THE SYSTEM UNIT

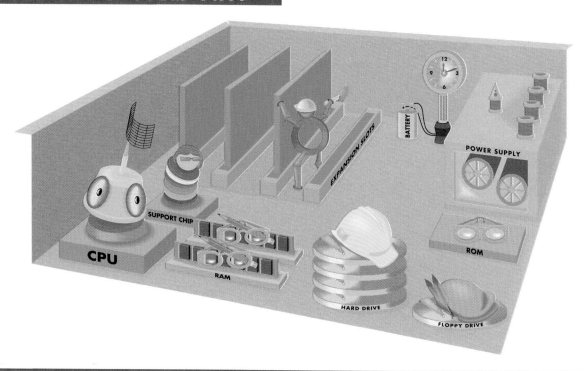

CHAPTER

3

YOUR COMPUTER'S FILING SYSTEM

In order to use your computer effectively, you need to understand a bit about its filing system, namely, how it stores and organizes information on disks. This chapter begins by discussing files, the repositories of programs and data on disks and other long-term storage media. You will learn about rules for file names, about file formats used by various application programs, and about the organization of files into groups known as folders or subdirectories. The second half of the chapter delves into detail about the disks themselves—the medium on which files are generally stored. By the time you're through, you will know how to choose the right type of disks for your floppy-disk drive(s), protect floppies from accidental damage, prepare new floppy disks for use, care for your hard disk, use CD-ROMs, and ward off computer viruses.

WHAT ARE FILES?

All data on disks is stored in files. A *file* is simply a named collection of information stored on a disk. There are two basic types of files: *program files*, which contain instructions to your computer, and *data files*, which contain data that you enter through an application program. In the worlds of Macintosh computing and Windows 95, data files are usually referred to as *documents*, regardless of their actual contents. A spreadsheet or mailing list file is considered to be as much a document as is a wordprocessing file, for example.

Unless you delve into programming at some point, most of the files you create will be data files. Every time you enter data in an application program—be it text, numbers, pictures, or anything else—and then save it for the first time, you are creating a new data file. And since all files, by definition, have names, the first thing that happens when you issue the command to save is that the program asks you to assign a file name.

NOTE *In some programs, data is saved to disk automatically. Many database programs work this way. When you first set up a database, you create a file to hold your data. Then as you enter the information on each customer (or product or order placed or whatever you are storing in your database), that information is automatically saved to disk as soon as you move to the next customer (or product or order).*

In general, every file on a particular disk must have a unique name. (We'll explain the qualifications to this rule a little later in this chapter, after you learn about folders.) This way,

FILES ON A DISK

A file is a named collection of information stored on a disk.

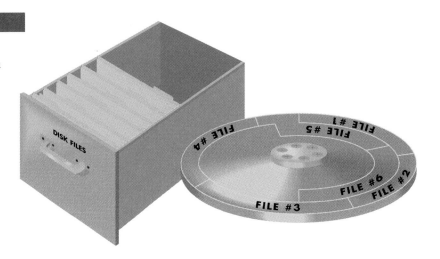

when you tell your computer to find the file LETTER.DOC and copy it into memory, it knows exactly which file you mean. It doesn't need to determine *which* LETTER.DOC.

You must keep this law of unique file names in mind when copying files. If you copy a file named Letter to Fred from disk 1 to disk 2, and disk 2 already has a file named Letter to Fred, the old version of the letter is completely and permanently replaced by the new one. If you are using a Macintosh or Windows, you will be asked to confirm that you want to replace the existing file. If you are working directly with DOS, however, you receive no warning at all. The file is simply replaced, and there is nothing you can do to rescue it afterwards.

SAVING, RETRIEVING, AND RESAVING FILES

As you learned in Chapter 2, once something is stored on disk, you can always copy it back into memory when you want to use it again (just as you can fetch a particular document from your file cabinet). This is known as *retrieving* data or *opening* a file.

Just as when you load a program from disk to memory, when you retrieve data, the original copy of that data remains in place and intact on the disk. If you then change the copy in memory, you end up with two different versions: an older version on disk and a newer version in memory. The same situation occurs when you save a new document to disk but continue working on it. You might, for example, get halfway through writing a letter and then save your data to disk. You then have two separate and independent versions of the same letter: one (the older one) on disk and another (the current one) in memory.

COPYING A FILE ONE ON TOP OF ANOTHER

When you copy a file to a disk, that file replaces any existing file with the same file name.

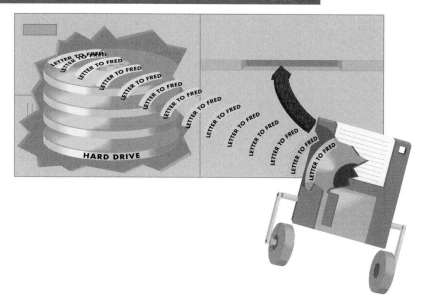

This has a couple of implications:

▶ *First, if you like the new version better than the old one, you must remember to save it before you leave the application program. Otherwise you'll have only the old version of the document (the one on disk) and your changes will be lost.*

▶ *Second, if you decide that you prefer the older version, you can close the document (remove it from memory) without saving it. When you do so, the version of the document currently in memory is erased. You can then retrieve the old version (the one on disk) and start amending it again. This can be extremely convenient when you completely bungle an edit and want to start all over.*

Whenever you decide to save a file that has already been saved once, you need to decide whether to use the same file name as last time or a new file name. As mentioned, you cannot generally store two files with the same file name on the same disk. In fact, if you copy a file to a particular disk and the disk already contains a file of that name, the new one replaces the old one. The same issue arises when you resave a file. Suppose you create a budget in your spreadsheet program, for example. Halfway through the process, you save your data, then you revise it, and save it again. If you resave it under the same name that you used the first time, the new version will replace the old one on disk. Most of the time, this is exactly what you want. If you want to retain the old version of the file as well as the newly revised one, however, you must assign a different name to the new version.

In Windows and in the Macintosh operating system, there are separate commands for resaving a document under its existing name and for saving it under a new name. (You use the Save As option on the File menu rather than the Save command when you want to save something under a new name.) In some DOS programs, there's only one save command, and you need to remember that saving a file under the same name means replacing the old version. Many application programs also ask for confirmation when you try to save a file under an existing file name.

FILE FORMATS

Most application programs have their own unique format for storing data, a format that only makes sense to that one program. For example, the format in which the Lotus 1-2-3 spreadsheet program stores data is not the same as the format used by the Excel spreadsheet. The format that the Word for Windows word processing program uses is not the same as the format that WordPerfect uses.

In general, if you want to see what's inside a particular data file, you need to look at the file from inside the program in which it was created. For example, if you want to see what's inside an Excel spreadsheet file, you need to look at it from within the Excel program. If you try to look at it from within a word processing program or even from within another spreadsheet program, you will probably just see a lot of nonsense characters on your screen.

Special codes that tell the program how to arrange and format the data distinguish the file format used by one program from that used by another. Each word processing program has its own code for representing italics or page breaks, for example.

Many programs have commands for importing and exporting data in the formats used by other programs. Word for Windows can import WordPerfect files, for example, translating all the WordPerfect formatting codes to their Word for Windows equivalents.

ORGANIZING A HARD DISK: FOLDERS/SUBDIRECTORIES

Hard disks often hold thousands of files. Rather than piling this entire collection of files in a single heap, most people organize their files into groups. These groups are generally known as *folders* in the world of Macs and Windows 95 and as *subdirectories* in DOS and

ASCII AND TEXT-ONLY FILES

Occasionally, a program does not have any tools at all for importing a file created by another program and interpreting the special codes that file contains. In this case, you can save the file in a generic format, without any of the special formatting codes specific to one particular program. The most commonly used generic format is one known as *ASCII* or *text-only*. (ASCII stands for American Standard Code for Information Interchange, and is a set of standardized codes used to represent all the characters you can produce on a typewriter, plus a few others.) When you save a file in ASCII or text-only format, your program strips out any proprietary codes—that is, codes that only it knows how to read—leaving you with plain-vanilla text; any special attributes such as underlining or unusual typefaces will be lost in this translation process. Once you have saved a file in ASCII or text-only format, you can open it in almost any other program, although you may need to specify the file format when you open the file or issue a special import command. Consult your program documentation for information on saving and using ASCII or text-only files.

older versions of Windows. You can think of folders/subdirectories as manila folders in a file drawer, each one of which can hold several individual files.

Just as when you set up a manual filing system, when you organize a hard disk you decide for yourself how many folders you need and what to store in each. Often you will place each application program and its associated files in a separate folder. For example, you might have one for your spreadsheet program, another for your word processing program, and a third for your accounting program. Many people prefer to create two separate folders for each application—one to hold the program itself (this one is usually created automatically when you install the program) and another to hold the data files created in that program. You might, for example, have one folder for your word processing program and another for your word processing documents. Since in most operating systems it is fairly easy to copy to a floppy disk all the files in a particular folder, storing nothing but data files in a folder makes it easy to create a backup copy of your data.

If you have many different types of data, you might also create separate folders for each type. You might create one folder for business correspondence and another for letters to friends, or one for correspondence, another for reports, and a third for invoices.

You can also create folders within folders if you like. For example, you might create a folder for word processing that contains your word processing program and then, within that folder, create another folder for the documents you have created and saved.

In short, the filing system you create on a disk is as individual as the one you create in a filing cabinet.

The process of actually creating and manipulating folders varies a bit from one operating system to the next, and is therefore covered in later chapters. For now, just be aware that creating a new folder always involves entering a unique name. The rules for naming folders are the same as the rules for naming individual files in your particular operating system. (You'll learn the rules for naming files and folders in Windows 95 and the Mac operating system in Chapters 5 and 6, respectively.)

Now that you know about folders, we can modify an earlier rule: Files in the same folder must have unique names. You can, however, have files of the same name in two different folders on the same disk.

WORKING WITH FLOPPIES

As you learned in Chapter 2, there are two basic types of disks: floppy disks and hard disks. Hard disks serve as the primary repository of data. Floppy disks are mainly used for copying data to and from your hard disk, acting as a kind of gateway between your computer and the outside world.

Floppy disks come in two sizes: 5¼ inch and 3½ inch. Which size disk you use depends on the type of floppy-disk drive you have in your computer. The floppy-disk drives in Macintosh computers always use 3½-inch disks. On PCs, drives designed to read 5¼-inch disks used to be the norm, but 3½-inch drives are becoming increasingly standard and the 5¼-inch variety is now almost obsolete. Some PCs have two floppy-disk drives, in which case one may take 5¼-inch disks and one 3½-inch disks.

As described in the last chapter, the part of the disk that you see and touch is the outside cover—the disk's jacket. Inside this jacket is a flimsy piece of plastic on which data is magnetically recorded. The reason that disks have jackets is that they are extremely sensitive: Scratches and spilled liquids are enough to permanently destroy them, and the oils on your fingers are enough to wreck the magnetic patterns used to record data on their surface.

On 5¼-inch floppies, the jacket contains an oblong read-write hole through which the surface of the disk itself is exposed. When you place the disk in the drive, the drive's read/write head (the part that reads and records data) is positioned right above this hole. When you handle 5¼-inch disks, you therefore need to be careful not to touch this exposed portion of the disk. To be safe, hold the disk jacket by the label. You should also avoid writing on a disk label with a ballpoint pen, since the pressure of the point can damage your data.

A FILING SYSTEM WITH FOLDERS/SUBDIRECTORIES

You can create folders within other folders. A word processing folder, for example, might contain separate folders for reports, memos, and letters.

You don't need to worry about accidentally touching or scratching the surface of 3½-inch disks, because the disk remains protected until it is actually inserted into the drive. When you insert a 3½-inch disk into a drive, the metal shutter is pushed to the side, exposing the disk's surface so that the read/write heads can read and record information.

With both sizes of disks, you do need to be wary of magnets. Any exposure to magnets can scramble or erase the information recorded on the disk.

Protecting your disk from magnets may take more vigilance than you realize. Magnets lurk in many unsuspected places, including many paper clip holders (that's why the clips stick to the rim of the holder) and various other office accessories, including some document holders. Since the coil for your telephone becomes magnetized every time your phone rings, it's wise to keep disks at least a few inches away from the phone. In addition, metal detectors in airports and government buildings sometimes use magnets to detect the presence of metal in your luggage, so you may want to remove disks from your luggage and show them to the attendant, just as you do with film.

You should also avoid storing floppy disks in extreme heat. (Do not, for example, leave a disk on your dashboard on a hot summer day.)

WARNING *When the read/write head is reading or writing to a disk, a small LCD (liquid crystal display) on the front of the drive lights up. Do not remove the disk until this light goes off, indicating that the process is complete.*

Occasionally, you may want to guard the files on a disk against accidental erasure or overwriting. (You may find this particularly useful for disks that contain programs.) You can do this by *write-protecting* or *locking* the disk—making it impossible for anyone to copy new files onto the disk or erase files already on it. (The term "write-protect" is generally used in the PC world; "lock" is used in the world of Macs.)

The procedure for write-protecting a disk depends on the disk type. 3½-inch disks have a tiny latch in the upper-right corner, which is usually closed. To write-protect such disks, turn the disk over and slide the latch downward so that a small window appears in the corner of the disk.

5¼-inch disks contain a notch in the upper-right corner. To write-protect such disks, you simply put something over this hole. When you buy disks, the box includes write-protect tabs (small sticky labels) designed for this purpose. If you don't have any write-protect tabs, just use part of a gummed label to cover up the notch.

NOTE *Some program disks are permanently write-protected—that is, they do not have a write-protect notch or latch. This prevents you from accidentally erasing the disk. You can often reuse these disks by taping over the notch.*

Whenever you buy floppy disks, you also need to decide whether to buy them already prepared for use with your type of computer and disk drive. Before you can store data on a disk, the surface of the disk needs to be subdivided in some way, so that data can be stored in specific, easily locatable spots. Otherwise, your computer would have an awful time finding

THE TWO TYPES OF FLOPPY DISKS

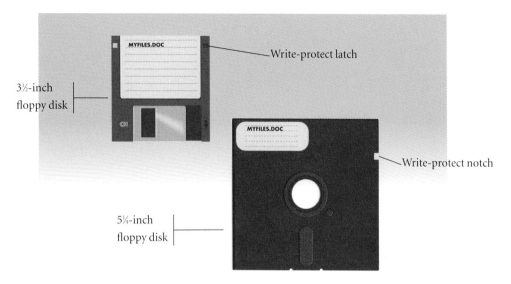

Write-protect latch

3½-inch floppy disk

Write-protect notch

5¼-inch floppy disk

files when you needed them. The process of subdividing a disk into sections by embedding magnetic codes on the disk's surface is known as *formatting*, or in the Mac world, *initializing*.

When you format a disk, your computer subdivides the disk in two different ways: drawing concentric circles (known as tracks) around the disk, and drawing straight lines (known as sectors) that divide the disk radially. It then uses these subdivisions to identify where your data is located on a disk. Just as people identify the seats in a stadium or a theater by section and row number, your computer identifies where files are "seated" by sector and track.

DISKS AND MAGNETS

In case you are interested, you need to keep disks away from magnets because of the way in which information is recorded on the surface of the disk. When your computer writes (records) information on a disk, electricity is sent through a coil of wire that is wrapped around a piece of iron within the read/write head. As you may remember from grade school science classes, whenever you happen to send electricity through a wire that is wrapped around a piece of iron, the piece of iron becomes magnetized. In effect, the read/write head is temporarily turned into a magnet. This magnet is then used to magnetize tiny particles of iron oxide (in a word, rust) on the disk's surface. As they become magnetized, different sets of particles are aligned in one of two configurations: one configuration represents ones, and the other, zeros. (Remember that computers store all types of information as numbers consisting entirely of zeros and ones.) Now since one magnet—a magnetized read/write head—is used to record the information on a disk, any other magnet has the capacity to realign the iron oxide particles and thereby scramble your computer's record of your data.

INSERTING FLOPPIES

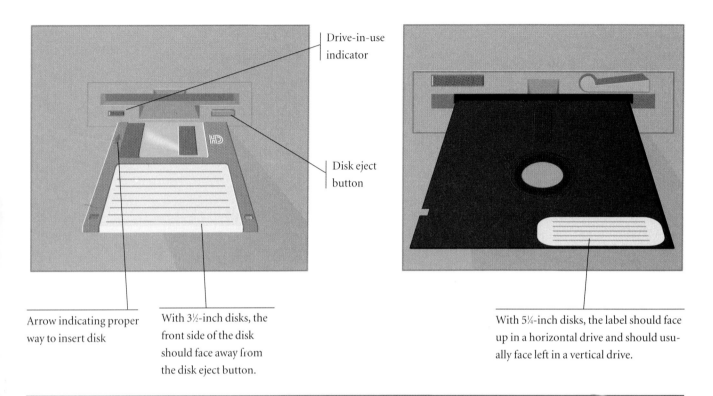

Drive-in-use indicator

Disk eject button

Arrow indicating proper way to insert disk

With 3½-inch disks, the front side of the disk should face away from the disk eject button.

With 5¼-inch disks, the label should face up in a horizontal drive and should usually face left in a vertical drive.

The process of formatting a disk is quite simple, but it may take a minute or two. On Macs and in Windows 95, whenever you insert an unformatted disk, you're asked whether you'd like to format/initialize it. To format a disk in DOS and older versions of Windows, you need to explicitly issue a format command. (For details, see your DOS or Windows manual.)

In most cases, it makes sense to buy disks that are preformatted for your type of computer and disk drive. These days, they cost little (if any) more than unformatted disks, and they save you the time and trouble of formatting disks yourself. The only real reason to buy unformatted disks is if you have both a Mac and a PC and want to be able to use the disks in either machine.

N O T E *Hard disks also need to be formatted before use, but they're almost always formatted when you buy them. If, for some reason, yours is not, find an expert to do it for you; the process is a bit too complicated for a novice.*

Different disk drives are designed to read different types of disks. The physical size of the disks is only part of the story. You also have to consider how closely the drive packs data

A FORMATTED DISK

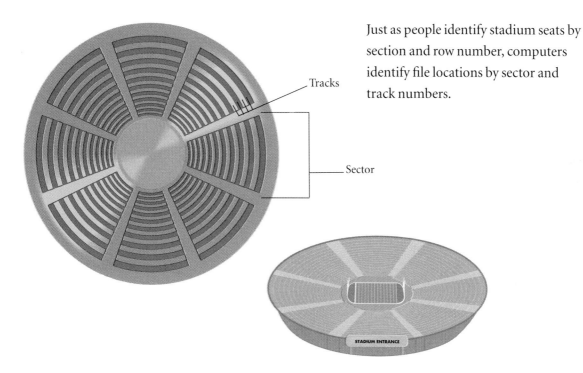

Tracks

Sector

Just as people identify stadium seats by section and row number, computers identify file locations by sector and track numbers.

on the disk. Some disk drives, known as high-density drives, store two or more times as much data on the same size disk as other, low-density drives.

You should be able to determine the type of disk drive you have by looking at your computer manual. If you can't find the manual, try getting a list of the files on a high-density disk. (You'll learn to do this in the chapter on your operating system.) If your drive can read the disk, it's a high-density drive. If it can't, you'll see an error message. Most new computers have only high-density drives. The whole issue of disk density is therefore slowly becoming moot as low-density drives become less and less common.

When you buy disks, you need to be sure to get the right type for your disk drive—not only the right size, but the right density as well. If you have a high-density drive, you should generally buy high-density disks (usually labeled as either double-sided high-density, or simply high-density). If you have a low-density drive, you should buy low-density disks. (Such disks are generally labeled as double-sided double-density disks since, unlike the disks used in some earlier computers, they can store data on both sides, twice as densely as some older-model disks.)

It is possible to use low-density disks in high-density drives. This allows you to trade floppy disks with computers that have low-density drives, even if you only have a high-density drive. However, some older high-density drives are not as well-behaved in handling low-density disks as you would like: While they read low-density disks beautifully, once you save any data on the disk, you may no longer be able to read the disk in a low-density drive. (In other words, as soon as you write to the disk using the high-density drive, you can only read it using a high-density drive.) If you have this problem with your high-density disk drive, try to limit your activity with low-density disks to reading (retrieving information) rather than writing (recording information). Low-density drives can neither read nor write to high-density disks.

THE CARE AND FEEDING OF HARD DISKS

Hard disks are not as vulnerable to dust and liquids as floppies are because they are sealed inside metal cases. They are, however, far from indestructible (as many discovered during recent California earthquakes). Knocking a computer off your desk or dropping it on the floor is an almost sure fire way to lose some data if not permanently damage the disk. Some hard disks are more sensitive than others, and may respond poorly to being repeatedly moved from desk to desk.

The basic rules of thumb for caring for a hard disk are

▶ *Don't drop your computer.*

▶ *Unless you have a laptop or other computer designed for travel, don't move it any more often than you have to.*

▶ *If you're relocating to another office or building, try to pack the computer in its original packing materials to cushion it during the move.*

▶ *Most importantly, back up your data regularly. Operate on the assumption that sooner or later, your disk will fail (probably a day or two before some crucial deadline).*

I've been representing each file as occupying a single discrete area of a disk. In reality, files are sometimes stored in segments scattered across the disk. The first part of a file may be wedged in between two other files, for example—perhaps in the space previously occupied by a file that you later deleted. Since not all of the file can fit in that space, your computer simply makes a note of where the next piece is stored (rather like the next clue in a treasure hunt). If there isn't enough room for the rest of the file in that second spot, your computer

FLOPPY DISK DENSITIES

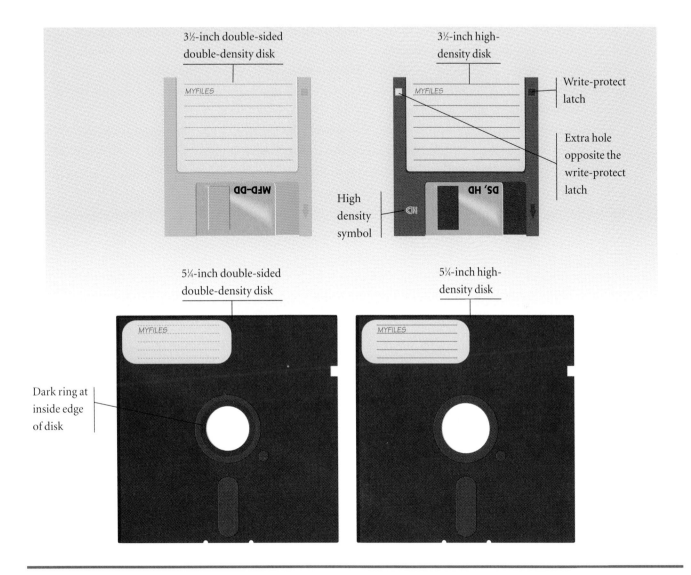

3½-inch double-sided double-density disk

MYFILES

MFD-DD

3½-inch high-density disk

MYFILES

DS, HD

Write-protect latch

Extra hole opposite the write-protect latch

High density symbol

5¼-inch double-sided double-density disk

MYFILES

5¼-inch high-density disk

MYFILES

Dark ring at inside edge of disk

makes a note of where the third piece is stored, and so on. Files stored in this way are said to be *fragmented*.

Over time, your hard disk will accumulate many of these fragmented files. Every time you load a fragmented file into memory, your computer has to jump from one part of the hard disk to another collecting all the file's different pieces. You can improve your computer's efficiency by periodically *defragmenting* your hard disk—that is, running a special program that rearranges data so that all the parts of each file occupy contiguous areas on the

MORE ABOUT HARD DRIVES

Most hard drives spin at a rate of somewhere between 3600 and 5400 revolutions per minute, generating the equivalent of gale-force winds at the edges of disk platters. While the disk is spinning, the read/write heads on hard disks do not actually touch the surface of the disk. Instead, they hover above or below the disk's surface, at a distance of millionths of an inch. (To make it a little more concrete, the distance between the read/write heads and a spinning disk is less than half the width of a particle of smoke.) When your computer is turned off, the read/write heads do come to rest on the surface of the disk, but only within a specified parking area that is reserved for this purpose and is never used for storing information.

If your hard drive malfunctions for some reason or you drop your computer on the floor, the read/write heads may fall onto the disk, permanently damaging it. This event, which is actually quite rare in modern-day hard drives, is known as a *head crash*. If someone tells you that their hard disk "crashed," they probably mean it underwent a head crash.

The small but essential gap that exists between the surface of the disk and the read/write heads explains why hard disks always live inside sealed containers, safe from such hazards as smoke, dust particles, and soda pop. Since the distance between the disk and the read/write head is half the size of a smoke particle, any encounter with such a particle would be like a high-speed go-cart running into a boulder.

disk. (You can compare this process to a bunch of people trading seats so a group of friends can sit together.)

Windows 95 has a built-in utility for defragmenting a hard disk; try looking up defragment in the Help system for details. (You'll learn to use the Windows 95 Help system in Chapter 5.) DOS started including a defragmentation utility with version 6; see your manual for details. If you are using a Mac or a version of DOS prior to 6, you'll need to purchase a disk defragmentation program.

USING CD-ROMs

CD-ROM stands for Compact Disc-Read Only Memory. A CD-ROM is a CD designed to be "played" by a computer. Although CD-ROMs look just like audio CDs, they only work in a computer and, more specifically, in a CD-ROM drive that you either install inside your system unit or attach to your system unit with a special cable. You can think of a CD-ROM drive as a computer-friendly version of a CD player. Unlike music CDs, which only contain audio information, CD-ROMs can hold graphics, text, and full motion video (movies), as well as sounds.

CD-ROMs have become increasingly popular in the last few years for a simple reason: they pack a huge amount of information into a small space at a low cost. A single CD-ROM can contain up to 660MB of data, enough to comfortably house an entire encyclopedia.

Because they can accommodate so much data, CD-ROMs are ideal for storing multimedia applications which tend to take up quite a lot of space—often more space than you might have or be willing to spare on your hard disk. CD-ROMs are also becoming a popular way of distributing large applications that you will actually copy to your hard disk. An application that might fill 10 or even 20 floppy disks will fit easily on a single CD-ROM, and installing it from a CD-ROM will take a lot less of your time (not to mention sparing you the bother of changing disks 10 or 20 times).

As their name implies, CD-ROMs are read-only—most CD-ROM drives allow your computer to read the information the discs contain but not to use them to store new information. (In other words, you can copy files from CD-ROMs to your hard disk, but not the other way around. You can also load programs from a CD-ROM into your computer's memory, but not save the contents of memory back to the disc.)

Recently, the cost of special CD-ROM drives that can record data on CDs has begun to drop dramatically. (As of this writing, these drives, which are called CD-Recordable or CD-R drives, can be had for as little as $1,000.) This has made it possible for even fairly small businesses to start using CD-ROMs to archive large amounts of old data or to make backup copies of current data. The price is still a bit steep for most individuals, however. So for most of us, CD-ROMs remain still truly "read only." They house only the data or programs the CD-ROM's publisher put on there originally—now and forever.

CD-ROM drives come in two basic flavors: internal and external. The only difference between the two is their location: internal drives fit into your computer's system unit and external ones sit in their own little boxes, which are connected to the system unit with cables. (An external CD-ROM drive is about the size of a phone book.) Internal drives are more common and slightly less expensive.

NOTE *Most multimedia CD-ROMs feature sound as well as pictures. In order to fully enjoy such CD-ROMs, you'll need a sound card and a set of speakers as well as a CD-ROM drive. You'll learn more about sound cards, speakers, and multimedia in Chapter 9.*

CD-ROM drives are generally categorized by speed: dual-speed, triple-speed, and quad-speed. The first CD-ROM drives spun exactly as fast as a stereo's CD player. This tempo turned out to be a bit slow for running programs, however, so manufacturers created double-speed CD-ROM drives, which transfer data from the CD-ROM to your computer twice as fast. More recently, they've started manufacturing triple-speed drives, which transfer data three times as fast as the original CD-ROM drives, and quad-speed drives which transfer data four times as fast. As of this writing, there are CD-ROM drives that transfer data at six times the rate of an audio CD player.

Which speed is right for you depends on your needs and your budget. If you're buying a drive mainly to install new software and to look things up in an encyclopedia on occasion, double-speed may be sufficient. Playing games is another story, however. If you spend hours on your computer tracking down Carmen Sandiego or slaying monsters in Doom, go for a quad-speed drive.

CD-ROM DRIVE SPEED

The speed at which the CD-ROM drive can read information from the disc and transfer it to your computer is known as its *data transfer rate*. The data transfer rate is 150K per second for single-speed drives, 300K for double-speed drives, 450K for triple-speed drives, and so on. (Remember that K stands for kilobyte, which is slightly more than 1,000 characters worth of data.) The other important benchmark for CD-ROM drives is *access speed*—the number of milliseconds (abbreviated as ms) it takes for the drive to locate a piece of data on a disc. You want a drive with an access speed of 200ms or less. When you're shopping for a CD-ROM drive, don't confuse the access speed with the data transfer rate. Data transfer rate is always measured in kilobytes (K) since it refers to the amount of data that can be transferred in a second; access speed is measured in milliseconds (ms).

Because information is recorded on CD-ROMs using light rather than magnetic read/write heads, CD-ROMs are not sensitive to magnets or magnetic fields the way disks are. They are susceptible to other hazards, however, such as dust, errant fingerprints, and soda pop. While a thumbprint or dust particle on an audio CD may not make much of a difference, the same thing on a CD-ROM can make the disc unusable or cause the CD-ROM's program to freeze when you try to run it. This means that you need to take special care not to touch the surface of the disc, especially the part near the middle that contains the data and programs. Be particularly leery of touching the unlabeled side of the disc, since that's where the CD-ROM drive reads the data. Instead, hold the disc by the edges or put your finger through the hole in the middle.

Because it's important to keep CD-ROMs clean, many CD-ROM drives employ devices known as caddys. A *caddy* is a plastic CD-ROM case with a metal door that slides back when you insert the disc into the CD-ROM drive. In most cases, you'll receive a caddy when you purchase either a CD-ROM drive or a computer that contains a CD-ROM drive. If not, you can buy one at computer supply stores. Always keep your CD-ROMs either in caddys, in CD-ROM holders, or in the plastic holders they came in; never leave them lying around on

HANDLING CD-ROMS

a desk or other surface. Try to keep them out of the sun as well: They don't fare well in high temperatures.

N O T E   *Although you can use one caddy for all your CD-ROMs if you load and unload them carefully, the best way to protect them is to purchase a separate caddy for each disc that you use often. Then you can reserve one caddy for escorting all your less critical discs into your CD-ROM drive. (You can mail order caddys for under $10; check the ads in computer magazines for details.)*

If one of your CD-ROMs becomes dusty, try blowing the dust off. Then wipe the disc using a clean, soft cotton cloth, wiping from the center out to the sides rather than in a circle. If the disc is actually dirty or you've spilled something on it, try either plain water or CD-ROM cleaner. (You should be able to find the latter at most computer stores.)

If your CD-ROM gets scratched, try one of the products designed to repair scratches on audio CDs. (You can usually purchase such products in stereo stores.) Make sure the disc dries completely before you insert it in your CD-ROM drive. If you can't repair the disc, contact the company that produced it. Many CD-ROM publishers will send you a replacement disc in exchange for the damaged CD and a small fee.

Inserting and removing CD-ROMs is a fairly straightforward matter. As mentioned, many CD-ROM drives employ caddys. Assuming that yours does, open the caddy by pressing the tabs on its sides (look for arrows labeled "Open") and then flipping up the lid. Next place the disc in the caddy with the label side facing up. Remember not to touch the surface of the disc. Close the caddy's lid. Next, open the CD-ROM drive's door and carefully insert the caddy. An arrow at the edge of the caddy itself will indicate which sides goes in first. After you've inserted the disc, close the drive door (if it doesn't close automatically). With a little practice, you'll be able to open the drive door and insert the disc with one hand—just use the edge of the caddy to open the drive door before you slip it in. To remove the caddy and the disc it contains, push the eject button on the front of your CD-ROM drive. (If you can't find the button, check your CD-ROM drive manual.)

If your CD-ROM drive does not use caddys, you press the open/close button on the front of the drive to elicit a plastic or metal tray. Place the disc on the tray and press the button again to cause both disc and plate to withdraw into the drive. To eject the disc, press the open/eject button again or, if you're using a Mac, drag the disc's icon to the Trash can. (You'll learn about dragging and icons in Chapter 6.)

NOTE *If your disc gets stuck in the drive (meaning that nothing happens when you press the eject button), check the drive's documentation to see if your drive has an emergency eject hole. If it does, turn off the power to the drive. (If you have an internal drive, this means turning off the computer.) Then insert a paper clip into the emergency eject hole. If that doesn't work, contact a computer repair person or at least a technically minded friend. If you do manage to get the caddy out of the drive, make sure that there's nothing wrong with the caddy itself before you use it again.*

If you are using Windows 95, your computer will often attempt to play the CD-ROM as soon as you insert it into the drive. If you are using a Mac, you'll see an icon representing the CD-ROM's program as soon as you insert the disc and you can use that icon to launch the program itself. For more information on launching programs, see the chapter on your operating system. For information on multimedia CD-ROMs and on playing music CDs in your CD-ROM drive, consult Chapter 9.

INSERTING A CADDY INTO YOUR CD-ROM DRIVE

COMPUTER VIRUSES

Even people who've never touched a computer have heard ominous tales about computer viruses. A virus is a program, generally designed by a bright but maladjusted computer nerd, that in one way or another interrupts or undermines the normal workings of your computer. Viruses work by copying themselves into legitimate files, called *hosts*. From there, they often branch out, replicating themselves in more and more files on the disk. While some viruses infect almost every file in sight, others are more picky: Some viruses only infect application programs, other infect data files, and still others invade the operating system itself.

The level of destructiveness among viruses varies widely from one program to the next. Some viruses simply display pictures or messages on the screen periodically. Others erase or destroy both programs and data. They also wreak their havoc at very different speeds: for example, some viruses spread through your system fairly quickly but don't actually do anything for days or even months.

Viruses are usually passed via disk: you buy or are given a disk that already has the virus on it. Some PC viruses are only passed if you boot (start your computer) from an infected disk—meaning you turn your computer on with the disk already in the floppy drive. Others

FILE FRAGMENTATION AND DEFRAGMENTATION

Over time, files on a hard disk tend to become fragmented (stored in clusters that are scattered across the disk). You can improve your computer's performance by periodically defragmenting the disk—that is, running a program that puts all the parts of each file in adjacent clusters.

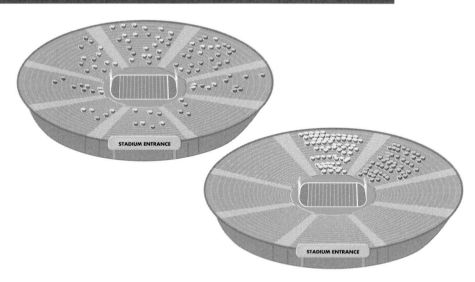

can infect your system when you copy a file from an infected disk or even when you attempt to erase an infected disk. Viruses can also be passed when you use a modem to download (copy) a file from a computer bulletin board or access data or programs on a network.

Before you get too paranoid about viruses, you should know that most computer users never actually encounter one. In over a dozen years of working with personal computers, I have yet to contract a virus (although I have a few clients and colleagues who've been less fortunate). The chances of contracting a virus are particularly small if you only install commercially available, shrink-wrapped programs and rarely exchange disks with anyone else. The more computers your system comes in contact with—via modem or via floppy disks— the greater your risk.

There are several steps you can take to protect your system from viruses:

▶ *Back up your data religiously, and don't discard or overwrite all of your older backups. (As mentioned in Chapter 2, you usually back up data by copying it to floppy disks.) It may take you days or weeks to notice and diagnose a virus, and many of your files may be damaged in the meantime. Backing up your data every day may not help in this case—you may just be backing up damaged files. What you need is an older copy of the data, a copy made before your computer was infected.*

▶ *Write-protect floppies whenever possible. Since viruses cannot infect write-protected (locked) disks, you should write-protect any disk that you don't need to copy files to. In particular, always write-protect your original copies of program disks before you insert them into your computer. That way, if you install the program and the copy that resides on your hard disk becomes infected, you can always reinstall from your write-protected floppies.*

▶ *Use antivirus programs. Some antivirus programs only detect and eliminate viruses on command. Others are what is known as "terminate-and-stay-resident" programs, or TSRs, meaning that they remain in memory throughout your work session, automatically hunting down viruses on every disk you insert into your computer. If you're very worried about viruses, you may choose to use the terminate-and-stay-resident type, in which case, the program will check your hard disk for viruses as soon as you turn on your computer, as well as scoping out any floppies you use over the course of the day. If you don't like the idea of waiting for all this virus-checking, you may prefer a less aggressive approach. In this case, simply use a nonresident virus scanning program whenever you suspect that a disk might be infected. One reasonable approach is to use such a program to scan any floppies you get from other people (as opposed to from computer stores) before you insert them into your floppy drive. For good measure, you might also scan your hard disk once a month and then create an infection-free backup copy of everything on that disk. You should create these monthly backups in addition to daily or weekly backups of any new or revised data files. That way if you discover that your hard disk has been infected for a week and that you have been backing up infected files, you will have the older, infection-free backup to fall back on.*

NOTE   *Some antivirus programs may conflict with some of your application programs. If you install an antivirus program and then start experiencing problems with your other programs, see if uninstalling the antivirus program solves the problem.*

One final note: Now that you know what viruses are, don't start blaming them for everything that goes wrong with your computer. Most of the problems you encounter on computers will be due to hardware problems, program bugs (mistakes within the program), or typos and other "user errors." If your computer starts displaying messages about being stoned, or if you keep encountering little happy faces in your word processing documents, by all means, investigate virus protection programs. But consider some of the other possibilities first.

NOTE *At best, antivirus programs can prevent or repair damage caused by already known viruses. Since new viruses are invented all the time, however, antivirus programs need to be updated to deal with each new menace to your computer's health. In most cases, you can buy updates to your antivirus program for a fraction of the program's original cost.*

CHAPTER 4

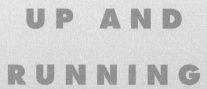

UP AND RUNNING

Starting Up Your Computer

■

What Happens When You Turn On Your Computer

■

Keyboards and Keyboard Layouts

■

What to Do When You Get Stuck

■

Using a Mouse or Trackball

■

Turning Off Your Computer

■

Ergonomics: Taking Care of Your Body While You Use a Computer

In this chapter, you will learn the proper way to turn on and off your computer, and to communicate with and control your computer via the keyboard and mouse. You'll also learn some tips for arranging the different parts of your computer system for maximum comfort and minimum back, wrist, and eye strain.

STARTING UP YOUR COMPUTER

Many personal computer systems are set up so that all the components, including the system unit and the monitor, are plugged into a single power strip. In this case, you turn on your computer (and everything else in sight) by throwing the switch on the power strip itself. If you don't have a power strip, you'll have to turn on the components one at a time.

MAC If you have a Macintosh system with external devices such as an external disk drive or a CD-ROM drive, turn those on first. Then locate the power switch on the system unit. The switch may be a regular looking switch located on the side or back of the machine, or it may be a button—often on the front of the unit—that you press in. Instead of an on/off switch, many Macintosh systems have a power button located either at the top of the keyboard, above all the other keys, or in the upper-right corner of your keyboard. (It is a largish button with a leftward-pointing arrowhead.) Many Macintosh monitors have on/off buttons of their own, so if you turn on the computer and the monitor stays dark, look for a button on the front of the monitor or a switch on the side or back.

PC If you are using a PC with a laser printer, it's a good idea not to turn on the printer at the same time you turn on the computer. Laser printers draw so much electricity that they can cause the power to fluctuate, which can put a particular strain on the computer during its start-up process.

WHAT HAPPENS WHEN YOU TURN ON YOUR COMPUTER

As you learned in Chapter 1, your computer hardware can't do much of anything without instructions from a program. When you turn on a computer, the first thing it does is go searching for a program that can tell it what to do next. (You might think of someone with extremely poor eyesight fumbling around for their glasses in the morning.)

The program the CPU is looking for is a very small part of the operating system known as the *boot program*. This program is stored in ROM (read-only memory) and is known as the boot program because it essentially helps the computer "pull itself up by its own bootstraps," by loading the rest of the operating system into memory. This process is known as *booting.*

Under the direction of this boot program, the CPU performs what is known as a *Power-On Self Test* (POST for short). During this stage, the CPU tests to see whether the various parts of the system are still alive and well.

If you have a PC, you will see a progress report during this phase. At a minimum, you will probably notice the computer counting up its memory. You may also see messages as the CPU checks out various peripherals and you may witness little lights on your keyboard and/or printer turn on and off. Finally, you'll hear a beep, indicating that everything seems to be okay. The same self-testing process occurs on the Macintosh, but with less running commentary.

Once the CPU has finished its internal inventory, it goes hunting for the rest of the operating system: the part that is stored on disk. The first place it looks is in the floppy-disk drive. (If you have a PC with two floppy drives, it looks to the drive named drive A—which is usually the leftmost or uppermost drive. If you have a Macintosh with two drives, it looks on the internal one first and then on the external one.)

If the floppy-disk drive is empty, the CPU continues its search on the hard drive. If there is a floppy in the drive, however, your computer checks to see whether it contains the operating system. Now Macintosh computers are a bit smarter about this process than PCs: If the floppy in the floppy drive does not contain the operating system, the Macintosh simply ignores it and looks to the hard drive. On a PC, if there is a floppy without the operating system in the floppy-disk drive, the computer stops and informs you that you have an invalid system disk or a non-system disk or disk error. At this point you have to open the floppy-drive door or eject the disk, and then press any key on your keyboard. The CPU will then resume its hunt for the operating system and, since it will no longer find a disk in drive A, will look to your hard drive. The moral of this story is that if you plan to work with a floppy disk, postpone inserting it until your system is done booting.

NOTE *The term for a disk that can be used to start up your computer is a* start-up disk, system disk, *or* boot disk. *(The term "boot disk" is almost exclusively used in the PC world.) All of these terms refer to the same thing: namely, a disk that contains the essential operating system files that your computer has to load before it can do anything else. In most cases, the start-up disk* *you will use is your hard disk. But you might use a floppy start-up disk if something goes wrong on your hard disk.*

As soon as the CPU locates the operating system, it loads it into memory. If you are running Windows 95, you'll see the message Starting Windows 95 and then a more colorful screen with the Microsoft Windows 95 logo. If you have your own computer and are not part of a network, you'll probably go immediately to a screen known as the Windows desktop. (You'll learn all about the desktop in Chapter 5.) If you are on a network, however, or if you share your computer with other people each of whom has a different user profile, you'll need to enter your name and password before you arrive at the desktop. (A *user profile* is a collection of information about a user's preferences regarding the appearance of the screen, the items on menus, and so on.) This process is known as *logging in*. (For more information on networks, see Chapter 8.)

If you're using DOS on a PC, you will see something known as the DOS prompt, which usually looks like C:\>.

On a Macintosh system, you will briefly see the Happy Macintosh Face, followed by a Welcome to the Macintosh screen, and finally the Macintosh desktop screen. If your computer is part of a network, you'll be asked to log in (enter your name and password) before you reach the desktop. You may then see icons (pictures) at the bottom of the screen as your computer loads various INITs. (INIT is short for initialization resource. INITs are special programs that either customize the Mac environment in some way—by displaying the current time at the top of your screen, for example—or allow the computer to communicate with various peripherals.) You'll learn what to do from there in Chapter 6.

KEYBOARDS AND KEYBOARD LAYOUTS

Before you can use your computer effectively, you need to know your way around the keyboard. The first thing to know about your computer keyboard is that it is very sensitive; you don't need to bang or lean on the keys. Banging on the keys simply places unnecessary stress on both your own wrists and the keyboard's innards. And since your computer recognizes and responds to the lightest key press, leaning on keys is the equivalent of screaming at your machine. If you hold down a key for more than a second, your computer will respond as if you had pressed it several times in rapid succession. The effect will depend on what that key actually does in the program you are currently using, but it's unlikely to be the result you intended. If you are used to using a manual typewriter or if you're not used to typing

BOOTING YOUR COMPUTER SYSTEM

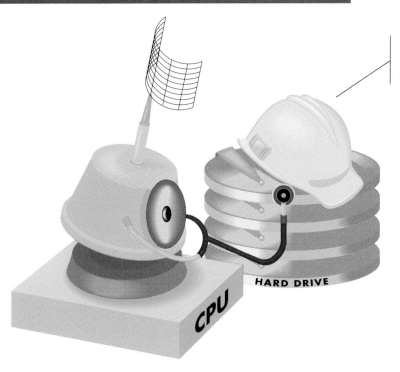

1. The CPU makes sure the disk drives and other components are working.

HARD DRIVE

CPU

2. The CPU takes an inventory of memory.

MEMORY MAILBOXES

0 1 2 3 4 5

6 7 8 9 10 11

12 13 17

INVENTORY
MEMORY ✓

CPU

3. The read/write head locates the operating system on the hard disk.

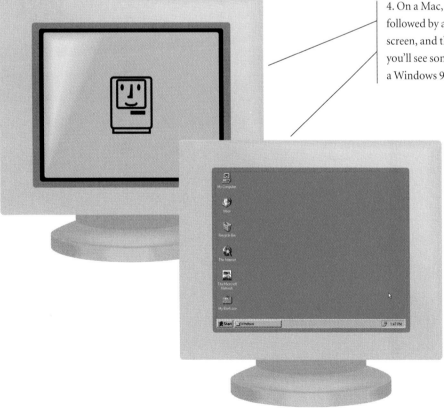

4. On a Mac, a happy Macintosh face appears, followed by a Welcome to the Macintosh screen, and then the desktop. In Windows 95, you'll see some hardware tests, a DOS prompt, a Windows 95 screen, and then the desktop.

at all, your first challenge will therefore be cultivating a lighter touch. Experiment to find the lightest touch that will work on your machine. Then try to use exactly that amount of pressure.

There are close to a dozen different styles of computer keyboards. There are keys on PC keyboards that you won't find on most Macintosh keyboards and vice versa, and even within the Mac and PC families, there are several keyboard layouts available. Different brands of keyboards may also have a very different feel. On some the keys click when you press them and on some they don't; the keys feel stiffer on some keyboards and mushier on others. The nice part about this variety is that you can choose the feel and the layout you like. The unfortunate part is that if you switch computers at some point, you may well need to spend some time getting used to the feel of the keyboard and hunting down keys.

The figures called "A Standard PC Keyboard" and "A Standard Macintosh Keyboard" depict what most computer keyboards have in common.

THE TYPEWRITER KEYS

All keyboards contain a section with the same keys that you find on a typewriter. Although these keys usually have the identical position and effect that they have on a typewriter, there are a few differences worth noting. First, if you are accustomed to using a typewriter, you may have a little trouble getting used to the position of the Shift keys (the keys that let you type capital letters) because they're slightly above the spacebar key rather than directly to the spacebar's left or right. (The spacebar is the long key near the bottom of the keyboard. It is used to enter spaces between words and, less frequently, to select items from a list.) Until you get used to the new layout, you may find yourself pressing the wrong keys—like the ones labeled Ctrl or Alt, or the Command keys on a Macintosh keyboard (the ones with a symbol of an apple, a cloverleaf, or both).

NOTE *The Caps Lock key on computer keyboards works a bit differently than the Shift Lock key on typewriters. Shift Lock on a typewriter affects punctuation keys and the number keys at the top of the keyboard, as well as letter keys. It allows you to type the character that appears on the top half of the key. Caps Lock on a computer keyboard affects letters only. This means that typing a dollar sign requires holding down the Shift key while you press the 4 at the top of your keyboard, even if Caps Lock is on.*

A STANDARD PC KEYBOARD

Your keyboard may have a different arrangement of keys. If you are using an older computer or laptop, or a notebook computer, you may have fewer keys altogether.

Function keys

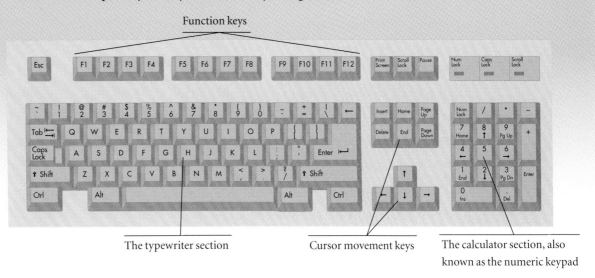

The typewriter section · Cursor movement keys · The calculator section, also known as the numeric keypad

A STANDARD MACINTOSH KEYBOARD

Some of the older models may not have all of these keys.

Fkeys

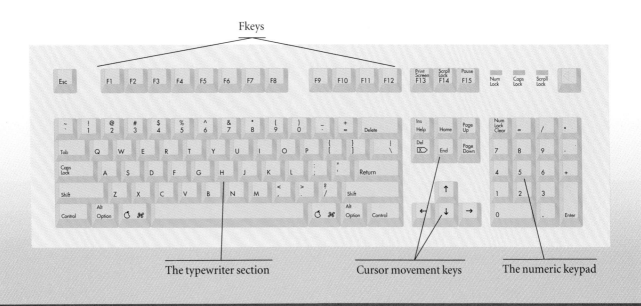

The typewriter section · Cursor movement keys · The numeric keypad

Caps Lock is what is known as a toggle key. A *toggle key* is a key that you use to alternately enable and then disable a particular feature. Like the power button on many stereos and TVs, you press it once to turn the feature on and again to turn it off.

The Enter or Return key works something like a carriage return on a typewriter: You press it to move to the next line when you get to the end of a paragraph. (In general, this key is labeled Enter on most PC keyboards and Return on Mac keyboards. Both PC and Mac keyboards may also have an additional Enter key, at the right side of the numeric keypad, to use when you're entering numbers.) As you'll learn in Chapter 7, you don't need to press Enter/Return at the end of each line in word processing programs because the program automatically "word wraps" text to the next line when you reach the right margin. You still need to press Enter/Return to force the cursor to a new line before you reach the right margin, however. You also sometimes use Enter/Return to select options from a menu (onscreen list of options) or to indicate that you are done entering instructions or data and want the program to go ahead and respond.

NOTE *On some PC keyboards, the Enter key is labeled with the ↵ symbol. This symbol is also used to indicate "Press the Enter key now" in many software manuals.*

The Tab key doesn't actually say Tab on some older PC keyboards and many laptops. It just has two arrows pointing in opposite directions, like ⇆ .

On PC keyboards and some of the newer Macintosh keyboards, there are two keys that contain slashes. One of these keys contains a question mark and a slash. The slash on this key is simply called a slash and is occasionally called a forward slash. The other key contains a vertical bar character, which looks like | or ¦ . The type of slash on this key is called a backslash. It is rarely used as an actual character; most often it is used to precede a special formatting code, depending on the program. Just remember, if you're told to press slash, press the key with the question mark. If you're told to press the backslash, press the key with the vertical bar character. (The location of the backslash/vertical bar key varies from keyboard to keyboard.)

THE CURSOR MOVEMENT KEYS

In most programs, there is some symbol that indicates where you are on the screen at the moment—kind of like a "you are here" indicator on the map for a park or shopping mall or the bouncing ball that you are supposed to follow in old cartoons. In some cases, the symbol is a little blinking line or rectangle, known as a *cursor.* Sometimes it will be a larger bright rectangle, often referred to as the highlight or cell pointer. When you are entering text

THE TYPEWRITER KEYS

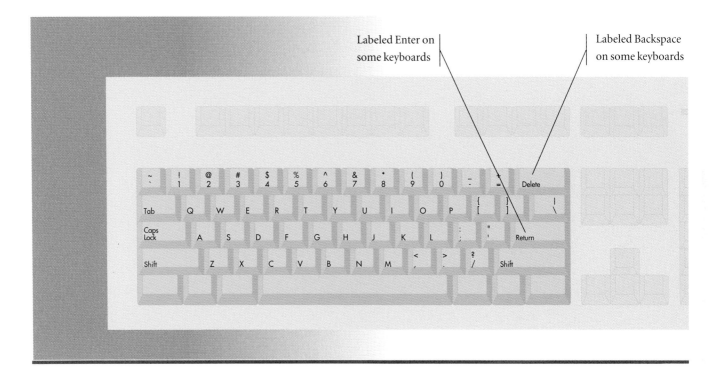

Labeled Enter on some keyboards

Labeled Backspace on some keyboards

in Windows or on a Mac, the "you are here" symbol is a blinking vertical line known as the *insertion point.*

N O T E   *You'll never have both a cursor and an insertion point. You always have one or the other, depending on the type of computer and the program you are using.*

On most keyboards, there are two groups of keys designed to move the cursor or insertion point around the screen.

The arrow keys move the cursor/insertion point one character or one unit at a time in the direction of the arrow. To move one character to the left when you are entering text in a word processing program, for example, you press the Left Arrow key. On most keyboards, the arrow keys occupy keys by themselves.

The other cursor movement keys (Home, End, Page Up, and Page Down) let you make larger jumps across the screen. Their effects vary at least slightly from one program to the next. On some older PC keyboards and laptop keyboards, there are no separate cursor movement keys: They are always part of the numeric keypad (the calculator section). You'll discover how to use these dual-purpose keys when you learn about the numeric keypad. You can also move the cursor or insertion point using a mouse, if you have one.

THE SPECIAL KEYS

The special keys include all the keys other than the normal typewriter keys, cursor movement keys, numeric keypad (the set of keys that resembles a calculator), and function keys. These keys are scattered around the keyboard and are generally used to perform some operation other than displaying a particular character on the screen.

Most keyboards include two keys for erasing. The Backspace key on PC keyboards or the Delete key on Macintosh keyboards deletes the character to the left of your current position. (This key is labeled Backspace on some older Macintosh keyboards. On some PC keyboards, it doesn't say Backspace at all; it simply shows a leftward pointing arrow.)

The key labeled either Delete or Del on PC keyboards and labeled Del on Macintosh keyboards generally deletes the character immediately to the right of the insertion point (in Windows or on Macs) or immediately above the cursor (in DOS). Note that only the extended Macintosh keyboard includes a Del key.

In most programs, it's also possible to select a group of characters to erase using either your keyboard or the mouse. Pressing either the Backspace/Delete key or the Del key will delete any currently selected characters.

PC There are a few other special keys on PC keyboards.

The Insert key (often abbreviated as Ins) is a toggle key that determines what happens when you type new characters within existing text or numbers. If the Insert feature is on and you type new characters in the middle of a paragraph, for example, the old characters are pushed to the right to make room for the new ones. When the Insert feature is off, the new characters simply replace the old ones. In some programs, the Insert feature is off by default,

---

THE BACKSPACE KEY VERSUS THE LEFT ARROW KEY

On PC keyboards, don't confuse the Backspace key and the Left Arrow key. Both of these keys contain leftward pointing arrows. (On older PC keyboards, the word Backspace doesn't even appear on the Backspace key; there's just an arrow.) Although both of these keys move the cursor to the left, the Left Arrow (like all arrow keys) moves the cursor nondestructively; it doesn't change anything. In contrast, the Backspace key moves and erases at the same time. Every time you press the key, the character to the left of the cursor is deleted and the cursor moves left one space to take up the slack. (If you've ever seen or played the game Pac Man, you can think of Backspace as the Pac Man key: it's like a little creature gobbling up the characters in its path.)

THE CURSOR MOVEMENT KEYS

You can move the cursor or insertion point using either the cursor movement keys or your mouse.

The *insertion point* or *cursor* indicates your current position on the screen.

Untitled

Dear Aunt Alice,

Thanks so much for the birthday prese never too many ties!

Life here York continues to go

YOU ARE HERE

The Home key is often used to move to the beginning of some set of data—such as the top of a document, the beginning of a line, or the upper-left corner of a spreadsheet.

The Page Up key is usually used to move up one page or one screenful of data. (This key is often labeled PgUp.)

The Page Down key is usually used to move down one page or one screenful of data. (This key is often labeled PgDn.)

The End key is often used to move to the end of some set of data—such as the bottom of a document, the end of a line, or the last number or character in a particular block of data in a spreadsheet.

On PC keyboards without a separate set of cursor movement keys, you use the arrows on the numeric keypad to move the cursor.

The arrow keys move the cursor one character or one unit at a time in the direction of the arrow.

Home | Page Up

End | Page Down

7 Home | 8 ↑ | 9 Pg Up

4 ← | 5 | 6 →

1 End | 2 ↓ | 3 Pg Dn

↑

← | ↓ | →

DELETING CHARACTERS

The Backspace key on a PC or Delete key on a Mac gobbles characters to the left of the cursor or insertion point.

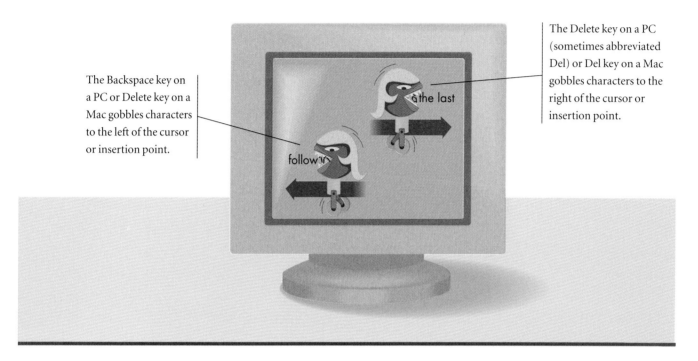

The Delete key on a PC (sometimes abbreviated Del) or Del key on a Mac gobbles characters to the right of the cursor or insertion point.

and pressing Insert the first time turns it on. In other programs, it is on by default, so pressing Insert turns it off. On certain PC keyboards, Insert shares a key with the number 0 on the numeric keypad.

On most PCs, the Print Screen key (often abbreviated to PrtScrn) sends an image of the screen directly to the printer—producing a "hard copy" (that is, a paper copy) of whatever currently appears on your monitor. On some systems, you need to hold Shift while you press the Print Screen key. In Windows, the Print Screen key sends an image of the screen to the Windows Clipboard (which you'll learn about in Chapter 5).

Scroll Lock is a toggle key that, in a few application programs, changes the effect of cursor movement keys. When Scroll Lock is on, pressing the cursor movement keys makes the display appear to scroll while the cursor stays put. Normally, the cursor moves as far as it can and only then does the display start scrolling.

Pause doesn't do anything in most currently available application programs.

THE MODIFIER KEYS

All PC and Macintosh keyboards contain three or more types of special keys that you use almost exclusively in combination with other keys and that don't do anything by themselves.

THE SPECIAL KEYS

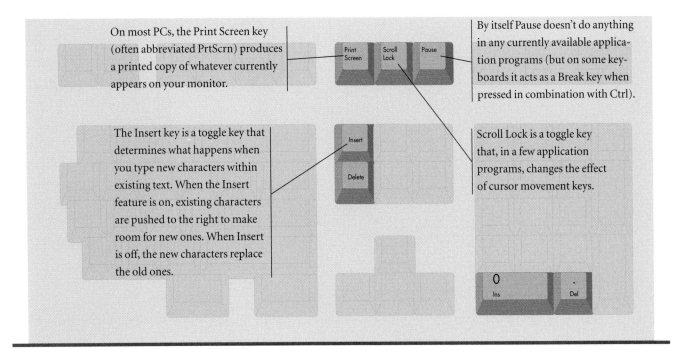

On most PCs, the Print Screen key (often abbreviated PrtScrn) produces a printed copy of whatever currently appears on your monitor.

By itself Pause doesn't do anything in any currently available application programs (but on some keyboards it acts as a Break key when pressed in combination with Ctrl).

The Insert key is a toggle key that determines what happens when you type new characters within existing text. When the Insert feature is on, existing characters are pushed to the right to make room for new ones. When Insert is off, the new characters replace the old ones.

Scroll Lock is a toggle key that, in a few application programs, changes the effect of cursor movement keys.

(Many keyboards contain two keys of each type—that is, two Shift keys, two Control keys, and so on.) Since these keys' only function is to modify the effect of other keys, this book will refer to them as *modifier keys*.

PC For those of you who've used typewriters, the Shift key on a typewriter is an example of a modifier key. Pressing the Shift key by itself does nothing. But if you hold down Shift while pressing the letter *A*, you get an uppercase *A* instead of the lowercase *a* you get by pressing the *A* key by itself. Similarly, on a PC keyboard, nothing happens when you press Shift, Control (often abbreviated as Ctrl), or Alt (short for Alternate). But in many application programs, holding down a modifier key while pressing another key is a way of issuing a command. In some word processing programs, for example, holding down the Ctrl key while pressing *U* issues the command to underline any currently selected text (while pressing *U* by itself would simply generate a letter *U* and pressing Ctrl by itself would do nothing).

N O T E *Some PC keyboards are designed specifically to work with Windows 95 and applications designed to run under Windows 95. These keyboards contain two extra types of keys—known as Application keys and Windows Logo keys—that provide fast keyboard alternatives to many operations you'd usually perform with a mouse. For example, you can use the Windows*

Logo keys to open the Start menu, an operation you'd usually perform by clicking the Start button located in the lower-left corner of the desktop.

If you're not sure whether your keyboard contains these keys, try looking a bit to the left and right of the spacebar. The Windows Logo keys contain the Windows logo (surprise). The Application key looks like a piece of paper with an arrow pointing to it. For information on using these special keys, see the documentation that came with your keyboard.

MAC Macintosh keyboards include three types of modifier keys in addition to the Shift keys.

▶ *Command keys (the ones with the four-leaf clover and, in most cases, an apple) are used in combination with letters to let you issue commands quickly. Once you learn one of these key combination shortcuts, using it is often faster than issuing the same command by selecting options from menus. If you press the Command key by itself, nothing happens.*

▶ *Option keys (which are generally located next to the Command keys) allow you to access special characters like a cent sign or an accent mark. They are often used in combination with the Command or Shift key.*

▶ *Control keys are used in combination with other keys in a few Macintosh programs. They are included on Mac keyboards largely to let you run Windows and DOS-based programs on your Mac.*

The term *key combination* means a combination of two or more keys (at least one of which is a modifier key) to perform some operation. Whenever you use a key combination, you press the modifier key first and hold it down while you press the other key. Don't try to press both keys at once. (If you do, you'll often press the second key slightly before you press the modifier key, which has the effect of pressing that second key by itself.)

When computer books or manuals refer to key combinations, they sometimes combine the names of the keys with commas, with dashes, or plus signs. In other words, if you're supposed to hold down Alt while you press the Backspace key, the manual might say Alt,Backspace, Alt-Backspace, or Alt+Backspace.

FUNCTION KEYS

The function keys are the keys labeled F1 through either F10, F12, or F15. They are frequently located at the top of the keyboard, although they sometimes live to the left of the keyboard keys in older PC keyboards.

PC In many PC application programs, function keys are used to issue commands. For example, F1 is frequently used to invoke an application's Help system, which provides you with information on how to use the program. F10 is sometimes used to activate the program's menu system.

MAC Function keys are generally known as Fkeys in Macintosh manuals; older Mac keyboards may not have them at all. Although Fkeys rarely serve a set purpose in Macintosh programs, you can purchase special programs, like QuicKeys, that allow you to program those keys to do whatever you like. Fkeys are included on Mac keyboards partly so that you can run PC programs from your Macintosh. (To do this, you must run a special PC-emulation program like Soft PC.)

THE NUMERIC KEYPAD

PC There are currently two basic layouts for PC keyboards: one, often called the *extended keyboard,* for desktop PCs, and another layout for laptops. The main difference between the two is that desktop keyboards generally have both a numeric keypad and separate groups of cursor movement keys, while laptops usually have a numeric keypad that doubles as a set of cursor movement keys.

On all PC keyboards, you can use the numeric keypad for either of two functions: typing numbers or moving around on the screen. The status of the Num Lock (number lock) setting—which you control by pressing the Num Lock key—determines which of these two hats the keypad is currently wearing. Num Lock is a toggle key, like the Caps Lock key (or Shift Lock on a typewriter): Each time you press it, the status of the Num Lock feature changes, from off to on or on to off.

When Num Lock is on, the keys on the numeric keypad generate numbers. When Num Lock is off, they change to cursor movement keys. The 7 key acts like a Home key, for example, and the 8 key serves as an Up Arrow key. The function of the each key is spelled out on the key itself. (The effect of the cursor movement keys was covered earlier in this chapter.)

The gray keys other than the Num Lock key around the outside of the numeric keypad work the same regardless of whether Num Lock is on or off. They let you enter mathematical symbols like + and – (the / symbol is often used to symbolize division and the * symbol is often used to symbolize multiplication). The Enter key works just like the Enter or Return key in the main section of the keyboard.

There are usually several ways to determine whether Num Lock is on or off. On most keyboards, there is a little light on the key itself or a light labeled Num Lock above the key. If the light is on, the feature is on. Many application programs also display the words Num Lock or Num on the screen when Num Lock is on. Worst comes to worst, you can just press one of the arrow keys and see whether the cursor moves or a number is generated.

Why, you may wonder, would you want to turn off Num Lock? On older style IBM keyboards and many laptops, there is no separate set of arrow keys. You therefore have to choose between using the cursor movement keys and using the numeric keypad to type numbers. If you don't need to do a lot of moving around at the moment, you might turn Num Lock on temporarily to enter a set of numbers, particularly if you're a wiz at touch-typing on calculators. Otherwise, you leave Num Lock off and use the number keys at the top of the keyboard to enter numbers. The Num Lock key was carried over to the newer keyboards primarily to accommodate all those people who had already grown used to navigating with keys on the numeric keypad (habits are hard to break). The Num Lock key also supports older programs not capable of recognizing the new keys. Some people also prefer the layout of arrow keys on the numeric keypad (with the up arrow key above the left arrow and right arrow keys).

NOTE *It's a lot easier to type arithmetic operators (like + and *) using keys at the side of the numeric keypad rather than keys at the top of the keyboard. If you use the keys at the top of the keyboard, you always need to remember to hold down the Shift key. If you forget, you get = when you mean + or 8 when you mean *.*

MAC Like PCs, most Macintosh keyboards contain a numeric keypad with keys for entering the digits 0 through 9, a decimal point, and the arithmetic operators: + for addition, – for subtraction, / for division, and * for multiplication. On Mac keyboards, unlike PC keyboards, the numeric keypad also includes an = key and a Clear key. In some programs, you can use the Clear key to clear, or undo, the last number you typed in case you made a mistake, just as you'd use the C or Clear key on many calculators.

WHAT TO DO WHEN YOU GET STUCK

Yಂou should never turn off your computer in the middle of an application if you can avoid it. (Turning off your computer is covered later in this chapter.) It can damage data and, at the least, cause you to lose any unsaved data in memory. Occasionally, however, you may just get stuck. There may be a "bug" (glitch) in the program you are using and you may get an error message that won't go away; or the program may stop responding to your commands.

PC Here are some techniques to try if you do get stuck on a PC, listed from the least drastic to the most.

▶ *In many application programs, the Escape key (usually labeled Esc) is a general-purpose "get me out of here" key—used to cancel or back up a step in the current operation.*

▶ *Although there is no key with the word Break on the top, on most PC keyboards either the Scroll Lock key or the Pause key has the word Break on its front edge. (If you don't find Break on either key, assume that you can use Scroll Lock for this purpose.) Holding down a Ctrl key and pressing this key will interrupt some programs or commands, although not all. This key combination is referred to as Ctrl+Break (pronounced "Control Break").*

▶ *If neither of the preceding techniques works, you can do what is known as rebooting your computer by holding down the Ctrl and Alt keys and then tapping the Del key. Rebooting means erasing memory and then reloading the operating system. When you do this, you lose any data currently in memory. In some programs, you may damage data as well, so only use this key combination when you can't think of any other way to get out of your current fix. Although fairly drastic, rebooting is still a bit safer than the next two options.*

If you are using Windows 95, pressing Ctrl, Alt, and Del invokes a Close Program dialog box. To close the currently running program, just click the End Task button. If that doesn't work, try clicking the Shut Down button. If you still have no luck, press Ctrl, Alt, and Del again.

▶ *Many PCs have a Reset button that lets you restart your computer without actually flicking the power switch. The only practical difference between pressing this button and turning your computer off and on is that the main power to the computer's components is not interrupted, resulting in less wear and tear.*

▶ *If all else fails and your computer doesn't have a Reset button, turn the computer off, wait at least ten seconds, and then turn it on again.*

MAC There are also a few different strategies you can try for getting unstuck on a Mac. Although the Escape (Esc) key is rarely used in Macintosh programs, in a few programs it undoes the last operation or cancels the current one. In some other programs, you can cancel an operation by holding the Command key and pressing the period.

Holding down the Command key and the Option key on a Mac and then pressing Escape executes what is known as a *forced quit*. This key combination will usually—but not always—get you out of an application program if nothing else will. Assuming it works, you will see a message asking if you really want to quit the program. Select Forced Quit if you do or Cancel if you don't.

USING A MOUSE OR TRACKBALL

Keyboards are only one of the tools available for talking to your computer. The other main tool, and one that's particularly important if you are using a Mac or running Windows, is a mouse or trackball.

A mouse is a hand-held pointing device that lets you point to, select, and manipulate objects on the screen. As you move the mouse around on your desk, a special symbol, known as the *mouse pointer*, moves in an analogous direction on the screen. If you move the mouse forward and backward, the mouse pointer moves up and down on the screen; if you move the mouse left and right, the mouse pointer moves left and right. Although the mouse pointer most often looks like an arrow, it can assume other shapes, depending on which program you are running and what operation you are performing.

You can hold the mouse in either hand. Most people prefer to use their dominant hand (the right if right-handed or left if left-handed). Make sure that the mouse cord is pointing away from you. Then just glide the mouse lightly over the surface of your desk.

If you reach the edge of your desk or your mouse pad before you reach the desired point on the screen, just lift your mouse up and move it. The mouse pointer only moves when the mouse is flat against a surface like a desktop, so that the ball underneath is rolled as you move the device. If you are trying to move the mouse pointer down to the bottom of your screen, for example, and you reach the front edge of your desk when the mouse pointer is still an

GETTING OUT OF TROUBLE ON A PC

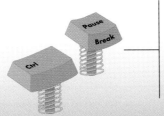

In programs that can't be interrupted with the Escape key, you can sometimes use the Ctrl+Break key combination to get "unstuck." Although there is no key with the word Break on the top, on most PC keyboards either the Scroll Lock key or the Pause key has the word Break on its front edge. (If you don't find Break on either key, assume that you can use Scroll Lock for this purpose.)

If all else fails, you can reboot your computer by holding down the Ctrl and Alt keys and then tapping the Del key. Since this erases the entire contents of memory, it often results in some loss of data.

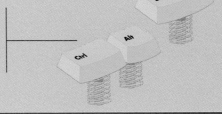

THE MANY GUISES OF THE MOUSE POINTER

In most programs, the mouse pointer assumes different shapes depending on what you are doing.

inch above the desired spot, just lift the mouse, move it back a few inches, and then continue moving it forward.

If you use a mouse often, you may want to purchase a mouse pad: a rectangular piece of nylon-covered rubber that you place on your desktop as a platform for your mouse. Many people find that their mouse gets better traction and therefore moves more smoothly on a pad than directly on a desktop, particularly if the surface of the desk is at all uneven.

A trackball is essentially an upside down mouse. Instead of having a ball on the bottom, it has a ball on the top, set inside a square cradle. Rolling this ball has the same effect as moving a mouse around on your desk.

TIPS ON CLICKING

When you want to click the mouse in a particular spot, move the pointer to the desired spot and then, continuing to hold the mouse with your whole hand, just use your index finger to press the mouse button. (Some beginners try to jab the mouse key from on high, which usually jettisons the mouse pointer away from the desired target.) If you're double-clicking, be sure to keep the mouse in the same spot between the first and second click.

Many people find double-clicking a bit of a challenge. If every time you try to double-click, the computer responds as if you'd only clicked once, chances are you're waiting too long between the first and second click. If you're using Windows, you can adjust the double-click speed—that is, the amount of time you're allowed to leave between clicks—by selecting the Mouse icon in the Windows Control Panel. (You'll learn how to get to the Control Panel in Chapter 5.) Similarly, on a Mac, you can adjust double-click speed using the mouse icon in the Control Panels folder. (See Chapter 6 or your Mac manual for details.)

Many of the operations that you perform using a mouse or trackball involve pushing buttons. Macintosh mice have a single large button. Mice designed for PCs have either two or three buttons: a left button, a right button, and occasionally a third button, known as the middle button. Although there are very few programs that use the middle button, you can often program that button so that pressing it once has the same effect as double-clicking the left mouse button. (For instructions on doing this, see your mouse manual.) When you see instructions to press or click the mouse button, assume that you should use the left mouse button unless explicitly told otherwise. If you are supposed to click the right mouse button, for example, the instructions will say "right-click" or "click the right mouse button" rather than just "click." The button(s) on trackballs are usually positioned at the far end of the device. You can press them using either your thumb or forefinger.

NOTE *If you're left-handed and are using Windows 95, you may want to reverse the effect of the left and right mouse buttons. You can do this by selecting the Mouse icon in the Windows Control Panel. (Again, you'll learn how to get to the Control Panel in Chapter 5.)*

Cleaning Your Mouse or Trackball

If your mouse pointer starts moving in fits and starts, or if it moves in one direction but not another, it's probably time for a mouse cleaning. Start by turning the mouse upside down. Next, you'll either need to slide the round lid down until it pops open or turn it counter-clockwise until it reaches the open position. Once the lid is open, the ball should drop out into your palm. Clean the rollers inside the mouse using a cotton swab dipped in alcohol. Clean the ball using a soft, dry cloth. Finally, replace the ball and the lid and you're ready to

U S I N G   A   M O U S E   I N   D O S

If you are using DOS, you may need to explicitly load your mouse software before you can use the mouse within most programs. If you are running Windows, you don't need to load mouse software first: Windows has its own program for dealing with the mouse. With most DOS programs, however, you need to load the mouse software yourself. If you're not sure whether you need to load your mouse software, you can try starting up the program and seeing whether a mouse pointer appears on your screen. (Try moving your mouse around and seeing if anything moves on the screen at the same time.) If you do see a mouse pointer, you can assume that either the program has its own tools for communicating with the mouse or that the person who set up your system has directed the computer to load the mouse software automatically as soon as you turn on your computer. If you don't see a mouse pointer, consult your mouse manual for instructions on loading your mouse software. (If you just bought the mouse, you'll probably need to install the software first. Again, see the mouse manual for instructions.)

go. To reassemble a trackball after cleaning, you may need to place the ball in one hand, use your other hand to place the mouse part on top of it, and flip your hands over.

TURNING OFF YOUR COMPUTER

The first thing to know about turning off your computer is that you shouldn't do it too often. In general, you should turn off your computer only when you don't plan on using it again for several hours. If you're simply going to lunch, leaving the computer on for an hour or two causes less wear and tear than turning it off and then on again. As explained in Chapter 8, however, you may want to turn off your monitor temporarily, both to protect the screen and to turn off the electromagnetic radiation.

When you are done using your computer for the day, save any unsaved data that you want to be able to use in future work sessions. Then follow this procedure:

PC If you are using Windows 95, save any data that you haven't already saved. (Don't worry, if you forget to save something, the program will double-check with you before discarding your changes.) Then click the Start button in the lower-left corner of the screen to display a Start menu. Click on the Shut Down option. When Windows displays a box with the title Shut Down Windows, leave the option "Shut down the computer?" selected and click the button labeled Yes. In a moment, you'll see the message "It's now safe to turn off your computer" and you can flip the on/off switch or press the power button.

If you are using DOS, be sure to exit any application programs you are running before you turn off your computer. If you're running an early version of Windows, exit from Windows too. You can tell that it's safe to turn off your computer if you see a symbol known as

THINGS YOU CAN DO WITH A MOUSE OR TRACKBALL

When you read software manuals, there are six terms you are likely to encounter for the various things you can do with a mouse or trackball.

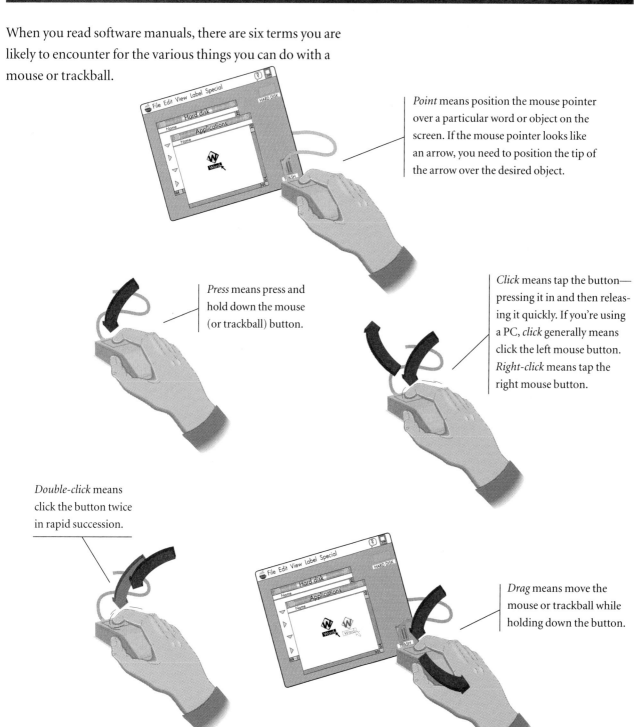

Point means position the mouse pointer over a particular word or object on the screen. If the mouse pointer looks like an arrow, you need to position the tip of the arrow over the desired object.

Press means press and hold down the mouse (or trackball) button.

Click means tap the button—pressing it in and then releasing it quickly. If you're using a PC, *click* generally means click the left mouse button. *Right-click* means tap the right mouse button.

Double-click means click the button twice in rapid succession.

Drag means move the mouse or trackball while holding down the button.

the DOS prompt—usually a capital C followed by one or more characters and then a greater than sign—followed by a cursor (a short blinking line).

MAC With Macs, you must shut down your computer by issuing the Special ShutDown command. To do this, point to the Special option on the menu bar at the top of the screen. Then press the mouse button to open the Special menu. Drag the highlight down to the ShutDown option, and then release the button. The Mac will update its information on the current state of the Desktop (its working environment) and then turn off automatically.

ERGONOMICS: TAKING CARE OF YOUR BODY WHILE YOU USE A COMPUTER

You'll never learn to love (or even tolerate) a computer if it causes you discomfort or pain. If you're planning to spend hours at the keyboard, it's therefore worth taking time to make the experience as comfortable as possible. Setting up your workstation properly isn't just about feeling good (although that's a worthy goal in itself). It's also a way of preventing painful and potentially debilitating conditions like carpal tunnel syndrome, tendonitis, repetitive motion disorder, or chronic back pain.

The figure "The Ergonomic Workstation" shows how to arrange your computer to cause minimum wear and tear on your body. The basic rules of thumb are as follows:

▶ *The top edge of your monitor should be at eye level or slightly below, so that you're looking down just slightly. (You may need to prop up the monitor with a large book or a monitor stand.) The front edge should be 20 to 30 inches from your eyes.*

▶ *Your wrists should never be higher than your elbows. Ideally, your elbows should be bent at a 90-degree angle and your wrists should be straight rather than flexed upward or bent downward. If you can't achieve this position given your desk height, your desk is too high (or your chair seat too low). You may want to get a typing desk or a keyboard drawer that allows the keyboard to sit lower than the desktop.*

▶ *Your feet should touch the floor or a foot rest and the angle between your thighs and spine should be 90 degrees or a bit more.*

▶ *Keep your mouse close to the keyboard so you don't have to reach far to use it. This will minimize strain on your shoulder. If you use the mouse even more than the keyboard, put the mouse directly in front of you and the keyboard slightly off to the side.*

One of the worst things you can do to your wrists is lean the heel of your hand on the desk, so that your wrist is flexed backward as you type. It's best to train yourself to hold your wrists up while you're typing (like your piano teacher always told you) and to rest them on a wrist rest when you're not. If you can't manage holding your wrists straight, use the wrist rest while you're typing as well. (You can purchase wrist rests in some computer or office supply stores, through office/computer supply catalogs, and often in stores that specialize in back problems.) Some mice are designed to conform to the shape of your hand and may result in less strain.

You can also alleviate wrist strain by adjusting the angle of your keyboard. You can angle most keyboards so that the back is slightly higher than the front. On some Mac keyboards, you adjust the angle by sliding a bar located in the middle of the front side of the keyboard. Most other keyboards have tabs underneath; swinging down these tabs raises the back end of the keyboard.

Part of the problem with most computer keyboards (and typewriters) is that they force you to hold your hands at an unnatural angle to your arms—so that your hands are both more horizontal to the desk than they'd like to be and rotated slightly outward at the wrist. Apple now makes a keyboard—named the Apple Adjustable Keyboard—that is split down the middle, allowing you to move the halves outward as much as 30 degrees. Microsoft also offers an ergonomic keyboard called the Natural Keyboard in which the left-hand and right-hand keys are slightly separated and angled outwards, although the angle between the keys cannot be adjusted. There are similar keyboards available from third-party vendors.

Many people also experience some eye strain after staring at a computer screen for a few hours. The best approach here is to rest your eyes periodically, by focusing on a distant object once in a while, blinking often, and taking short breaks every hour or two. You should also make sure that you have proper lighting. Avoid overhead lights whenever possible because they almost always reflect off your screen. The best source of lighting is probably a desk or floor lamp or track lights that are not directly aimed at your screen. Beautiful as it is, sunlight streaming in the windows usually leads to glare as well. If your computer resides in a room full of windows, make sure you have shades that you can draw when necessary. For about $20, you can also buy a glare screen, usually made of very fine wire mesh, to fit over the front of your monitor—cutting down on glare and, in many cases, sharpening the contrast between light and dark.

THE ERGONOMIC WORKSTATION

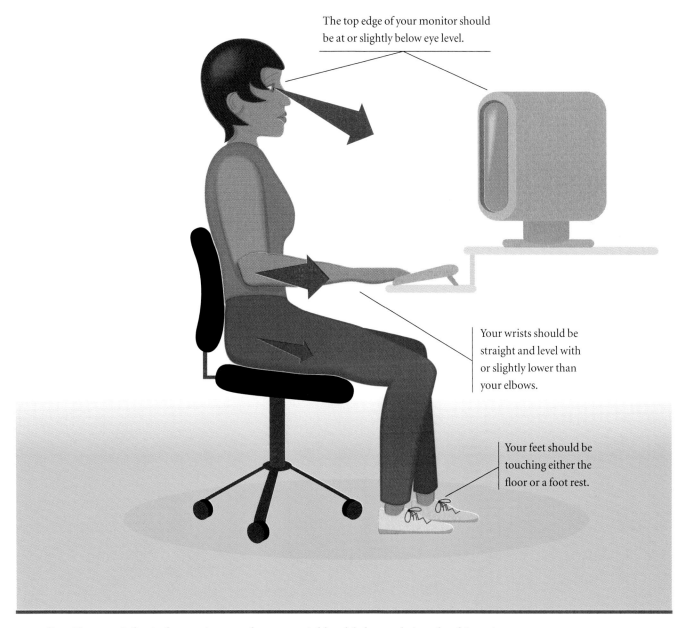

The top edge of your monitor should be at or slightly below eye level.

Your wrists should be straight and level with or slightly lower than your elbows.

Your feet should be touching either the floor or a foot rest.

See Chapter 8 for information on the potential health hazards involved in using computer monitors and what you can do about them.

Finally, if you have any back problems (or are determined to avoid them), a good chair is essential. Look for one that provides support for your lower back and that is fully adjustable. (You should be able to change both the height of the seat and the angle of the seat and the back.)

NOTE *Try not to get too paranoid about the health hazards of computers. There are hazards (including boredom) in most lines of work, and pianists and meat packers are about as prone to carpal tunnel syndrome as dedicated computer hackers. What's more, some people work on computers 8 to 10 hours a day, with lousy chairs, poor posture, and no ill effects. (Then again, some people smoke two packs a day and live into their 80s.) A good rule of thumb is that you should pay attention to how you feel after a day at your computer. If your neck, back, wrists, arms, or eyes are sore, respond accordingly, doing everything you can to minimize the strain. If all else fails, see a doctor—sooner rather than later.*

You have now learned everything you need to know about hardware in order to get started using your personal computer. You will learn more about hardware—particularly printers, monitors, and networks—in Chapter 8. In the meantime, the focus will move to software—the instructions that tell the hardware what to do.

As you learned in Chapter 1, operating systems are programs that, in effect, allow your computer to operate. They help control the flow of information from one part of the computer to another. They serve as an intermediary between application programs and your hardware. And they allow you to perform disk housekeeping operations like copying, erasing, and renaming files on disks.

Learning at least a little bit about your operating system is an essential step in learning to use your computer. At a minimum, you'll need to know enough to start up application programs to erase and copy files. But the more you learn about the operating system, the more you will understand both your hardware and the application programs that use the operating system as their base. The next two chapters cover two different operating systems: Windows 95 and the Macintosh operating system. If you are using DOS—either by itself or with a pre-Windows 95 version of Windows—an introductory book on the subject will be well worth the money. If you are using an early version of Windows, you'll probably want a book on DOS and a book on Windows. Or, better yet, consider upgrading to Windows 95.

CHAPTER

5

USING
WINDOWS 95

As you learned in Chapter 1, Windows 95 is an operating system for PCs. This chapter introduces the Windows environment and explains how to load application programs within Windows and how to use Windows to perform disk housekeeping operations like copying and deleting files. It also explores many of the features common to Windows application programs as well as to Windows itself—things like windows, dialog boxes, and menus.

Since most PCs are now sold with Windows pre-installed, I will assume that Windows is already installed on your computer. If this is not the case, see the documentation that came with your Windows disks or CD-ROM for installation instructions.

NOTE *This chapter covers Windows 95 only, which is quite different from earlier versions of Windows. Those earlier versions are not really operating systems in themselves; they always run as a separate layer on top of the DOS operating system. They also look and behave quite a bit differently from Windows 95. If your computer is running a pre-Windows 95 version of Windows (Windows 3.11, for example or if your computer is part of a network, Windows for Workgroups), you'll either need to find a good book on the subject or upgrade to Windows 95. (If you're considering upgrading, see the upcoming sidebar on Windows 95 Hardware Requirements.)*

WHAT'S SO GREAT ABOUT WINDOWS?

Windows is an operating environment created by Microsoft. It provides users of PCs with what's known as a *graphical user interface* (GUI); that is, an environment based more on pictures than on text. While issuing orders in text-based operating systems (such as DOS or Unix) is a matter of typing in commands, in Windows programs (and on Macs) it's a matter of clicking pictures on the screen or making selections from menus (on-screen lists of options). The advantage to this way of interacting with the computer is that it's less intimidating to new users and requires less memorization. If you forget how to perform a particular task, you can often refresh your memory simply by poking around on the screen, seeing which icons and menu options are available.

Another advantage of using Windows is that most programs designed to run within Windows look and behave similarly. Windows application programs are populated with entities such as icons (pictures that represent data files, programs, or folders), dialog boxes (frames that display information and/or ask you questions) and, as you might guess, windows (frames in which programs and data are displayed). Almost all Windows programs also feature similar menu systems and at least a few of the same commands. To leave any Windows application, for example, you choose the Exit option from a menu named File. Once you have mastered one Windows program, it's fairly easy to learn the next because Windows programs have so much in common.

Windows also allows you to run multiple programs at once. If you're just getting started with computers, this feature may seem of limited value: Why would you want to run two programs at once when you're still feeling overwhelmed by the first one? Once you get a little more comfortable with your system, however, you may find this feature invaluable.

Imagine getting a phone call about your latest sales figures when you're in the middle of typing a letter in your word processing program, for example. If you are using Windows, you can easily open your spreadsheet program and find the necessary information without leaving your word processing program. When you're done, a single mouse click or keystroke will take you back to your word processing document, and you can pick up exactly where you left off. (Windows also includes a feature known as the Clipboard that lets you easily copy or move data from one program to another. This means that you can copy those sales figures directly from your spreadsheet into your word processing document without having to use any special importing or exporting commands.)

Windows not only allows you to open two (or more) programs at once, it also allows you to carry out work in both programs simultaneously. If you need to perform a time-consuming task in one program—such as downloading a large file from the Internet—you can simply start the process and then switch to a different program. The task you started in the first program will continue unattended while you continue working in the second one. People refer to this ability to work on two things at once as *multitasking*. It's the computer equivalent of patting your head while rubbing your stomach.

NOTE *As you'll soon see, Windows is almost infinitely flexible and usually provides at least two or three ways to accomplish any task (sometimes as many as half a dozen). Once you get familiar with the Windows environment, you'll appreciate having the range of options. In the meantime, try not to get overwhelmed with all the alternatives. As you begin to use Windows, you'll undoubtedly develop your own favorite ways of doing things (and ignore all the rest).*

THE WINDOWS CAST OF CHARACTERS

Icons are pictures that represent programs, folders, or data files.

Dialog boxes are used to display information, ask questions, and/or allow you to change settings.

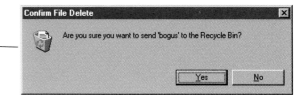

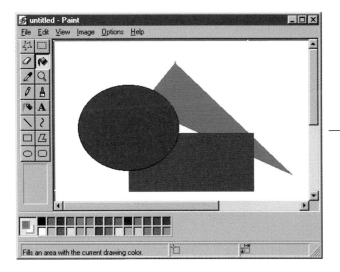

Windows are rectangular frames in which programs and/or data are displayed. (This is the window for the Paint program that comes with Windows.)

WINDOWS 95 HARDWARE REQUIREMENTS

In order to run Windows 95, you need a fairly powerful PC, one with both a reasonably fast CPU (an 80386 is the barely adequate minimum, an 80486 or Pentium is better) and a substantial amount of memory (at least 8MB). You also need a monitor and video adapter card capable of displaying graphics. (A video card is an expansion board that lets your computer "talk to" your monitor. You'll learn more about monitors and video adapter cards in Chapter 8.)

MULTITASKING

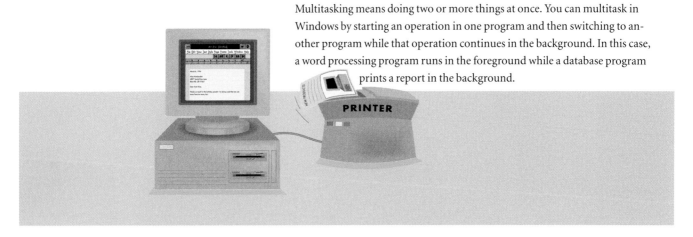

Multitasking means doing two or more things at once. You can multitask in Windows by starting an operation in one program and then switching to another program while that operation continues in the background. In this case, a word processing program runs in the foreground while a database program prints a report in the background.

PRINTER

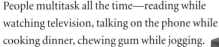

People multitask all the time—reading while watching television, talking on the phone while cooking dinner, chewing gum while jogging.

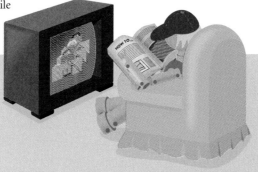

THE WINDOWS DESKTOP

As soon as your computer finishes loading Windows into memory, you'll arrive at a screen known as the Windows *desktop*. The desktop is a metaphor for your workspace—the surface on which you spread out any file folders, programs, and documents you wish to use. Technically, the desktop is the area behind all the objects on the screen, including any windows that you open. No matter what you do in the Windows environment, you can always get back to the desktop. Even if you open an application program and expand it to fill the whole screen, you can return to the desktop with a click or two of your mouse.

NOTE *Windows 95 can be configured to launch a particular program as soon as you reach the desktop. If your computer has been set up this way, you'll only see the desktop momentarily and then you'll see the chosen application program. You can return to the desktop by either* *minimizing or closing the application, both of which you'll learn to do shortly. Depending on how your system has been set up, you may also see a dialog box (a window with various option buttons) with the heading Welcome to Windows 95 and a tip on using the operating system. If you grow tired of the tips, just uncheck the box in the lower-left corner labeled "Show this Welcome Screen next time you start Windows." (You can uncheck the box by clicking it with your mouse.)*

The figure labeled "The Windows Desktop" shows a typical Windows 95 desktop. (Your desktop will probably differ at least slightly, but you should see the same types of objects.) As you can see, this desktop is populated with the little labeled pictures known as *icons*.

N O T E   *If Microsoft Office is installed on your computer, you'll probably see something known as a toolbar near the edge of the screen. A toolbar is a collection of buttons you can click to perform various tasks in a program. The Microsoft Office toolbar contains buttons that let you create and manipulate documents in the programs that are part of the Microsoft Office program "suite." (See the documentation on Microsoft Office for details.)*

Think of icons as doorways, each of which leads to a particular document, program, or folder. When you double-click an icon, you open it up into a rectangular frame called a *window*. The icons that appear on your desktop when you first start Windows provide quick access to the "places" on your computer that you visit most often. (If not, you can add or subtract icons as necessary until your desktop suits you better.)

The most common types of icons include

▶ *Folder icons—open up into folder windows, revealing the contents of particular folders in your computerized filing system.*

▶ *Program icons—open up into application programs, that is, they load the associated programs into memory and start them running.*

▶ *Document icons—open up into documents. When you double-click a document icon, Windows starts up the application (word processing program, spreadsheet, database, whatever) in which the document was created and then opens the document (data file) itself.*

▶ *Shortcut icons—provide alternative entryways to programs, documents, and folders. Shortcut icons always have arrows on them and their labels frequently contain the words "Shortcut to." You'll learn all about shortcuts, and about how they differ from other icons under "Creating and Using Shortcuts" later in this chapter.*

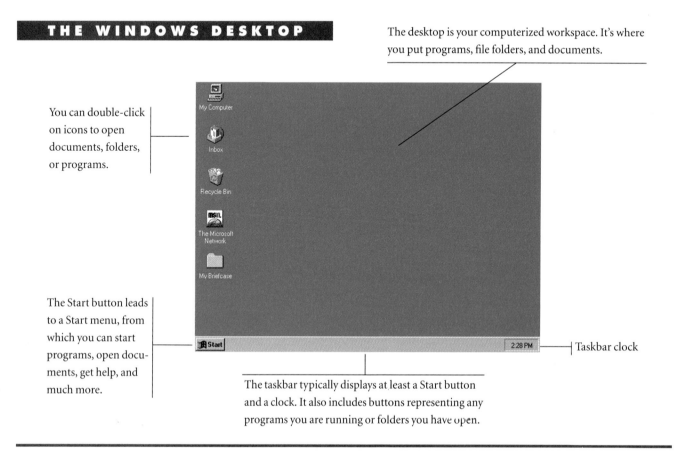

THE WINDOWS DESKTOP

The desktop is your computerized workspace. It's where you put programs, file folders, and documents.

You can double-click on icons to open documents, folders, or programs.

The Start button leads to a Start menu, from which you can start programs, open documents, get help, and much more.

The taskbar typically displays at least a Start button and a clock. It also includes buttons representing any programs you are running or folders you have open.

Taskbar clock

Your desktop may also contain a few specialized icons, including The Recycle Bin, which is used for discarding files and folders, and possibly Microsoft Network, My Briefcase, and Inbox. The Recycle Bin is discussed later in this chapter. The Microsoft Network and Inbox are discussed briefly in Chapter 10. The others are too specialized to be covered in this book; see the Windows Help system for further details. (You'll learn to use the Help system later in this chapter.)

THE TASKBAR

The Windows taskbar is a gray bar with the word Start at one end. It is usually located at the bottom of the desktop but you can move it elsewhere. The taskbar is "control central" for Windows 95. Unless you go out of your way to hide it, the taskbar usually stays on screen all the time, regardless of whether you're looking at the desktop or at an application program. It tells you which programs are currently running, which folder windows are open, and, in most cases, what time it is. It also gives you access to a list of options known as

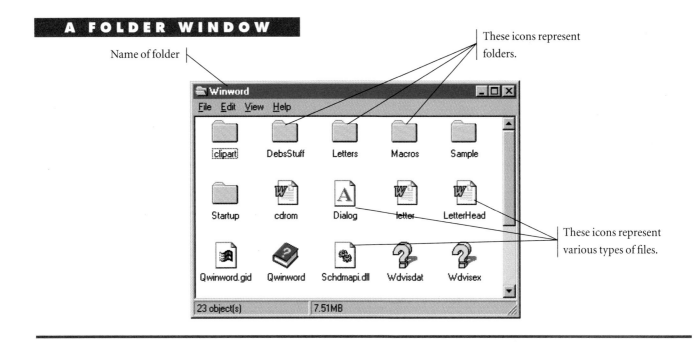

A FOLDER WINDOW

Name of folder

These icons represent folders.

These icons represent various types of files.

the Start menu, which you can use to launch programs, find files, activate the Windows Help system, change the way Windows behaves, and shut down your computer.

The taskbar can be divided into three sections. At the left or top edge is the Start button (the button with the word Start and the Windows logo). Clicking this button opens the Start menu, which you can use to start up Windows applications.

In the center of the taskbar you will see one button for each program that your system is currently running, and one for every folder that's currently open on your desktop. This collection of buttons (known as *task buttons*) not only provides a running status report on your working environment, it also gives you a quick means of switching from one folder and/or application to the next: Whenever you click a task button, Windows immediately activates the associated window or program. When you first start Windows, this middle section of the taskbar will probably be empty. As you begin opening folder windows and starting programs, however, the taskbar will grow a bit more crowded. In the figure titled "The Windows Desktop," there are two task buttons on the taskbar, indicating that Microsoft Word (a word processing program) and Paradox for Windows (a database program) are currently up and running.

The third section of the taskbar is a clock which usually appears at the right edge of the taskbar and displays the current time (or at least the time your computer thinks it is). To display the current date, hold the mouse pointer over the clock for a moment. You can

A TASKBAR WITH PROGRAMS RUNNING

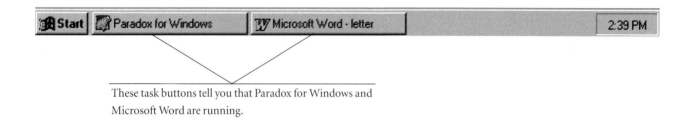

These task buttons tell you that Paradox for Windows and Microsoft Word are running.

change the time and/or date by double-clicking the clock. As described in the following sidebar, you can also get rid of the clock altogether.

WORKING WITH WINDOWS

The Windows program gets its name from its most ubiquitous feature: the rectangular frames, called windows, that you encounter at every turn. Just about everything that happens in the Windows environment takes place inside a window.

There are two types of windows in Windows. An *application window* is a window that houses either a program or a folder. A *document window* is a window that you open inside an application window. It contains data specific to that program. If you load the word processing program Word for Windows, for example, a Word for Windows application window appears on the screen. Then, every time you open or create a document, it is displayed in its own document window within this main window. Document windows always reside inside of application windows and cannot exist without them. If you close an application window, any document windows it contains are closed as well.

MANAGING CROWDED TASKBARS

Once the taskbar becomes full, Windows starts shrinking task buttons every time you open a new folder window or application. Eventually, you won't be able to see the full names of the windows and applications on the buttons. When this happens, you have a few options. You can expand the taskbar by dragging its innermost edge. (The innermost edge is the edge closest to the middle of the screen. If your taskbar is positioned at the bottom of the screen, as it usually is, the innermost edge is the top edge.) Alternatively, you can point to a button and let the mouse pointer hover over it for a second. A small ToolTip window will appear with the full text of the item. You can also make room by getting rid of the clock by right-clicking the taskbar, choosing Properties, clicking the box labeled Show Clock to remove the check mark inside the box, and then selecting OK.

APPLICATION WINDOWS AND DOCUMENT WINDOWS

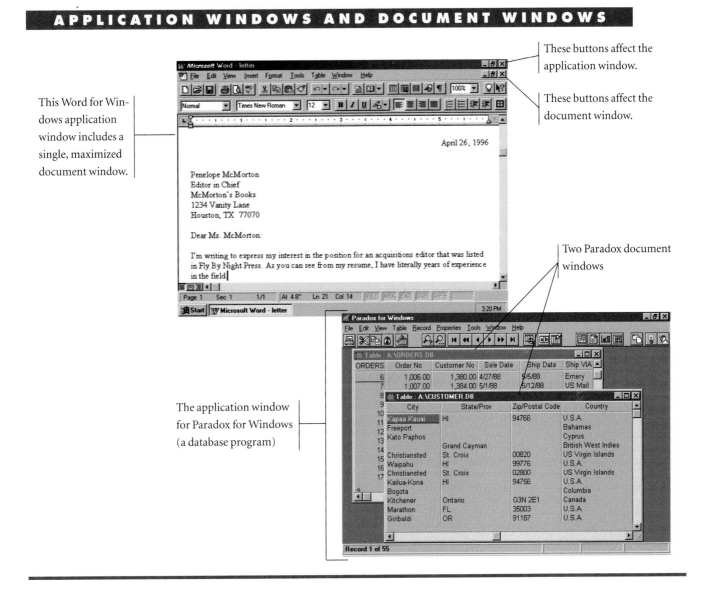

These buttons affect the application window.

These buttons affect the document window.

This Word for Windows application window includes a single, maximized document window.

Two Paradox document windows

The application window for Paradox for Windows (a database program)

NOTE *In case you're wondering where the two types of windows get their names, in Windows-speak, programs are usually called* applications, *and* document *means any set of data, regardless of whether it contains text, pictures, numbers, or anything else. The term "document" is therefore roughly equivalent to file, except that a document has not necessarily been named and saved to disk. If you are using a spreadsheet program, each spreadsheet is a document. If you are using a drawing program, each drawing is a document.*

Both Windows itself and most Windows applications let you arrange your electronic desktop in any way you like. You can work with one window at a time or several. You can move the windows around, shrink them, expand them, arrange them side by side, pile them on top of each other, and so on. In short, you can keep your electronic desktop as spartan or as cluttered as your other desk. (As with a physical desk, however, the more chaotic your Windows desktop, the harder it becomes to find what you need when you need it.)

NOTE *Although most applications let you open multiple document windows at once, only one of those document windows can be active at any moment. In Windows terminology, this window is said to have* focus. *The document window with focus is the one that will respond to your next keystrokes or commands. Its title bar is always the same color as the title bar of its application window. (See the next section for information on title bars.) If the document windows are overlapping, the one with focus is always on top of the stack. In the bottom half of the figure Application Windows and Document Windows, the document window entitled Table: A:\CUSTOMER.DB has focus.*

ANATOMY OF A WINDOW

Application windows (including folder windows) and document windows have several common features, as shown in the figure entitled Anatomy of a Window.

▶ *They have title bars at the top which usually tell you something about the purpose or contents of the window.*

▶ *At the left edge of the title bar, they feature a Control menu icon (it looks like a miniature version of the icon for the program or document displayed in the window).*

▶ *At the right edge of the title bar, they have sizing buttons, which you can use for expanding and shrinking the window (you'll learn more about these shortly), and a Close button (which contains an X), which you can click to close the window.*

▶ *Most application windows also contain status bars along their bottom edges, which serve to display information on the current environment.*

Whenever a window is not large enough to display its contents fully, Windows provides *scroll bars* that let you scroll through the window's contents with your mouse. If the window isn't tall enough to display its contents, you'll see a vertical scroll bar; if it's not wide enough, you'll see a horizontal one. Each scroll bar contains a box known as a *scroll box*. The size of the box indicates how much of the folder or document's contents you're actually seeing in the window. If the scroll box occupies 25 percent of the scroll bar, for example, you're seeing

ANATOMY OF A WINDOW

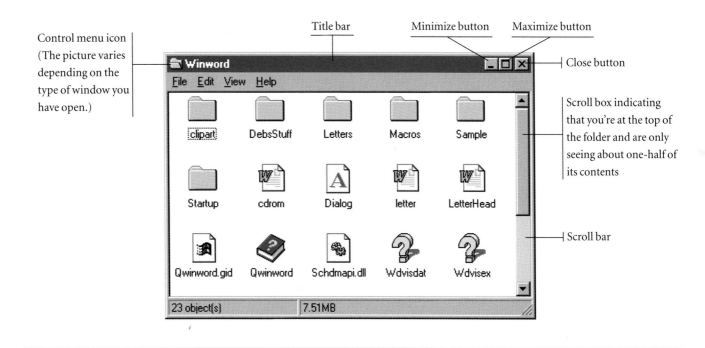

roughly one-quarter of the contents. The position of the scroll box tells you where you are, relative to the entire contents of the folder or document. If the scroll box in a vertical scroll bar is in the middle of the scroll bar, for example, roughly half the contents lie above your current position in the window and half below.

There are several ways to use scroll bars to move through a window's contents.

▶ *To move up or down one line at a time, click the arrow at either end of a vertical scroll bar. To move sideways a character at a time, click the arrow at either end of a horizontal scrollbar. To scroll continuously, point to one of the arrows and keep holding your mouse pointer.*

▶ *To move by approximately one windowful, click within the scroll bar on either side of the scroll box.*

▶ *To move to a specific location, drag the scroll box. Dragging the scroll box to the middle of the scroll bar, for example, takes you to the middle of your document or folder.*

HAVING YOUR WAY WITH WINDOWS

All the windows you'll encounter in Windows are very malleable: You can expand, shrink, push, pull, and rearrange them to your heart's content. When you first open a window, it may occupy less than the entire screen or, in the case of a document window, less than its entire application window. If you want more room to work in, you can expand the window as far as possible by clicking its Maximize button.

NOTE *When you maximize a document window, its title bar merges with that of the application window—so that the title reflects both the program and document names. You also get two sets of Control menu icons and two sets of sizing buttons, which can be a little confusing. (See the figure called "Maximizing, minimizing, and resizing windows" for an example.) The Control menu icon and sizing buttons at opposite ends of the title bar affect the application window. The ones on the next row, to the left and right of the menu bar, control the document window. In many applications, document windows are maximized by default.*

Once you have maximized a window, the Maximize button itself is replaced by a Restore button, which contains a picture of two overlapping windows. Clicking on this button restores the window to its previous size—that is, the size it was just before you maximized it.

NOTE *You can also maximize and restore windows by double-clicking their title bars. If the window is not maximized, double-clicking the title bar expands it to full screen; if it's already maximized, double-clicking the title bar restores it to its previous size.*

To minimize a window, you click its Minimize button. When you minimize an application window, it disappears from the screen but its task button remains on the taskbar. When you minimize a document window, it shrinks to a miniaturized version of the title bar, containing only a Control menu icon, the window title (or some portion thereof), and Restore, Maximize, and Close buttons. Minimizing a window is rather like placing it in a corner of your desk, somewhere in your "to do" pile. You're not putting it away completely; you're just removing it from the center of your attention, with the aim of returning to it later. (In more technical terms, when you minimize a window, you shrink it on the screen but leave it in memory.) You can restore a minimized window in an instant just by clicking its task button (in the case of application windows) or double-clicking its miniaturized title bar (in the case of documents).

MAXIMIZING, MINIMIZING, AND RESTORING WINDOWS

To restore a minimized document window, either double-click it or click it and choose Restore. To maximize a minimized application window, click its task button.

Minimized document window

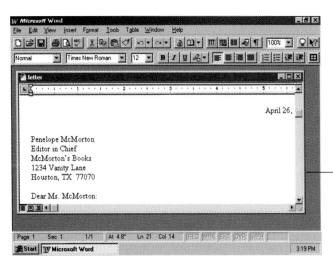

To minimize a restored window, click its Minimize button. To maximize it instead, click its Maximize button or double-click its title bar.

Restored window

To restore a maximized window, click its Restore button or double-click its title bar. To minimize the window, just click its Minimize button.

Maximized window

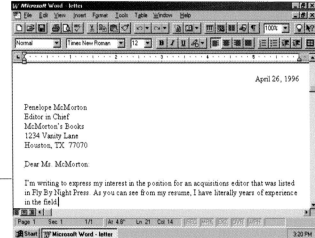

MOVING, RESIZING, AND CLOSING WINDOWS

Y ou can move a window (assuming it is not maximized) by dragging its title bar with the mouse. You also use your mouse to resize a window. Start by slowly moving the mouse pointer across the border until the pointer changes into a double-headed arrow. Then press the left mouse button, drag the border until the window is the desired size, and release the mouse button. If you want to change both the height and width of a window, drag one of its corners.

There are several ways to close a window:

▶ *You can click the Close button (the button with the X) in the window's upper-right corner.*

▶ *You can open the window's Control menu (by clicking the Control menu icon in the upper-left corner) and select Close.*

▶ *You can close a document window by pressing Ctrl+F4, or an application window (including a folder window) by pressing Alt+F4.*

▶ *You can close an application window by opening the File menu and selecting the last option. (You'll learn to work with menus shortly.) This option will be named Close if you're in a folder window; otherwise it will be called Exit. You can close a document window by opening the File menu and choosing Close.*

Bear in mind that closing a window means removing its contents from memory. In the case of document windows, this just means removing data from memory as well as from the screen. (Don't worry: It's not erased from the disk.) In the case of application windows, it means leaving the program.

If you want to manipulate a sample window, just double-click on the My Computer icon to open a folder window. Then try dragging the folder window around the screen, resizing it, maximizing it, minimizing it (notice that it disappears from the screen and appears as a button on the taskbar), restoring it (by clicking the button on the taskbar), and then closing it.

WORKING WITH MENUS

A s you have seen, you can perform many operations in Windows just by clicking, double-clicking, or dragging with your mouse. But other tasks require you to work with menus, telling the computer what you want it to do by selecting options from onscreen lists.

RESIZING AND MOVING WINDOWS

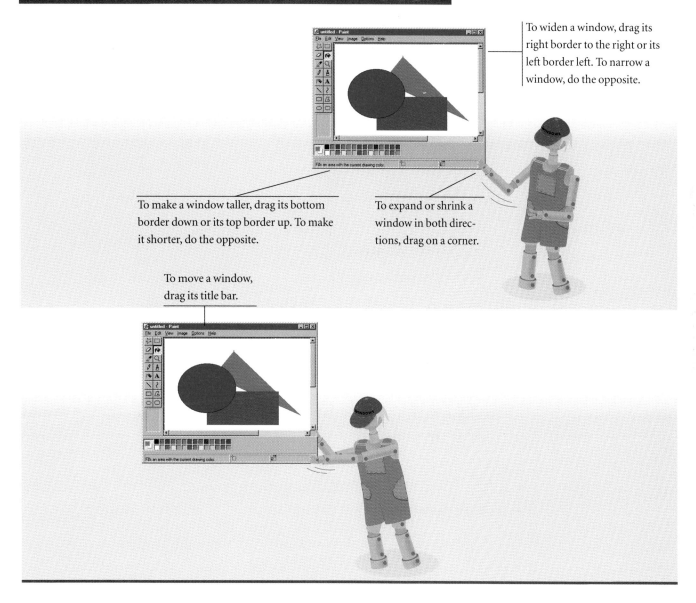

To widen a window, drag its right border to the right or its left border left. To narrow a window, do the opposite.

To make a window taller, drag its bottom border down or its top border up. To make it shorter, do the opposite.

To expand or shrink a window in both directions, drag on a corner.

To move a window, drag its title bar.

There are four main types of menus in Windows and in most Windows applications: menu bars, pull-down menus, submenus, and context menus. Most application windows (including folder windows) sport menu bars just below their title bars. (The menu bar generally looks like a set of words—such as File, Edit, View, and Help—laid out horizontally starting at the left edge of the screen.) To select an option from a menu bar, you can either:

▶ *Click the option with your mouse (for example, to select File and thereby open the File menu, you simply click on the word "File") or*

TYPES OF MENUS

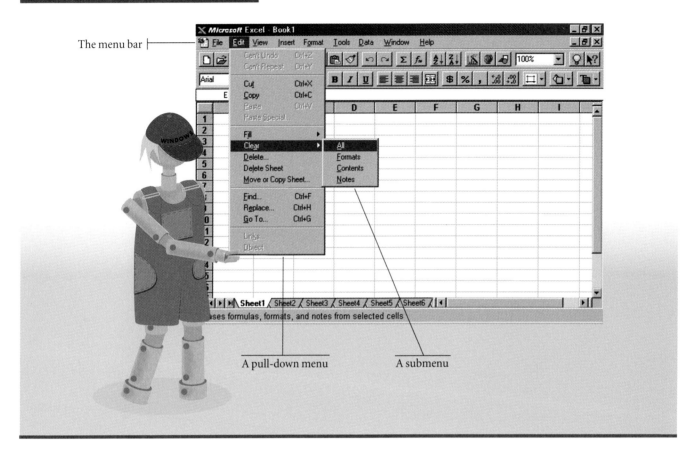

The menu bar

A pull-down menu

A submenu

▶ *Hold down the Alt key and press the underlined letter in the option name. To select File, for example, you would press Alt+F.*

NOTE   *If you start to select either a menu option or a button on the screen and then change your mind, move the mouse pointer to a blank area of the screen before you release the mouse button.*

In some cases, selecting an option from one menu evokes another menu with a more specific set of options. Whenever you point to a menu option that leads to a submenu, the menu automatically appears to the right of the current menu or, if there is no room to the right, to the left. To select an option from that submenu, slide your mouse pointer directly to the right (or left if the submenu is to the left). Then, once your pointer is positioned on the submenu, move up or down as necessary to point to the desired option. You can also select options from pull-down or submenus by using the Up Arrow or Down Arrow key to highlight the option and then pressing Enter, or by typing the underlined letter in the option name.

MENU CONVENTIONS

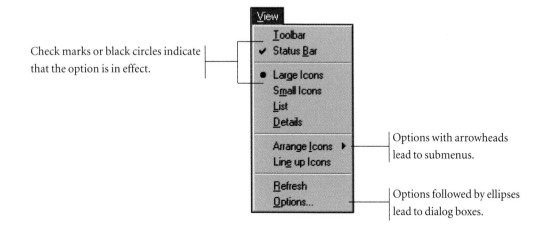

Check marks or black circles indicate that the option is in effect.

Options with arrowheads lead to submenus.

Options followed by ellipses lead to dialog boxes.

NOTE *Menus are often referred to by the name of the option you select to open them, and the phrase "opening a menu" means displaying a pull-down menu. Hence "open the File menu" means click on the File option on the menu bar (or press Alt+F) to display the pull-down menu associated with that option.*

To close a pull-down menu, simply click anywhere outside the menu or press Esc twice. To close a submenu, point to another option on the menu to its left or press Esc.

NOTE *In most Windows programs, when you point to an option on a pull-down menu or submenu, a short description of that option appears in the status bar at the bottom of the window.*

There are several conventions used in Windows menus to convey information about particular menu options. Some of these conventions are shown and explained in the figure entitled Menu Conventions. In addition, on many menus you will notice the names of keys or key combinations displayed to the right of some menu options. You can use these keys, which are known as *accelerator keys*, as an alternative to using the menu system—pressing the accelerator key has exactly the same effect as selecting the associated menu option. Three of the most useful accelerator keys are Ctrl+C (equivalent to opening the Edit menu and choosing the Copy option), Ctrl+X (equivalent to choosing the Cut option from the Edit menu), and Ctrl+V (equivalent to choosing the Paste option from the Edit menu). Once you memorize these key combinations, you'll use them constantly to copy and move files and folders as well as to copy and move data within application programs.

Context menus are menus that appear when you right-click an object on the screen. (Such menus are sometimes called object menus or shortcut menus as well.) Remember that right-clicking means pointing to an object and then clicking the right mouse button. Each context menu is essentially a list of the operations you can perform on the associated object. The content of the menu therefore varies from one type of object to the next. If you right-click a folder icon, for example, you'll see a menu with options like Open, Copy, Delete, and Rename. If you right-click the icon for a floppy disk, you'll get an context menu that includes Copy Disk, Format, and Eject.

USING THE CONTROL PANEL

The Windows Control Panel is a special folder that contains tools for customizing the Windows environment. You can use these tools (most of which are actually little programs) to do everything from adjusting the speed at which your mouse moves across the screen, to resetting the date and time, to adding new hardware or software to your system. To access the Control Panel, click the Start button, select Settings, and choose Control Panel. Then double-click the appropriate icon. (Feel free to explore the various tools: You can always bail out by either closing the resulting folder window or clicking a Cancel button.)

TALKING TO DIALOG BOXES

Dialog boxes are special windows that appear whenever a program needs more information before it can complete an operation you've requested. (Think of them as computerized questionnaires.)

Sometimes expressing your preferences in a dialog box is a simple matter of clicking command buttons labeled Yes or No, OK or Cancel. Other times, it involves stating your preferences via onscreen devices such as list boxes, drop-down list boxes (aka combo boxes), check boxes, spinners, text boxes, sliders, and option buttons (aka radio buttons). Most of these items are shown and described in the figure "Dialog Box Elements."

When you're done with a dialog box, you usually leave it by selecting a button labeled either OK or Close (if there is one) or by clicking the Close button in the Window's upper-right corner. In many cases, the OK button will be the default choice, so you can also select it by just pressing Enter. (The button that will be selected if you press Enter has a darker border than the other buttons and may have a rectangle of dots surrounding the button's label.) If you decide to cancel the operation the dialog box is asking you about, click the button labeled Cancel or press Esc. If there is no Cancel button, try clicking the Close button.

DIALOG BOX ELEMENTS

These are option buttons (sometimes called radio buttons). Clicking on one button selects that option (the button darkens) and deselects any other selected option button in the group. In other words, the options are mutually exclusive.

Click these tabs to move to a different page of the dialog box, with a whole new set of options.

Check boxes (not shown here) are boxes that you can click on to select or deselect. (Selected check boxes usually display an X or a check mark.)

Click these command buttons to carry out an action or to display another dialog box.

These are spinners. You can click the up arrow to increase the value or the down arrow to decrease it. You can also type values in the box if that seems easier.

You can click on the downward pointing arrow to display a drop-down list box of options from which you can choose. Regular list boxes are similar but show more than one option at a time.

You can enter text or numbers in text boxes. For example, you could type **10** here to have 10 be the first page number.

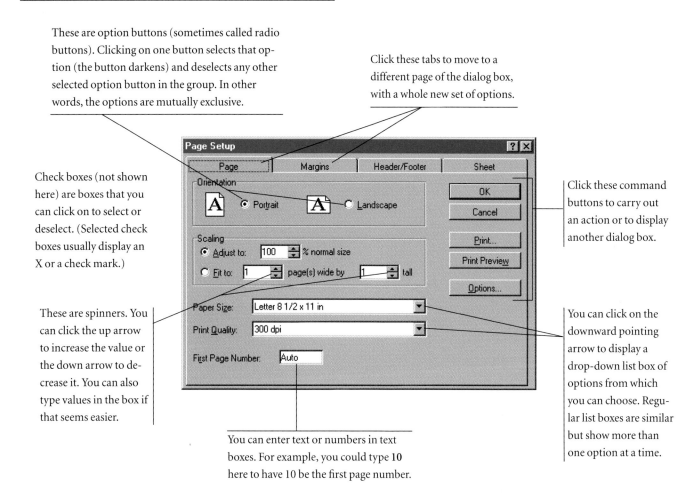

Some dialog boxes feature tabs, much like the plastic tabs in many notebooks. For example, the dialog box in the figure "Dialog Box Elements" has four tabs: Page, Margins, Header/Footer, and Sheet. You can switch from one of these "pages" of options to another by clicking the appropriate tab.

FINDING OUT ABOUT YOUR COMPUTER SYSTEM

You can elicit basic information about your computer by right-clicking the My Computer icon and choosing Properties. You will see a System Properties dialog box, which describes the version of Windows you are running, who it's registered to, and the type of CPU chip and amount of RAM your computer contains. When you're done reading this information, click OK or Cancel to close the dialog box. For information about the amount of available space on your hard disk, double-click My Computer, right-click the icon for your hard disk, and select Properties. The resulting dialog box includes a pie chart diagramming the amount of used and free disk space.

GETTING TO WORK

Windows's main purpose is to serve as a platform for applications software, a launch pad for more goal-oriented word-processing, database, and spreadsheet programs (among others). There are two approaches to getting to work in Windows.

▶ *You can open an existing document or create a new document from the desktop and Windows will automatically launch the appropriate application. If you open a document created in WordPerfect for Windows, for example, Windows will launch Word-Perfect and then open the specified document.*

▶ *You can start the program you want to use and then either open an existing document or create a new one.*

Not all applications require or even allow you to create documents. For example, playing a game or using the Windows calculator does not involve creating a document. In both cases, you'll always start the program directly. But much of your work will involve creating documents (data files). And you may find it more intuitive to open a particular document and let Windows worry about which program you used to create the document.

To get to work by opening an existing document, you can do any of the following:

▶ *Locate the icon for the document you wish to use—in a folder window, in the Windows Explorer (which you'll learn about shortly), or on the desktop itself—and double-click it.*

▶ *If you opened the document any time recently, open the Start menu and choose Documents. (There are at least three ways to activate the Start menu. You can click the Start button in the lower-left corner of your screen; you can press Ctrl+Esc, or, if you have a Windows 95 keyboard, you can press one of the Windows logo keys.) You will see a list of the most recently opened documents. To open one of them, just click it.*

▶ *If you are using Microsoft Office, open the Start menu and choose New Office Document. You'll see a dialog box in which you can specify the type of document you'd like to create. Later, when you save the document, you'll get to specify both a name and a location for the file.*

To create a new document, try either of these techniques:

▶ *Right-click the desktop or an empty area in a folder window and choose New. You will see a menu that includes options for Folder and Shortcut (in case you want to create items of those types) as well as several types of documents. (The types of documents that appear in the list depend on which programs you have installed on your computer.) As soon as you pick one, Windows will create a new icon for the document and assign it a name such as "New Microsoft Word Document." This document name will still be selected after the dialog box disappears. This means that you can change it just by typing in something else. Then you can open the new document by either double-clicking the icon or right-clicking it and choosing Open.*

▶ *If you are using Microsoft Office, open the Start menu and choose Open Office Document from the top of the menu. You'll soon see a dialog box you can use to search for and select the desired document. (See the program documentation for details.)*

If you prefer to start a program directly, do any of the following:

▶ *Open the Start menu, select Programs, and then select the program you wish to use. Often when you select a program from the Programs submenu, you'll see another submenu including both the main program and other little programs or documents. For example, if you choose the option for Myst (a computer game), you'll see a submenu with the options Myst and The Making of Myst. You'd choose Myst to open the program itself.*

▶ *Locate the icon for the program you want to use—in a folder window, in the Windows Explorer, or on the desktop—and either double-click it or select it and press Enter.*

NOTE *Some CD-ROMs have an auto-play feature, so that all you need to do to launch the programs they contain is insert the disc in the drive. If nothing happens when you insert the disc, you'll need to launch the program in the usual way: opening a folder window for the CD-ROM drive and then double-clicking the program icon.*

There's actually one final way to open documents and applications. Windows lets you create special icons, known as *shortcuts*, that allow you easy access to a frequently used program or document. To use a shortcut, you simply double-click the icon. Although you can place shortcuts in folder windows, they're usually placed on the desktop itself (since the whole point is to spare you the trouble of hunting around in folders or on menus). You'll learn to make your own shortcuts under "Creating and Using Shortcuts" later in this chapter.

NOTE *It's entirely possible to load two or even more copies of the same program into memory at once, although there's rarely a good reason to do so. When you want to use a program,* *remember to check whether a copy is already running by reading through the task buttons on the taskbar. If you do find a task button for the program, use that rather than starting another copy of the program. Otherwise, you'll be filling up memory unnecessarily, and slowing your computer in the process.*

SWITCHING APPLICATIONS

As mentioned, one of the benefits of using Windows is that you can run several applications at once. No matter how many applications you open, however, only one of them is active at one time. The active program is the one that is affected by any commands you issue or data you enter. It is sometimes called the foreground application, because it always sits on top of the stack of application windows—in front of all the others. (Depending on whether the window is maximized, you may or may not see part of the other application windows underneath.) The foreground application is also the one that receives most of your

RUNNING DOS PROGRAMS IN WINDOWS

A program does not need to be designed for Windows in order to run inside the Windows environment; regular DOS programs will work in Windows as well. As you might guess, there are several ways to launch a DOS program under Windows.

- If your DOS application appears on the Start menu's Program submenu, select it from there.
- Find the icon for the program in a folder or Windows Explorer window and double-click it.
- Select Programs from the Start menu and then select MS-DOS from the program list, and then start up the program as you normally would in DOS.

You can also create shortcuts for DOS programs just as you would for a Windows program.

If you launch a DOS program using either of the first two methods, terminate the program by exiting as you normally would in DOS. If you've launched a DOS program by going first to the MS-DOS Prompt, when you exit the program you'll be returned to the DOS prompt. From there, either click the window's Close button or type EXIT and press Enter to return to Windows.

All but a few DOS-based programs can be run either in a window, just like a Windows application, or in "full-screen mode." (A few DOS programs can only run in full-screen mode.) When you run a DOS program in full-screen mode, the desktop temporarily disappears and the DOS program fills the screen. You can switch back and forth between full-screen and windowed modes by pressing Alt+Enter. If you are running a DOS application in full-screen mode, use Alt+Tab to switch to other applications.

If you want to work exclusively at the DOS prompt, press the function key labeled F8 while your computer is booting. When a menu of startup options appears, type 6 for "Command prompt only" and press Enter. If you want to run Windows later, you must type WIN at the DOS prompt and press Enter. If you're already in Windows and want to work exclusively in DOS, choose Shut Down from the Start menu. Then select Restart the Computer in MS-DOS mode. When you're done working in DOS, either turn your computer off or type EXIT and press Enter if you want to return to Windows.

CPU's attention. Other open applications are said to be running in the background, meaning that they continue to plod along at any tasks you have assigned to them, but they do so slowly, since they are receiving a relatively small part of your CPU's brain power.

Whenever you run more than one application at a time, you'll need a method of switching from one to the next. Your options for doing so include

▶ *Clicking the application's button on the taskbar.*

▶ *If any part of the other program's application window is visible, clicking in that window.*

▶ *Pressing Alt+Tab. When you do this, Windows displays a window in the center of the screen that contains icons representing each program you're running. If you hold down Alt and continue to press Tab, Windows cycles through the programs, enclosing one after another within a box, and listing its name at the bottom of the window. When the program you want is selected, release both keys to switch to that program.*

If you want to return to the desktop without closing applications, you can minimize all your application windows by right-clicking a part of the taskbar that isn't covered by a task button and choosing Minimize All Windows. This allows you to take advantage of your desktop shortcuts or wander through folder windows. (Be sure to right-click the taskbar, which is usually located all the way at the bottom of the screen, rather than the status bar of your application program, which may appear just above the task bar.) If you want to reverse this action later, just right-click the taskbar again and choose Undo Minimize All. Or you can return to particular programs by clicking the appropriate task button on the taskbar. Bear in mind that you don't need to return to the desktop to launch new programs: You can always use the Start menu.

WORKING WITH FOLDER WINDOWS

As you know, folders are the building blocks of your computerized filing system. You can think of the desktop as the top or outermost layer of this system. The desktop contains megafolders entitled My Computer and, if you're part of a network, Network Neighborhood. Those megafolders contain folders for individual disk and CD-ROM drives. (My Computer is the container for all the drives on your local computer and Network Neighborhood provides access to drives on your network file server and other computers on your network.) And those drive folders, in turn, contain a combination of file folders, representing groups of program and document files, and individual files. The filing system can continue indefinitely—folders can contain folders (often called subfolders) which can contain additional folders, and so on. The figure titled "The Folder Hierarchy" shows the basic structure of the filing system on most standalone (non-networked) PCs.

The My Computer folder serves as your point of entry into your own computer's filing system. It is the first folder you'll open and, in most cases, the last one you'll close. (If you're part of a network, you'll use Network Neighborhood to enter the filing system of the network server.)

As mentioned, you can open a folder window by double-clicking on a folder icon. If the folder you want to reach is more than one level down in the folder hierarchy—that is, is anywhere below the My Computer or Network Neighborhood level—you'll need to open two or more folder windows to get there—rather like those Russian nesting dolls in which one doll contains another, which contains another, and so on.

When you open one folder window from inside another, the first window (often called the *parent window*) usually remains open on the desktop, partially covered by the newly opened *child window*. If you want to leave the child window open, but activate the parent window, you can either click somewhere in the parent window or press the Backspace key.

CUSTOMIZING WINDOWS

For the interior decorators among you, Windows provides some simple tools for dressing up your desktop and changing the Windows color scheme. To customize the desktop, right-click an empty spot on the desktop and choose Properties to invoke a Display Properties dialog box. At this point, you can use the Pattern list to choose a geometric pattern with which to fill the desktop, or use the Wallpaper list to select a graphic, which you can either tile (repeat across the desktop) or center. (Look at the monitor to see your results.) If you select wallpaper and then choose the Tile option, the effect is similar to selecting a pattern from the Pattern list. You can't display tiled wallpaper and a pattern at the same time: If you select both, the tiled wallpaper takes precedence, covering up the pattern completely. If you center the wallpaper (by clicking the Center option button), you'll see a single copy of the selected image in the center of your desktop. You can also create your own wallpaper, by saving a graphic image—such as a picture you create in a drawing program or a photograph on a photo CD—as a .BMP file. Then you can use the Browse button in the dialog box to find and select that file. (The .BMP file format is Windows's standard graphics format. For information on photo CDs, see Chapter 9.)

To change the Windows color scheme, right-click an empty spot on the desktop, choose Properties, and select the Appearance tab in the Display Properties dialog box. Click the arrow at the right edge of the Scheme drop-down list to display a list of schemes. As soon as you pick one, Windows displays a sample in the upper half of the dialog box. When you've located a scheme that you like, click OK to close the dialog box and put your new scheme into effect. To return to the standard Windows color scheme, repeat this procedure and select Windows Standard from the Scheme drop-down list.

THE FOLDER HIERARCHY

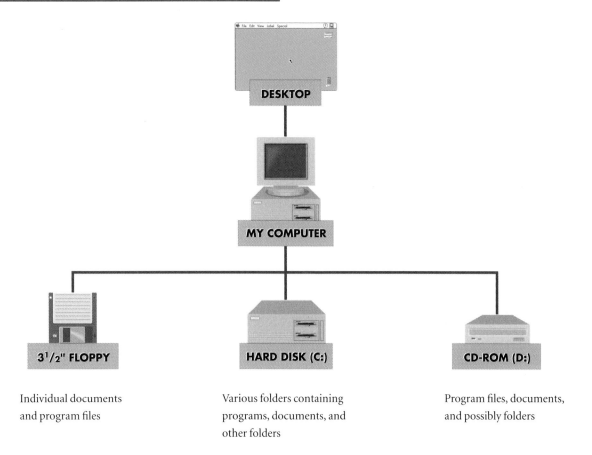

DESKTOP

MY COMPUTER

3¹/₂" FLOPPY

Individual documents
and program files

HARD DISK (C:)

Various folders containing
programs, documents, and
other folders

CD-ROM (D:)

Program files, documents,
and possibly folders

N O T E *If you insert a floppy disk or CD-ROM into a drive while a folder window for that drive is open, you will need to open the folder window's View menu and choose Refresh to see the contents of the newly inserted disk.*

When you open a folder window, the left section of the status bar at the bottom of the window indicates the number of items in the window; the right section indicates the amount of disk space occupied by those items. As soon as you select one or more items in the window, the status bar tells you the number of items selected.

N O T E *To find out the amount of room left on your hard disk, double-click the My Computer icon on the desktop, click the icon for the hard disk, and look at the right side of the folder window's status bar.*

As mentioned, when you open a folder from within another folder window, the "parent" window normally remains open on the desktop even as a new folder window is opened. Although this makes it easy to see how you arrived at the current folder window, it can also lead to a very cluttered desktop, particularly if you burrow several levels down in the folder hierarchy. Fortunately there's a trick for closing several folder windows at once. If you hold down the Shift key while you open a window's File menu and choose Close, Windows closes not only that window but all of its "ancestors" (that is, its parent window, its parent's parent window, and so on).

You can also change Windows's behavior so that only one folder window is open at a time. If you opt for this single-window mode, whenever you open a new folder, the folder window changes to reflect that folder's contents. Although this makes it a little harder to see at a glance where the current folder falls in the folder hierarchy, it also makes for a much neater desktop. To switch to single-window mode, open the View menu in any folder window and choose Options to display an Options dialog box. Select the second option button (the one labeled "Browse folders by using a single window that changes as you open each folder") and click OK. (To change back to multiple-window mode, select Options from the View menu in any folder window and select the first option button.) In single-window mode, you can still return to the parent folder if you like by pressing the Backspace key. If you do, however, Windows displays the parent folder's contents in the folder window rather than opening up a separate window.

CREATING NEW FOLDERS

You can create new folders by right-clicking a blank spot on the desktop or within a folder window, and selecting New from the context menu. (Alternatively, you can open the File menu and select New.) Next, you select Folder from the resulting submenu. Windows will create a new folder icon with the label New Folder. Since the label will already be selected, all you need to do to rename the folder is type in the name you want and press Enter. Once you have created a folder, you can either store new files in it as you create them, or you can copy or move files or folders from other, older folders.

When you install a new program, a folder for that program is created automatically.

DESIGNING YOUR FILING SYSTEM

If you've just purchased a computer, spend some time thinking about how you want to organize your files. Which programs are you likely to use most often? Would it be helpful to group programs, creating one folder for game programs and another for work programs, for example, or one folder for kid programs and another for adult programs? What kinds of data files are you likely to create? Would it be helpful to separate word processing documents by person (if more than one person is using your computer) or by subject? You can always change your mind later, but when you do, you'll need to take some time moving files from one place to another. The more organization you can institute up front, the better.

RULES FOR FILE AND FOLDER NAMES

In Windows 95, the names you assign to files and folders can be up to 255 characters long. They can include spaces and periods. The only characters that file and folder names cannot include are

$$* \mid < > ? / \text{"} :$$

The names for most files include short last names known as *extensions* which are usually used to identify the file type. Programs that use extensions add them to your filenames automatically. If you name a file "Letter to Sally," in Word for Windows, for example, the full filename becomes "Letter to Sally.doc" (the period and the doc extension are added by the program itself). Windows maintains its own registry of file types and the associated extensions. By default, Windows does not display any extensions it recognizes. This means that even though your full filename is "Letter to Sally.doc," it still appears as "Letter to Sally" in folder and Explorer windows. If you prefer to see the extensions in folder or Explorer windows, open the View menu, choose Options, and select the View tab. In the resulting dialog box, deselect the check box labeled "Hide MS-DOS file extensions for file types that are registered." This change applies to all folder and Explorer windows, not just the one that's active at the moment.

The rules for file and folder names in Windows 95 are far more lenient than the rules in DOS. In DOS, files can have a first name of up to eight characters followed by a period and an optional extension. Spaces are not allowed and the characters = , . ; [ ] are prohibited, in addition to the characters that are prohibited in Windows 95.

Windows 95 actually keeps track of two filenames for every file: the filename that you assign and a DOS-compatible version called the MS-DOS filename. (If your Windows filename respects all DOS file-naming rules, the two filenames will be identical.) If you give copies of your files to people who are using DOS or an older version of Windows, they'll need to use the MS-DOS filenames when opening the files. If you want to see the MS-DOS filename for a file, right-click the file icon and select Properties. Windows will display a Properties dialog box with information on the file, including its type, location, size, the dates on which it was created, last modified, and last accessed, and its MS-DOS filename. It also contains information about file attributes, which you don't need to worry about at this point.

MS-DOS FILENAMES

When devising MS-DOS filenames, Windows takes the first six characters of the Windows filename, excluding any spaces, and then adds a tilde character (~) plus a single numeric digit. (But remember that it doesn't have to go through these contortions if the Windows filename matches DOS file naming conventions.) If there is no other file in the folder with the same first six characters in its MS-DOS filename, the digit at the end of the filename is 1. If there's already a file with those first six characters, followed by a tilde and the number 1, then the final digit is 2, and so on. For example, if you create a file with a Windows filename of "Note to John," the MS-DOS filename will be NOTETO~1. If you create another file in the same folder named "Note to Sally," its MS-DOS filename will be NOTETO~2. If you plan on giving a file to someone who uses MS-DOS or an earlier version of Windows, try to convey something about the contents of the file in the first six characters of the filename. In addition, if that person changes the file and returns it to you, the original Windows 95 filename will be lost: The Windows 95 filename will be the same as the MS-DOS filename.

CHANGING YOUR VIEW OF A FOLDER WINDOW

Windows provides four different ways of representing the items in a folder window. By default, most folder windows display the items in a folder window in what's known as the Large Icons view. You can change to a different view, using the View option on the window's menu bar. When you open the View menu, you'll see options for Large Icons, Small Icons, List, and Details. The figure "Four Views of a Folder Window" shows all the possibilities. The only difference between Small Icons view and List view is that items are arranged horizontally in Small Icons view and vertically in List view. Details view gives you more information than the other three views, displaying each item's size, item type (folder or file), and the date last modified, as well as the name.

FOUR VIEWS OF A FOLDER WINDOW

Large Icons view. Each drive, folder, or file is shown as a large icon with a name or description underneath.

Small Icons view. Each drive, folder, or file is shown as a small icon with a name or description to its right.

List view. This view is just like Small Icons view, but the icons are arranged vertically rather than horizontally.

Details view. This view not only lists item names, but also indicates the size and type of the item, as well as when it was last modified.

You can change the widths of columns in Details view by dragging the borders between the column headings with your mouse. To narrow the Type column, for example, you could drag the border to the right of the column heading "Type" to the left.

NOTE *The Details view tells you when a file was last modified. To find out when it was created or when it was last opened, right-click the filename or icon and choose Properties from the context menu.*

To sort icons, open the View menu and choose the Arrange Icons option. Then you can choose to sort by name, file type, file size, or date last modified. If you want to straighten up the icons without actually changing their order, choose Line up Icons. To sort the items in Details view, just click a column heading. Clicking on Size, for example, sorts the list in order by file size. Clicking on Name sorts it alphabetically by filename. The order you establish in one view carries over to any other view you choose. If you sort items by Size in Details view, for example, they remain sorted by size when you switch to Large Icons view.

If you want Windows to automatically preserve a particular arrangement of icons in Large Icons and Small Icons view, open the View menu, choose Arrange Icons, and then se-lect Auto Arrange. Once Auto Arrange is turned on (that is, appears checked on the menu), any new items you add to the folder are instantly escorted to their proper place in the order you've specified. If you drag an icon out of position, it snaps right back. If you delete an icon, the remaining ones immediately close ranks. The one advantage of leaving Auto Arrange off is that it allows you to create your own clusters of icons within a folder window.

MANIPULATING FILES AND FOLDERS

The more you use your computer, the more files and folders you are likely to accumulate. Learning to handle these files and folders—to copy or move them from one disk to an-other or one folder to another, to change their names, and to delete ones you no longer need—is an essential part of using your computer well. When it comes to files, you can carry out some of these types of operations inside your application programs. But if you need to work with folders, or if you want to manipulate several files at once, you'll need to work with Windows itself.

There are actually two environments in which you can carry out file system mainte-nance in Windows. For now, we'll focus on using folder windows. Later, you'll learn to per-form the same operations using the Windows Explorer.

The first step in manipulating (copying, moving, renaming, or deleting) a file or folder using folder windows is to drill down through the folder hierarchy until you reach the win-dow that contains the associated icon. (You should already know how to do this.) The next step is to select the icon, which you can do with any of the following techniques.

▶ *To select one item, just click its icon.*

▶ *To select multiple items, click one and then hold down Ctrl while you click on others.*

▶ *To select multiple items using your mouse, you "lasso" the items. To do this, move the mouse pointer to a spot slightly above and to the left of the group of items and then drag to a point just below and to the right of the items. As you drag, Windows displays a dotted rectangle around the group of items you are lassoing. As soon as you release the mouse button, all the items inside the rectangle become selected. (This technique is hard to use in anything other than Large Icons view.)*

▶ *If the items you want to select happen to be contiguous, click the first (highest) one you want to select and then hold down Shift while you click the last (lowest).*

▶ *To select everything in the window, choose Edit from the menu bar and then choose Select All (or you can use the accelerator key Ctrl+A).*

To deselect a group of files, click the mouse anywhere else, without holding down Ctrl or Shift.

There are several different ways to copy or move selected files and/or folders. The method that's probably the easiest and safest for beginners involves three steps:

▶ *Select the items you want to copy or move in a folder window. If you want to copy files from a floppy disk, insert the disk in the drive, open a folder window for My Computer, double-click the icon for your floppy disk drive, and then select the desired files.*

▶ *Issue a command to "cut" the items if you plan to move them, or copy the items if you plan to make duplicates. You can do this either by opening the Edit menu and choosing Cut or Copy or by using accelerator keys: Ctrl+X cuts the selected items and Ctrl+C copies them. You can also just right-click the selected item and choose Cut or Copy from its context menu. (If more than one icon is selected, right-click any one of them.)*

N O T E   *When you cut items, the icons don't disappear right away; their outlines become dotted so that they look a little ghostlike. As soon as you paste the items in their new location, these ghost icons disappear.*

▶ *Open a folder window for the folder into which you want to copy the items (you may need to root around in your folder hierarchy again to find the folder). Then either right-click a blank spot within the window and choose Paste from the context menu or open the Edit menu again and choose Paste (or use the accelerator key Ctrl+V). You'll immediately see the items you pasted appear in the window. Alternatively, you can locate the icon for the folder into which you want to copy or move the items, right-click the icon itself, and choose Paste from the context menu.*

If you want to copy files from your hard drive to a floppy disk, there's an even easier method. Just find and select icons for the file(s) you want to copy. Then right-click any one of the selected icons and choose Send To. When Windows displays a menu of places you can direct the file(s) to, choose the option for your floppy drive.

If you try to move or copy a file to a folder that already contains a file of the same name, you'll see a dialog box asking you if you really want to replace the other version of the file. Select Yes if you do or No if you don't. If you are moving or copying multiple files at once, the dialog box will offer the choices Yes (meaning replace this file and then ask me about any others), Yes to All (meaning yes, replace all files of the same names), No (meaning don't replace this file, but ask me about the others), and Cancel (meaning stop moving or copying altogether).

You can rename a file or folder by clicking the file or folder's label once to select it and then a second time to display an insertion point inside the label, or by right-clicking the icon and choosing Rename. Then type in the desired name.

To delete one or more files, start by selecting the items and then press Del, drag them to the Recycle Bin icon on your desktop, or issue the File, Delete command. If you press Del, Windows will ask you to confirm that you want to send the items to the Recycle Bin.

DRAG AND DROP

You can also move and copy items between folders using a feature known as *drag-and-drop*—that is, by using your mouse to drag selected items from one folder window to another, or from a folder window to the icon for another folder. If you want to try this, it's safer to right-drag the items rather than left-drag (that is, to drag using the right mouse button rather than the left). That way, when you release the mouse button, Windows will ask whether you want to copy or move the selected items. (If you drag using the left mouse button rather than the right, Windows will decide whether you intend to copy or move depending on whether you're dragging between folders on the same disk or on different disks.)

Be wary of dragging icons within folder windows that are in List, Small Icons, or Details view: It's all too easy to rearrange your folder hierarchy by mistake. If you accidentally drag one folder on top of another, for example, you make it a subfolder of that folder. Since I've found it easier to do this by accident than on purpose, I'd avoid dragging icons around inside a folder window, particularly if you're using anything other than Large Icons view. If you want to move a folder, use any of the cut or copy and paste methods described above. You're much less likely to make a mistake.

If you do drag something to the wrong place by accident, try right-clicking a blank spot in the folder window or on the desktop and choosing Undo Move. If you misplace either a file or folder, you can also use the Find command to ferret it out. (The Find command is described later in this chapter under "Finding Files in Windows.")

NOTE *If you delete one or more files and then change your mind before you've deleted, copied, renamed, or created any other file, you can reverse the deletion by right-clicking a blank spot on the desktop or in a folder window and selecting Undo Delete from the context menu. If it's too late for that technique, you can also undo deletions using the Recycle Bin folder, as described in the next section.*

USING THE RECYCLE BIN

The Recycle Bin icon on your desktop is actually a folder icon. When you select one or more files or folders and either press Del or drag those items to the Recycle Bin icon, Windows does not actually erase them. Instead, it simply stores them in the Recycle Bin folder. If you have a change of heart, you can open that folder and retrieve some or all of the items you previously recycled.

Items deleted from either floppy disks or network servers are not stored in the Recycle Bin. When you delete such items, Windows asks you to confirm the deletion. If you delete a file from within an application program, it may or may not get stored in the Recycle Bin—you'll need to try deleting one and then check.

When you delete a folder, Windows moves its contents, but not the folder itself, to the Recycle Bin. If you restore any of the folder's contents, Windows will ask if you want to recreate the folder. If you want to restore all of a folder's contents, sort the list by Original Location (by clicking on that column heading), then select all the items in the folder by clicking the first and then holding Shift as you click the last item, and finally select Restore from the File menu.

To retrieve items from the Recycle Bin, double-click the Recycle Bin icon to open it into a folder window. This window differs from other folder windows only in that it uses Details view by default and the view includes columns for the item's original location and the date the item was deleted. To recover an item, just select it, open the File menu and choose Restore.

By default, Windows lets you keep adding items to the Recycle Bin until it's full. (By default, the Recycle Bin is considered full when it consumes 10 percent of the space on the hard disk on which Windows was installed.) Then Windows automatically empties the Recycled Bin, erasing its contents from your disk.

If you are running low on disk space, you may want to empty the Recycle Bin yourself by right-clicking the Recycle Bin icon and choosing Empty Recycle Bin from the context menu. If you're already in the Recycle Bin window, choose Empty Recycle Bin from the File menu.

You might also empty the Recycle Bin if you want to make sure that no one can easily retrieve some of the items inside (the equivalent of paper shredding.)

Dealing with Disks in Windows

You learned the reason for formatting disks in Chapter 3. The mechanics of doing so are simple: You just place the disk in the drive, double-click the My Computer icon, right-click the icon for your floppy disk drive, and select Format from the context menu. When you see the Format Disk dialog box, change the Format type to Full and then click Start. (If you try to access an unformatted disk, Windows asks if you want to format it and, if you say Yes, takes you to this same dialog box.)

The Format Disk dialog box offers three levels of formatting:

- *Full for unformatted disks and disks that your disk drive is having trouble reading*

- *Quick for erasing disks that have already been formatted*

- *System Files Only to turn a disk that's already been formatted into a "boot disk"—a disk that you can use to boot up your computer in case there's a problem on your hard disk*

The Quick option provides a fast way of erasing all the files on a disk at once. (It's a little easier than opening a folder for the disk, selecting all its contents, and then pressing Del.) You'll rarely use the System Files Only option.

Although you won't need to format your hard disk, you will eventually want to defragment it. As explained in Chapter 3, the files on hard disks tend to become fragmented after the disk has been used for a while. (This means that various parts of files are stored in separate sections of the hard disk, causing extra work for your computer whenever you access those files.) To defragment your hard disk, double-click the My Computer icon, right-click the icon for your hard disk, and select Properties from the context menu, displaying a Properties dialog box. Then click the Tools tab and click the button labeled Defragment now.

Exploring the Windows Explorer

The Windows Explorer is a utility program that is part of Windows. You can accomplish the same tasks in the Explorer as you do in folder windows—launching programs, opening documents, and copying, moving, deleting, and renaming folders and files. The main advantage of using the Explorer is that it features a graphic representation of the folder hierarchy, which makes it easy to figure out where you are in the hierarchy and to move from one location in the hierarchy to another.

To launch the Explorer, you can either click the Start button, highlight Programs, and then choose Windows Explorer, or you can right-click the Start button and choose Explore from the resulting context menu. In either case, you'll see a window with the word Exploring in the title bar. Unlike most other windows you encounter in Windows programs, the Explorer window is divided into two sides, or *panes*. The left pane contains the diagram of your folder hierarchy; the right pane looks much like a folder window.

When you first start the Explorer, you'll see four levels in the folder hierarchy:

▶ *The desktop itself*

▶ *The folders and other icons on the desktop (such as My Computer and the Recycle Bin)*

▶ *Subfolders of the folders on the desktop (underneath My Computer, for example, you'll see icons for the various drives on your computer)*

▶ *Subfolders of the subfolders of the folders on the desktop (such as the folders on drive C)*

You can expand and contract levels by clicking the plus and minus signs that appear next to some of the icons. Any icon that contains additional folders not currently shown in the hierarchy will be preceded by a plus sign. Clicking the plus sign reveals the folders inside.

MICROSOFT BACKUP

If you want to make a backup copy of one or more files that can fit on a single floppy disk, you can do so by simply copying them from your hard disk to a floppy, as just described. Creating backup copies of a file or group of files that is too large to fit on one floppy disk is a little more complicated. Either you need to use a device, such as a tape drive, that can store a lot of data at once, or you need to use a backup program that's capable of splitting a file or group of files across two or more floppy disks. Windows 95 comes with its own backup program, named Microsoft Backup. However, this program is not copied to your hard disk during the normal Windows 95 installation, so if you want to use it you'll probably need to install it from your Windows disk or CD-ROM. If you have the CD-ROM, insert it in your CD-ROM drive and then select Add/Remove Software from the resulting screen. If you have the disks, open the Start menu, select Settings, choose Control Panel, and then choose Add/Remove Programs. In either case, you'll soon see an Add/Remove Programs Properties dialog box. Click the Disk tools check box and a checkmark will appear in the box. If you have a CD-ROM, just click OK. If you have disks, click Have Disk and then insert the disk as requested.

Once Microsoft Backup has been installed, you can run it by opening the Start menu, selecting Programs, choosing Accessories, picking System Tools, and finally choosing Backup. Then follow the instructions on screen, using the Help option in the Microsoft Backup window if you need further assistance. If something happens to the original copy of your data and you need to use your backup copy, you can't simply copy it from the floppy disks back to your hard disk. Instead, you need to direct Windows to restore the file. Look up "Restoring backed up files" in the the Windows Help index for details. (You'll learn to use the Windows Help system later in this chapter.)

AN EXPLORER WINDOW

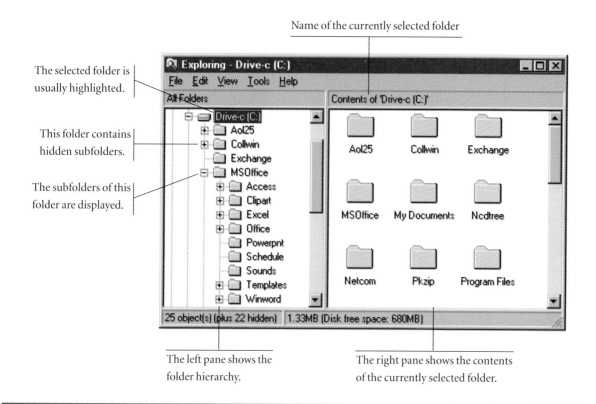

Name of the currently selected folder

The selected folder is usually highlighted.

This folder contains hidden subfolders.

The subfolders of this folder are displayed.

The left pane shows the folder hierarchy.

The right pane shows the contents of the currently selected folder.

Any icon preceded by a minus sign has already been expanded to reveal its contents. You can contract it (hide its contents) by clicking the minus sign. Icons that have neither a plus sign nor a minus sign don't contain any additional folders.

The right pane of the Explorer window shows the contents of the currently selected folder. The selected folder is highlighted in the folder hierarchy and its name appears in the window's title bar. (If you're at the desktop level, for example, the title bar will say Exploring - Desktop.) As soon as you select a different folder in the left pane, the contents of the right pane change to reflect that folder's contents. You can change the way items are displayed in the right pane by making selections from the View menu, just as you do in a folder window.

As in folder windows, when you first select a folder, the status bar at the bottom of the Explorer window tells you the number of items in the currently selected folder and the amount of free disk space left on the disk where that folder resides. As soon as you select one or more items in the right pane, the status bar tells you the number of items selected and the amount of space they occupy.

Each of the panes has its own scroll bar. You can also move up and down through a pane's contents by clicking somewhere in the pane to select it and then pressing the PgDn or PgUp key to move down or up a windowful at a time. You can also press the End key to move to the bottom of the list and Home to move back to the top.

NOTE   *When you start the Explorer, the current folder is the hard disk on which the Windows program itself was installed. To get to the top of your folder hierarchy (that is, to the desktop), you'll need to scroll up a bit in the left pane.*

To open a program or document from within an Explorer window, just double-click the associated icon in the right pane, just as you would in a folder window. You can copy or move files or folders using almost the same set of steps you use in folder windows:

▶ *In the left pane, select the folder that contains the items you want to move or copy.*

▶ *In the right pane, select the items themselves. (You can review the techniques for selecting icons under "Manipulating Files and Folders" covered previously in this chapter.)*

▶ *Issue the Edit, Copy or Edit, Cut command (or press its Ctrl+X or Ctrl+C accelerator key), or right-click one of the selected items and choose either Cut or Copy.*

▶ *Scroll the folder hierarchy in the left pane until you can see the folder into which you want to copy the files. (Expand any folders you need to.)*

▶ *Select the folder and then press Ctrl+V or select Paste from the Edit menu, or right-click that folder and select Paste.*

To copy files from your hard drive to a floppy disk, just select icons for the files you want to copy. Then right-click any one of the selected icons and choose Send To. When Windows displays a menu of places to send the files, select the option for your floppy disk drive.

If you're adventurous, you can also copy or move items using drag-and-drop. To do this,

▶ *Select the items you want to copy or move from the right pane.*

▶ *Scroll the folder hierarchy in the left pane until the folder into which you want to paste the items is visible.*

▶ *Right-drag any one of the selected items from the right pane to the desired destination folder in the left pane.*

▶ *When asked, specify whether you want to copy or move the items.*

Unless you know exactly what you're doing, avoid dragging icons around in the left pane of an Explorer window; by doing so, you are actually rearranging the folder hierarchy.

You can rename a file or folder in an Explorer window just like you would in a folder window: Either click the folder's label twice or right-click its icon and choose Rename from the context menu.

To create a new folder or file in an Explorer window, select the folder where you want the new file or folder to reside. Then right-click a blank spot in the right pane and select New.

FINDING FILES IN WINDOWS

It's easy to locate a particular file in either a folder window or the Explorer when you remember where you put the file in the first place. However, even the most organized Windows user will occasionally misplace a file. When all you know is that your file is "out there somewhere," you'll want to use Windows's Find command.

The Find command lets you locate documents, programs, and folders anywhere on your own computer or, if you're connected to a network, on any of the disk or CD-ROM drives on the network. When you use the Find command, you can look for files by their name, the date they were created or last modified, file type, size, content, or any combination of these attributes. You can, for example, use the Find command to locate all WordPerfect word processing documents that contain the word "budget." Or you might locate all the Excel spreadsheet files that haven't been modified in at least a year, in preparation for copying them to floppy disks and then deleting them. I'll focus on finding files by name or contents, since those are probably the types of searches you'll conduct most often. Once you've found the files or folders you're looking for, you can work with them in the Find dialog box just as you would in a regular folder window—opening them, copying them, deleting them, and so on.

You can issue the Find command by choosing the Find option on the Start menu. Windows will display a submenu with options for Files or Folders, Computer (if you're part of a network) and On the Microsoft Network. We'll be concentrating on the Files or Folders option. If you're on a network, the Computers option lets you locate other computers on your network. If you're a member of The Microsoft Network (an online service that you access via modem), you can also use Find to search the Network for information. (You'll learn more about The Microsoft Network in Chapter 10.)

Once you select Files or Folders, Windows displays a Find dialog box. Most of the time when you use the Find command, you'll probably be looking up files by name. To do this,

FINDING FILES BY NAME

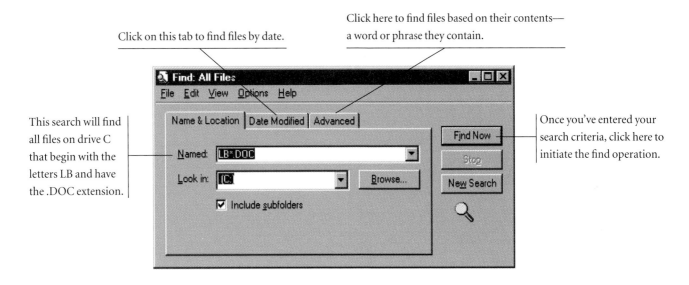

Click on this tab to find files by date.

Click here to find files based on their contents— a word or phrase they contain.

This search will find all files on drive C that begin with the letters LB and have the .DOC extension.

Once you've entered your search criteria, click here to initiate the find operation.

make sure that the Name & Location tab is selected and type the file name in the Named box. If you only know part of the name, or if you want to look for a group of files with similar names, you can use wildcard characters. An asterisk stands for any number of characters and a question mark stands for any single character. (If you've ever used DOS, these wildcards should be familiar.) For example, to specify all the files that start with the characters LB and have an extension of DOC, you would enter LB*.DOC. (lb*.doc would do fine as well, since, by default, the name search is not case-sensitive.) To specify all files that have the characters "brief" somewhere in their names, you'd enter *BRIEF* or *brief* or *Brief*. To search for files named INV followed by a single character only, enter INV?.

NOTE *If the search criteria that you enter include spaces, Windows locates all files and folders that contain the first word you enter in the Named box, ignoring the words after the space. This usually means you get a much longer file/folder list than you'd like. To prevent this, enclose the filename in quotes, entering "Letter to John", for example, rather than Letter to John.*

By default, content searches are not case-sensitive. If you only want to find items where the text uses a particular combination of upper- and lowercase, click on Options on the menu bar near the top of the dialog box and choose Case Sensitive. This might be useful if you're looking for letters to someone named Ng and you don't want all the files that contain words ending with "ing."

NARROWING THE SEARCH TO SPECIFIC FOLDERS

When you choose Find from the Start menu, Windows assumes that you want to look on the disk that contains your Windows system files (that is, the disk on which Windows was installed). If you have some idea where the file is located, you can accelerate the search by telling Windows to start searching further down in the folder hierarchy. To do this, you can type the folder's path in the Look in drop-down list box. (To look for files in a folder named "My Documents" which is on drive C, for example, you'd type C:\My Documents.) You can achieve exactly the same effect by right-clicking the icon for that folder or a shortcut icon for that folder (in a folder window or Explorer window) and selecting Find. If the folder you want to search is already open, you can also just press F3. In either case, Windows will immediately open the Find dialog box and put the path to that folder in the Look in drop-down list box. If you want Windows to search just the specified folder and not bother searching its subfolders, click the checkbox labeled Include subfolders to remove the check mark.

To search for a file by its contents, you need to select the Advanced tab in the Find dialog box. Then enter the word or combination of words you're looking for in the Containing Text text box. If you enter more than one word, Windows looks for exactly those words in exactly that order: It doesn't look for documents that contain both words somewhere, or that contain one of those words or the other.

As mentioned, you can also use the Find command to search for files by date modified, size, and file type. In the section entitled "Getting Help," you'll learn how to use the What's This option on the Help menu in the Find dialog box to learn about those other types of searches.

Once you've specified all your search criteria, you can start the search by clicking the Find Now button on the right side of the Find dialog box. Windows will list any files or folders that match your criteria in a list at the bottom of the dialog box. If the search is taking too long or if you decide to revise your criteria midstream, you can stop the search by clicking the Stop button at the right edge of the dialog box.

You can manipulate the items in the files and folders list just as you would items in a folder window or Explorer window. To open a file in the list, just double-click it. You can right-click one of the file names to display a context menu, select a file in the list and press Del to send it to the Recycle Bin, and so on. To open the folder in which a particular item is located, open the File menu by clicking the word File on the menu bar near the top of the dialog box, and choose Open Containing Folder.

NOTE *By default, each search builds on the criteria you specified last time. To get rid of all previously specified criteria and start from scratch, click New Search.*

CREATING AND USING SHORTCUTS

As you know, shortcuts are icons that provide you with quick access to a program, document, or folder, usually from the desktop. The easiest way to create a new shortcut is to right-drag an icon from a folder or Explorer window to either the desktop or the folder where you want the shortcut to reside. When Windows displays a menu of options, choose Create Shortcut Here.

If you have an elaborate hierarchy of folders, you may want to create shortcuts for frequently used folders on your desktop—so you don't need to burrow down to get to them.

NOTE *You can make it easy to print documents without opening them first by creating a shortcut for your printer. Then, to print a document, just drag the file to the printer shortcut. (If you frequently need to print the latest copy of your resume, for example, you could leave your resume on your desktop. Then to print, you'd just drag the resume icon to the printer icon and release.) To create a shortcut for your printer, open the My Computer folder, and then double-click the Printers icon. Then right-drag the icon for your printer to the desktop and choose Create Shortcut Here.*

There's a big difference between creating a shortcut to a file on your desktop and actually moving that file to your desktop. A shortcut is nothing more than a set of directions to a file. The file itself lives elsewhere. If you delete a shortcut, you're deleting only this set of directions; the file itself stays intact and in its usual location. If you copy a shortcut, you're copying just that set of directions, you're not copying the actual file.

If you want to be able to access a program quickly, it's generally better to create a shortcut than to move the program's icon to the desktop. Leaving the program in its own folder makes it easier for you to upgrade the program when a new version comes out. It's also just plain neater. The folders for most programs contain other files in addition to the main program file, including last-minute documentation files and sometimes additional utility programs, and it makes sense to leave the main program files in with these subsidiary files.

In the case of document files that you use all the time, there are arguments to be made for both creating shortcuts and moving the document itself to your desktop. The advantage of creating a shortcut is that the document itself stays in a logical place within your folder hierarchy. This can make it easy to find files and manipulate files as a group. (If all of your word processing documents are in one folder, for example, you can easily copy the entire folder to a floppy for backup purposes.) The one advantage of actually placing the document on the desktop is that this makes it easy to copy and, if you've created a printer shortcut, to print the file without opening any folders. To copy a document on the desktop to a floppy, for example, you just right-click it, choose Send to, and then select the option for your floppy drive. To print it, you just drag the icon of the document to the shortcut for your printer.

NOTE *Another way to provide easy access to programs you use often is to add those programs to the Start menu. To do this, locate an icon for the program in question in either a folder window or Explorer window. Then drag the icon over to the Start button. As soon as you release the mouse button, the program is added to the top section of the Start menu, above the Programs option.*

USING THE CLIPBOARD

Whenever you copy or move items by copying or cutting them from one location and pasting them to another, you are using a Windows feature known as the Clipboard. You can think of the Clipboard as a temporary holding pen, a place where you put things that you want to transport from one spot to another. So far, you've learned to use it for copying and moving files and folders. You can also use the Clipboard to copy and move selected data. Specifically, you can use the Clipboard to:

▶ *Move or copy files, folders, and shortcuts. (You've already learned to use it to copy files and folders.)*

▶ *Move or copy data to another location within the same data file. You might copy a paragraph from the third page to the fifth page of a report, for example, or move a set of numbers from one part of your spreadsheet to another.*

▶ *Move or copy data to a different document within the same application, copying a sentence or two from one letter to another, for instance.*

▶ *Move or copy data to a document in another application. You might copy part of a spreadsheet into a report you are creating in your word processing program, or copy a picture from a graphics program to a newsletter you are creating in a desktop publishing program.*

Bear in mind that you can only copy or move the data into a file or area that suits it—that is, in which that type of information makes sense. You can't just drop a photograph into the middle of a word processing document, for example, although if your word processing program supports graphics, you can create a special graphics box and place the picture inside of that.

Moving or copying data via the Clipboard involves four steps:

▶ *First you must select the data that you want to move or copy. (More on this in a moment.)*

USING THE CLIPBOARD

You can use the Clipboard to copy blocks of text between different types
of applications. In this case, data from a spreadsheet has been copied
from a spreadsheet to a quarterly report in a word processing program.

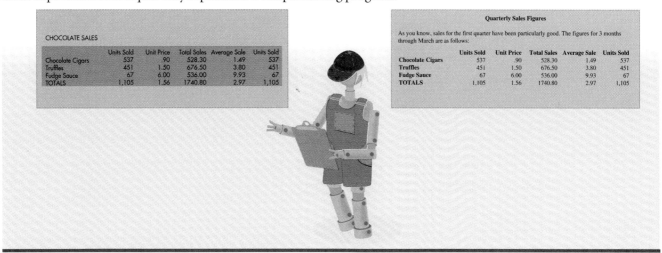

▶ *Then you either copy or "cut" (move) that data to the Clipboard, using the Edit, Copy
or Edit, Cut command, or their Ctrl+C or Ctrl+X accelerator keys. If you have trouble
figuring out whether to cut or copy, think about what you want to happen to your
original copy of the data. If you want the original to remain where it is, use Copy. If
you want the original to be erased, use Cut. In either case, the data will be copied to
the Clipboard so you can paste it somewhere else.*

▶ *Next, you move to the desired location—be it in the same file, a different file, or a file
in another application.*

▶ *Finally, you paste the data from the Clipboard using the Edit, Paste command or its
Ctrl+V accelerator key.*

NOTE   *When you paste data from the Clipboard, you do not erase it from the Clipboard. You
simply copy it to a designated spot. Anything you place in the Clipboard usually remains there
until you either place something else in the Clipboard or leave Windows. This means that you
can easily paste the same set of data into several different locations. (If you have a very long company name, for example, you might type it once, copy it to the Clipboard, and then paste it in
from the Clipboard every time you want to use it again.)*

As mentioned, the first step in copying or cutting data to the Clipboard is selecting the data that you want to manipulate. In most Windows programs, you can select data by dragging across it with your mouse. You can also often select data by clicking at one end of the set of data you want to select and then holding down Shift while you click on the other end. Double-clicking a word selects that word and clicking in the left margin next to a line of text usually selects the entire line. To select discrete items on the screen, you select one by clicking, and then hold Ctrl while you click others.

If you prefer to select data using your keyboard, try any of the following:

▶ *Shift+End selects from the insertion point to the end of a line.*

▶ *Shift+one of the arrow keys selects from the current position of the insertion point to wherever you move the insertion point. If you hold Shift while you press the Down Arrow key three times, for example, you'll select from your original spot to a spot three lines down.*

▶ *Shift+Ctrl+End selects from the current position of the insertion point to the end of the document.*

GETTING HELP

Windows features a very extensive and easy to use Help system—a series of informational screens and a set of tools for navigating them and finding the information you need. Not only is there a Help system for Windows itself, most Windows programs have Help systems of their own, which function in much the same way as Windows Help.

To get information on Windows, you can either open the Start menu and select Help, or you can open the Help menu in any folder window or Explorer window and choose Help Topics. To get help with an application program, select the Help option on the application window's menu bar. In some applications, you can also press the function key labeled F1, which is usually located in the upper-left corner of the keyboard, to the right of the Esc key.

NOTE *In some application programs, the F1 key leads to what is known as context-sensitive help, meaning a screen with information about whatever operation you are performing or object you are manipulating at the moment. If you open a menu, highlight an option, and then press F1, for example, you will see a screen with information about that menu option.*

The dialog box you see when you first enter the Windows Help system is called the Help Topics dialog box. This dialog box has three tabs:

▶ *Contents—presents information on general topics in outline form. It's the place to start when you need information on a broad topic, like using the Help system or printing.*

▶ *Index—features more specific topics, listed in alphabetical order, and lets you look up information by topic.*

▶ *Find—lets you search for particular words or phrases within a help topic.*

Most of the time, you can find the information you need using either the Contents tab or the Index tab.

If you're still getting your feet wet in Windows, you may want to take some time to investigate topics using the Contents tab. Information in the Contents tab is arranged in outline format—as in the table of contents in a book. Question mark icons always represent topics that can be displayed, either by double-clicking or by clicking once and then clicking the Display button at the bottom of the dialog box. Book icons represent headings that can be expanded or collapsed, revealing or hiding subtopics. To expand a heading, either double-click it or click it once and then click the Open button at the bottom of the dialog box. Sometimes expanding one heading leads to a bunch of more detailed headings. Keep going until you see a topic you're interested in. (Remember that topics are always preceded by question marks.)

To use the Index tab, just start typing the first few characters of the word or words you want to know about. As soon as you start typing, Windows will start displaying topics in the list area below your entry. When you see a topic you want to explore, either double-click it or click it once and then click the Display button.

Before you can use the Find tab, you need to let the Help system create a word list from all the entries in the help file. The first time you select the Find tab for a particular program (including Windows itself), you'll see a dialog box entitled Find Setup Wizard. Just click Next to direct Windows to create a relatively small word list (it will take up less disk space). On the next screen, click Finish. Once the word list has been created, you can look up words by typing them in the text box at the top of the dialog box. If the word or phrase you type isn't specific enough, you'll see a list of similar words or phrases in the middle of the dialog box. Double-click one of them to narrow your search. The list at the bottom of the dialog box will

THE HELP TOPICS DIALOG BOX

This tab lets you look up help topics in alphabetical order.

Use this tab to hunt for help topics that contain particular words or phrases.

This tab lets you look at lists of help topics laid out in a table of contents format.

Double-click question mark icons to see help screens.

Double-click book icons to display lists of topics or additional books. (The book icon will open; you can double-click it again to close it.)

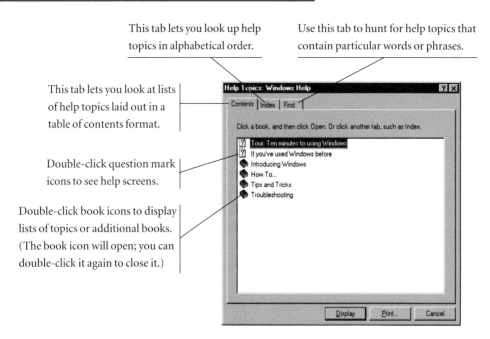

show a list of all the entries in the Help system that contain the word you specified. To display one of these entries, just double-click it or click it once and then click Display.

When you are done using the Help dialog box, either click the Cancel button or just activate another application.

For more information on using the Help system itself, select the Contents tab, double-click How To …, double-click Use Help, and then double-click any specific topic you're interested in. You can also look up the word "help" in the Help system's index.

NOTE *Windows includes several built-in applications (sometimes called applets) that let you do everything from drawing pictures to word processing. For information on these programs, activate the Windows Help system, double-click Introducing Windows, and then double-click Using Windows Accessories. Then double-click the heading you're interested in for a list of specific topics.*

Many dialog boxes offer little Help systems of their own which let you display descriptions of individual items in the dialog box. If the dialog box provides this feature, you'll either see a button with a question mark on it in the upper-right corner or you'll find a What's This option on the Help menu. When you either click a question mark button or select a

What's This option, your mouse pointer will acquire a question mark next to the usual arrow. To display a description of an item in the dialog box, just point to it and click.

SHUTTING DOWN OR RESTARTING WINDOWS

Before you turn off your computer, you should always open the Start menu and choose Shut Down. You'll see a dialog box with the options

▶ *Shut down the computer.*

▶ *Restart the computer.*

▶ *Restart the computer in MS-DOS mode.*

▶ *Close all programs and log on as a different user. (You'll only see this option if your computer is part of a network or if passwords have been defined for various users.)*

Since "Shut down the computer" is selected, just click OK or press Enter. If you have any open application windows with open and unsaved documents, Windows asks if you want to save your data. Once you have either saved or discarded any unsaved documents, you will see a screen informing you that it is now safe to turn off your computer.

If you are running any DOS (non-Windows) applications within Windows, you may need to close them before you can leave Windows. If so, Windows will display a dialog box that informs you of this and gives you the option of closing the program. To close the program, click OK and then exit the program as usual. When you're done, Windows will continue the shut down procedure.

NOTE *Windows remembers whatever state your desktop is in when you shut down your computer and automatically restores it the next time you load Windows. If one or more folder windows are open on the desktop when you leave Windows, you'll find them in the same spot when you return. While this behavior lets you customize and control your environment, it also means that you can't expect Windows to clean up after you. If you like to start your day with a clear desktop, close any open folders before you shut down your computer.*

THE MACINTOSH OPERATING SYSTEM

The Macintosh's main claim to fame is its operating system.

Compared to almost any other operating system in existence, it is extremely unintimidating to the new user, easy to learn, and even fun. It is also a very "intuitive interface," meaning that once you understand the basics, almost everything is pretty much the way you expect it or want it to be.

While some of the Mac's features—like the pictures of happy faces and trash cans—may strike serious DOS types as frivolous, the Macintosh operating system is actually extremely powerful. It provides multitasking abilities (the capacity to run two programs at once) and multimedia (picture- and sound-handling) talents that rival or surpass anything in the DOS world.

NOTE   *The latest version of the Macintosh operating system is known as System 7.5. I assume that you are using this version. If you are using an earlier version, a few of the features (like Macintosh Guide and Stickies) described in this chapter may not be available.*

THE FINDER AND THE DESKTOP

The Macintosh operating system actually consists of two parts: the system software itself and a program known as the Finder, which acts as the intermediary between you and the system software. The Finder is the first piece of software you encounter when you start up your computer. It is also the program that you use to:

▶ *Start other programs*

▶ *Install programs*

▶ *Find, list, delete, copy, and rename files, and organize them into groups known as folders*

▶ *Initialize, erase, and eject floppy disks*

You use the Finder to tell the Macintosh what to do—which disks you want to use, which programs you want to run, where you want to store your files, and so on. At its most basic level, learning to use a Macintosh involves learning about the Finder. The Finder is so called because one of its main roles is to help you find (and then utilize) programs and data. It does this by providing you with a graphic representation of the contents of disks and other storage media—that is, by displaying icons and windows you can use to view and manipulate your files.

The Finder is responsible for displaying and managing something known as the Macintosh desktop. The *desktop* is the gray or patterned background that appears behind all the other elements on the screen. Like its wooden or metal counterparts, the Macintosh desktop serves as a work space, a surface on which you spread whatever tools and documents you plan to use. Aside from the menu bar that stretches across the top of the screen, the main residents of the desktop are icons (little pictures) and windows (rectangular frames that serve as portholes, letting you view the contents of both disks and data files).

The desktop is only the first metaphor you will encounter in the Macintosh environment. In a sense, the entire Macintosh operating system is built around such analogies. Not only is the screen like a desktop, disks are also like file drawers filled with folders, which in turn contain programs and documents (data files).

The linchpins of the Macintosh filing system are folders. As described in Chapter 3, folders are repositories for files. Like paper folders in file cabinets, folders in the Macintosh world are used to organize information. A typical hard disk might contain folders for Work, Games, and Utility Programs. Within each of those folders, you might have additional folders for individual applications, and within those folders you might have folders for different types of data. Alternatively, you might have one folder for all your application programs and then separate folders for your word processing documents, spreadsheets, and graphics. Or, if the whole family is sharing one Mac, you might give everyone a folder of his or her own. The number of levels in your filing system is entirely up to you, and individual files can be stored at any level in disks, in folders, in folders that live within other folders, and so on.

As shown in the figure "Mac Iconography," there are different types of icons for the various elements in the Macintosh filing system. At a minimum, the desktop contains icons for your hard disk and any other storage device that is currently in use. (If you have a disk in your floppy drive, for example, you will see an icon representing that disk. If you put a CD-ROM into a CD-ROM drive, you will see an icon representing that disc.)

You may find it helpful to think of icons as containers. Disk and folder icons contain other icons. File icons contain either programs or data. To find out what's inside an icon, you double-click it with your mouse. The results will depend on the icon type:

▶ *When you double-click a disk or folder icon, the icon opens up into a window with a set of icons representing the disk's or folder's contents.*

THE MACINTOSH DESKTOP

The desktop serves as your workspace, a surface on which you spread the tools and documents you plan to use.

The Finder menu bar

The desktop

THE MAC'S FILING SYSTEM HIERARCHY

Disks and other storage devices contain…

folders, which contain…

documents, applications, and other folders.

MAC ICONOGRAPHY

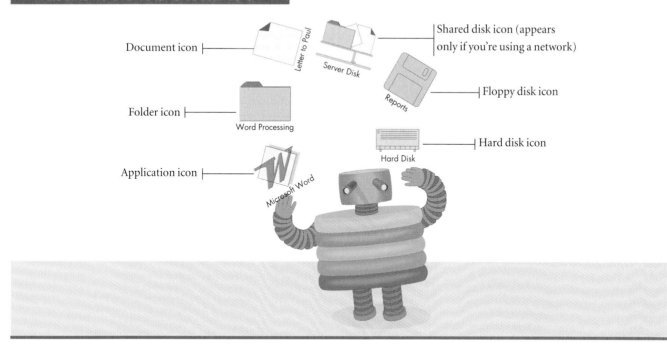

Document icon — Letter to Paul

Server Disk — Shared disk icon (appears only if you're using a network)

Reports — Floppy disk icon

Folder icon — Word Processing

Hard Disk — Hard disk icon

Application icon — Microsoft Word

STARTUP OR BOOT DISKS

Almost all hard disks contain a folder entitled System Folder. This folder contains the parts of the Mac operating system software, including the Finder, that are loaded from disk when you start up your computer (as opposed to the part that is stored in read-only memory). In other words, this folder contains the software that your computer needs in order to function. At this stage, all you really need to know about the System Folder is that you shouldn't delete it or even change it unless you know what you are doing.

▶ *When you double-click an application (program file) icon, the Macintosh starts up the program. (In some programs, an empty window immediately appears on the screen, waiting to be filled with data. In others, the only thing that changes is the menu bar.)*

▶ *When you double-click a document icon, the Macintosh starts up the program in which the document was created, and then loads the document.*

NOTE *The Trash icon (the picture of a trash can that usually resides in the lower-right corner of the desktop) is like a special kind of folder that contains objects you are planning to delete. As with other folder icons, double-clicking the Trash icon opens a window containing folders and file icons. You will learn to use the Trash icon later in this chapter.*

ICONS OPEN UP INTO WINDOWS

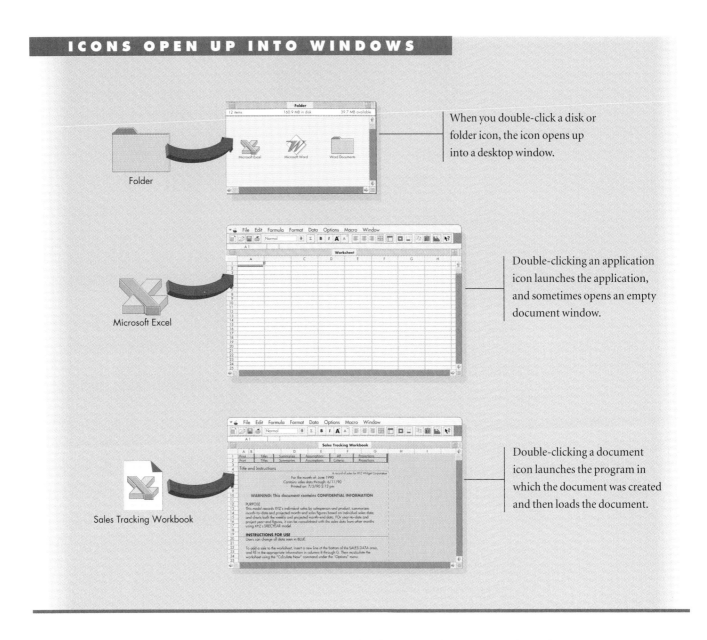

When you double-click a disk or folder icon, the icon opens up into a desktop window.

Double-clicking an application icon launches the application, and sometimes opens an empty document window.

Double-clicking a document icon launches the program in which the document was created and then loads the document.

In the Macintosh world, you can place the icons for both files and folders directly on the desktop rather than inside a disk or folder, just as you might move files and folders from a file drawer onto your wooden desk. You might do this on occasion to make it especially easy to find a file or folder that you intend to use again. Whenever you move an icon to the desktop, the file or folder itself retains information on where it belongs as if it had a built-in homing device. To return the file to its folder, simply click its icon to select it and then choose the Put Away option on the File menu. (Now if only paper files and folders knew their own way back to their proper spots in your file drawer.)

You can use the Control Panels option on the Apple menu to customize the Macintosh environment to your own tastes. (I like to think of it as the interior decorating option.) You can also use the General Controls panel to reset the date and time (something you'll want to do at least twice a year, as you reach and then leave daylight savings time). The details of using the control panels are beyond the scope of this book. The only reason I mention it is that if you are using a Mac already customized by someone else, your screen may look a little different from the ones shown in this chapter. For basic instructions on using control panels, see your *Macintosh User's Guide*.

USING THE MENU SYSTEM

Just about every Mac program displays a menu bar (a list of menu titles) at the top of the screen. When you point to any one of these menu titles and press down the mouse button, a pull-down menu appears. (Pull-down menus are so called because they pull down from the menu bar, almost like window shades.)

To issue a command, you generally point to a menu title on the menu bar, and then press and hold down the mouse button to open the associated pull-down menu. (You need to keep the mouse button pressed down or the pull-down menu disappears.) Then, you drag the mouse pointer downward until the desired option is highlighted. Finally, you release the mouse button to select the highlighted option.

Occasionally options on pull-down menus lead to *pop-out menus* (also known as *submenus*), which appear slightly lower and to the right of the pull-down menu. Whenever you highlight an option that has an associated pop-out menu, the pop-out menu will appear and you need to keep holding the mouse button while you drag to the desired option on that menu. Then you can release the button. (Pop-out menus are especially prevalent in the Page-Maker desktop publishing program.)

Menu titles or options that are gray rather than black are currently unavailable, usually because they don't make sense in the current context. For example, the Eject Disk option on the Special menu is only available if you have a disk in your floppy-disk drive.

To the right of many commands in the pull-down menus are little codes like ⌘ C. These are known as *keyboard shortcuts*: key combinations that you can use as an alternative to selecting the menu option. For example, ⌘ C is the keyboard shortcut for the Copy option on the Edit menu. Holding down the Command key (the one that has the cloverleaf and/or Apple symbol) while you press C therefore has exactly the same effect as opening the Edit pull-down menu and selecting Copy. (As detailed later in this chapter, this command

MAC MENUS

In the Finder and most Mac programs, you issue commands by selecting options from menus.

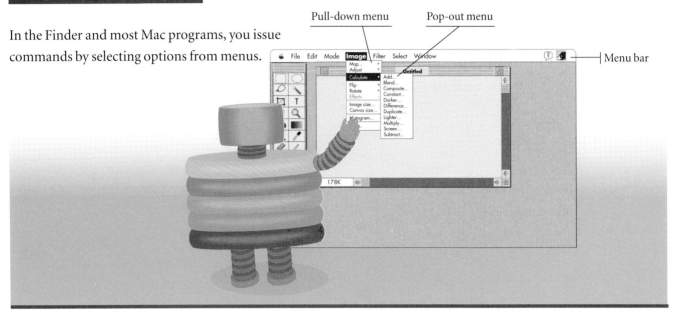

Pull-down menu   Pop-out menu

Menu bar

happens to copy whatever data is highlighted at the moment to a special area of memory known as the Clipboard.)

Any menu option that has three dots after its name leads to a dialog box: a rectangular frame in which you set options or express preferences. (Think of it as a tool for holding a dialog—that is, exchanging information—with the program.) Almost all dialog boxes contain a Cancel option. This makes it safe to wander into dialog boxes as you explore the menu system, because you can always click on Cancel to leave the box without actually doing anything.

The other type of menus that you will encounter in Macintosh programs are pop-up menus, which sometimes appear in dialog boxes. Pop-up menus usually look just like text boxes (little rectangular frames with words inside) except that they have shadows along their bottom and right edges and small solid triangles to the right of their names. To display the list of choices, just point to the menu name and hold down the mouse button. To select an option, drag to it with your mouse before you release the mouse button.

The menus available on the menu bar depend on which program is currently active. When you first turn on your Macintosh, the Finder is active, and the menu bar contains the titles of menus specific to that program. (You can always tell when the Finder is active because the word Special appears in the menu bar.) If an application program is active, the menu titles will change to reflect the menus available in that application.

THE FINDER MENU BAR

This is the menu that appears whenever the Finder is active.

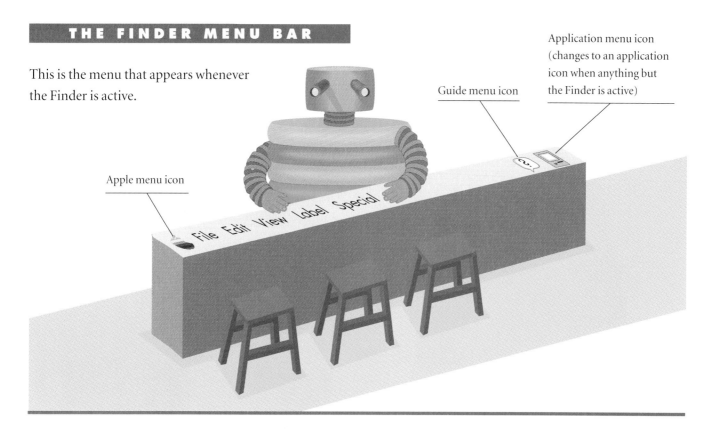

Application menu icon (changes to an application icon when anything but the Finder is active)

Guide menu icon

Apple menu icon

File Edit View Label Special

NOTE   *As mentioned in Chapter 4, the proper way to turn off your Mac is to select the Shut Down option on the Special menu. (Remember that the Finder is active.) On older Macs, you can then flick the on/off switch. On newer Macs, which have a Power On key rather than an on/off switch, the system shuts down automatically.*

WORKING WITH WINDOWS

As mentioned, all Macintosh icons lead to windows—either windows full of icons or windows full of data. The windows that open when you double-click a disk or folder icon are called *desktop windows* or *directory windows*. The windows that open when you double-click a program or document icon are called *document windows*.

As shown in the figure "Anatomy of a Mac Window," all Macintosh windows have several features in common. These features allow you to move, resize, scroll, and close the window using only your mouse. They include

▶ ***Title bar****. Displays the name of the window. Drag this bar to move the window to a different location. If you see horizontal stripes within the title bar, the window is active.*

A DIALOG BOX

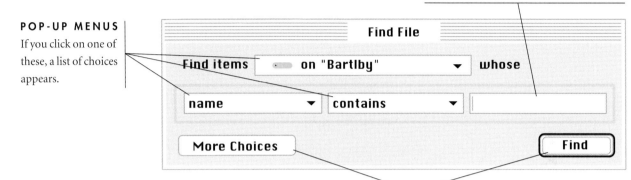

TEXT BOX
You usually type in a word or file name here (depending on the dialog box).

POP-UP MENUS
If you click on one of these, a list of choices appears.

BUTTONS
Click one of these to indicate what you want the computer to do next.

▶ *Close box. Click here to close the window.*

▶ *Information bar. This bar appears only in active desktop windows. It contains information on the number of items in the window, the amount of space used, and the amount of space available on the disk.*

▶ *Zoom box. Zooms (expands) or unzooms (shrinks) the window. When you zoom a disk or folder window, it expands only as much as necessary to display all the files and folders it contains. When you zoom a document window, it expands to fill the whole screen.*

▶ *Size box. Drag this box to resize the window. To make the window taller, for example, drag the size box downward. To make the window narrower, drag the size box to the left.*

▶ *Scroll bars. The color of the scroll bars indicates whether there is more data or more items than can fit within the window. When a scroll bar is gray rather than white, there are additional items or data in that dimension (that is, if the scroll bar is horizontal, there are other items to the left or right; if the scroll bar is vertical, there are other items up or down). To scroll one windowful at a time, click within the bar, somewhere in between the scroll box and the edge of the scroll bar that you want to move toward. If you want to move upwards, for example, click somewhere above the vertical scroll box. You can also scroll by dragging the scroll boxes or clicking the scroll arrows.*

▶ *Scroll boxes. You can scroll the contents of the window by dragging the scroll boxes in the desired direction. If you drag a scroll box all the way to the bottom of the vertical scroll bar, for example, you'll see whatever's at the very bottom of the document or collection of icons (in the case of desktop windows). Drag the scroll box to the middle of the scroll bar to see the middle of the icons or document.*

▶ *Scroll arrows. Clicking these arrows moves you in small increments in the direction of the arrow. In a word processing document, for example, clicking the up scroll arrow moves you up one line and clicking the down scroll arrow moves you down one line.*

As soon as you start working with your Mac, your screen tends to fill with windows. You may start by peeking inside your hard disk by double-clicking the hard disk icon. From there, you may open the window for a folder. Next you may open a window for another folder, which is contained within the first folder. Then you might open a document window by double-clicking a document icon. (This gives you four open windows already.)

FINDING FILES

Working your way down through the filing system hierarchy is not the only way to locate a particular program or document. You can also use the Find File option on the Apple menu. When you issue this command, the Macintosh displays a dialog box in which you can enter some or all of the name of the file you are looking for. As soon as you select Find, the Macintosh lists all the files that match your criteria. To open one, just double-click its name. (You will learn more about opening files under "Launching and Switching Programs.")

Only one window can be active at any given time. The active window is easy to locate because it has horizontal lines in its title bar and tools like the close, zoom, and resize boxes along its border. If you have several windows stacked on top of each other, the active window is also the one at the top. If no windows are currently active, the desktop itself is considered active.

To activate a particular window, just click anywhere inside its borders. To activate the desktop itself, click a spot outside of all the windows, or hold down the Option and Shift keys and press Up Arrow. You can also activate a window via the associated icon. Whenever you open a disk or folder icon, the icon itself turns dark gray or fills with dots. (Whenever you see such an icon, you know that a window for that icon is already open somewhere on the desktop.) If you double-click a grayed or dot-filled icon, the associated window becomes active and moves in front of any windows that are currently hiding it from view. (You will

ANATOMY OF A MAC WINDOW

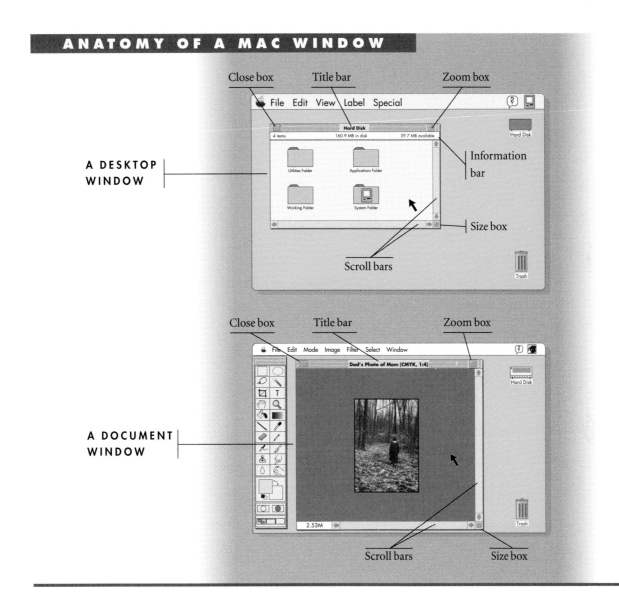

Close box   Title bar   Zoom box

A DESKTOP WINDOW

Information bar

Size box

Scroll bars

Close box   Title bar   Zoom box

A DOCUMENT WINDOW

Scroll bars   Size box

learn other means of activating document windows under "Launching and Switching Programs" later in this chapter.)

Given how easy it is to clutter the desktop, some of the first things you'll want to know about windows is how to move them around for better viewing, and how to close them. You can move a window simply by dragging its title bar. To close a window, click the close box in its upper-left corner. To close all open windows, hold the Option key while you click the close box in any one of the open windows.

As you create documents, install programs, and move icons from one place to another, your windows can grow both cluttered and disorganized. If you're the type who loves to straighten bookshelves or rearrange file cabinets, you'll love the Clean Up Window option on the Special menu. This option neatly arranges all the icons within an active desktop window. As soon as you select Clean Up Window, the icons in the active window snap to the nearest spot on an invisible grid that underlies the desktop. If an icon's name is particularly long, the adjacent storage spot will be left empty to keep the names from overlapping. (This is a good reason to stick with fairly short names for your files and folders.) You'll learn to sort icons as you straighten up in the next section.

To straighten up icons on the desktop itself, click any icon on the desktop, so that no windows are selected, and then choose Clean Up Desktop from the Special menu. All the icons on the desktop will fly to the nearest spot on the invisible grid.

When you shut down your Mac, the Finder remembers which windows were open when you left and where they were positioned on the desktop. When you turn your computer back on, the Finder automatically opens those same windows in the same spots. This is great when you want to pick up exactly where you left off, or if you always work with the same sets of windows. In some cases, however, you may prefer to start with an empty desktop. To do this, just hold down the Option key while you start your computer. (Don't release it until you see the desktop.)

CHANGING YOUR VIEW OF A WINDOW

By default, the Finder is set up to represent the contents of disks and folders as icons (pictures) on the screen. If you prefer, you can use various options on the View menu to have it display lists of file names instead. The figure "Different Views of a Window" shows the various possibilities. Two of the options (by Small Icon and by Icon) represent files and folders as pictures. The others (by Name, by Size, by Kind, by Label, and by Date) represent them as a list of file names with sizes, file type, label, and the date and time the file was last modified (much like a DOS directory listing). Labels, in the Mac world, are like little tags that you can attach to files or folders to organize them into groups by project or level of priority. If you have a color monitor, you can use them to control the color of file and folder icons.

N O T E   *If you see less than seven options on the View menu, it means that someone has limited your options using the Views Control Panel.*

The View menu is only available when a desktop window is active, and the option you select only affects the active window. The option that is currently in effect is preceded by a check on the menu itself.

DIFFERENT VIEWS OF A WINDOW

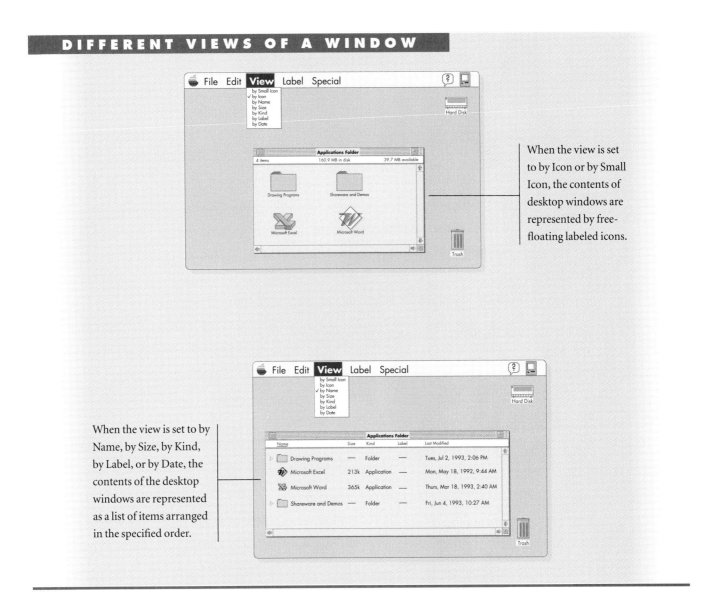

When the view is set to by Icon or by Small Icon, the contents of desktop windows are represented by free-floating labeled icons.

When the view is set to by Name, by Size, by Kind, by Label, or by Date, the contents of the desktop windows are represented as a list of items arranged in the specified order.

To sort icons, first select a view that sorts files and folders the way you want. (If you want to sort them by name, for example, select by Name from the View menu.) Then switch the View setting back to by Icons, and finally, hold down the Option key while you select the first option on the Special menu. The option will be something like Clean Up by Name or Clean Up by Size, depending on which View you used right before switching back to icons.

MANIPULATING FILES AND FOLDERS

The first step in copying, deleting, or renaming files or folders is selecting their icons. Once an icon is selected, it changes color and its name turns from black on white to white on black. You can always select a single icon by clicking on it once with your mouse, and if your plan is to drag that icon somewhere else, there's actually no need to click it first. (The moment you move the pointer to the icon and press the mouse button in preparation for dragging, the icon becomes selected.) If you are trying to select an icon in a crowded window, however, you may find it easier to use your keyboard: If you type the first character of the icon's name, the Finder will highlight the first icon in the active window that starts with that character. If that's not actually the icon you're looking for, press Tab to move to the icon that falls next in alphabetical order. Press Tab again to move to the next icon, and so on.

You can select a set of adjacent icons by drawing a rectangle around the entire group. To do this, move your mouse pointer to a spot just above and to the left of the first icon you want to include. Then press down the mouse button and drag to a spot below and to the right of the last icon. As you drag, you will see a dotted outline, known as a *marquee*, around the icons. (It's called a marquee because it's supposed to resemble the lights around the edge of a movie marquee.) When you release the mouse button, all icons inside the marquee remain highlighted.

To move one or more selected icons from one folder to another, you simply drag them with your mouse. As you drag, an outline of the icon(s) appears on the screen. As soon as you release the mouse button, the icon(s) themselves move, taking the place of the outline. Bear in mind that you can drag icons to other icons as well as to desktop windows or the desktop itself. If you want to move a file from one folder to another, for example, you can simply drag it to the other folder's icon. You don't need to open a window for that folder first. When you drag to an icon, you need to place the tip of the mouse pointer on top of the icon. (You can ignore the outline of the icon you are dragging.) As soon as the pointer crosses your destination, its icon name becomes highlighted. You can then release the mouse button.

If you want to copy rather than move one or more icons from one folder to another, simply hold down the Option key while you drag. (As always, you can drag to a window, an icon, or the desktop itself.) To create a copy of a file or folder within a particular disk or folder window, first select its icon and then choose Duplicate from the File menu. The object will be copied and the word Copy will be appended to its name.

To copy files or folders from one disk to another, you just select the icons of the desired files or folders and drag them to an icon or window that represents either the disk you want to copy them to or one of the folders on that disk. You don't need to hold down the Option key while dragging. To copy files from a floppy disk to your hard disk, for example, you open a window for the floppy disk, select the icons for the items you want to copy, and then drag

SELECTING MULTIPLE ICONS

You can select a set of adjacent icons by drawing a rectangle around the entire group using your mouse. Usually the easiest way to do this is to drag from a spot above and to the left of the group to a spot below and to the right of the group. As you drag, a flashing dotted line, called a *marquee*, appears around the group.

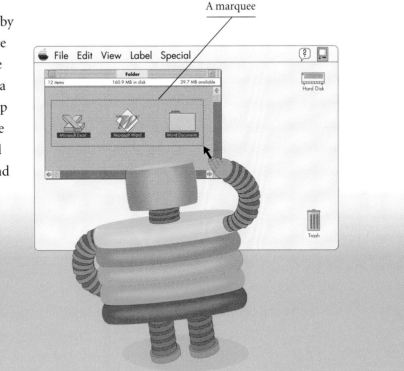

A marquee

to the icon or window representing either the hard disk itself or, more commonly, a folder on your hard disk. (You'll learn to copy entire floppy disks under "Handling Floppies and CD-ROMs.") To copy from your hard disk to a floppy, select the appropriate icons and then drag them to either a window or icon representing the floppy disk.

To rename an icon, click the icon name rather than the icon itself. (When the name is selected, it is both highlighted and enclosed in a box.) Then either type a new name or click within the existing name and edit it as much as you like. (Use the Delete or Del keys to erase characters. New characters you enter will be inserted into the text.) When you're done replacing or editing the icon name, press Return or click somewhere else.

To create a new folder, start by selecting the container in which you want the new folder to reside. (You can select either a disk icon, a disk window, or a folder window.) Next, select the New Folder option from the File menu. A folder will appear with the name "untitled folder" and the name will be selected. Finally, type in a new name for the folder. (If you accidentally select some other element on the screen before you type in a new name, just click on the folder's name to select it again, and then type in a new name.)

MANIPULATING ICONS

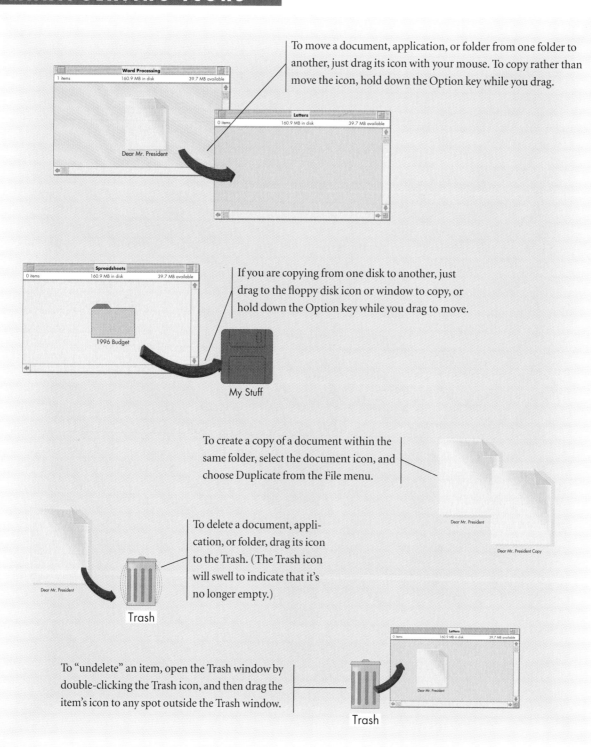

To move a document, application, or folder from one folder to another, just drag its icon with your mouse. To copy rather than move the icon, hold down the Option key while you drag.

If you are copying from one disk to another, just drag to the floppy disk icon or window to copy, or hold down the Option key while you drag to move.

To create a copy of a document within the same folder, select the document icon, and choose Duplicate from the File menu.

To delete a document, application, or folder, drag its icon to the Trash. (The Trash icon will swell to indicate that it's no longer empty.)

To "undelete" an item, open the Trash window by double-clicking the Trash icon, and then drag the item's icon to any spot outside the Trash window.

DELETING ICONS

Deleting files or folders on a Macintosh is a two-step process. The first step is to drag the file or folder icon(s) to the Trash icon (usually located in the lower-right corner of the screen). When the tip of the mouse pointer reaches the Trash icon, the icon itself will darken. You can then release the mouse button. The selected icon(s) will disappear into the Trash and the Trash icon will bulge to indicate that it is no longer empty. (If you delete a folder—that is, place it in the Trash and then empty the Trash—everything inside that folder is deleted as well.)

The second step in deleting is to "empty the trash" by choosing the Empty Trash option from the Special menu. When you do this, you will probably see a warning box asking if you really want to discard the items in the Trash. Select OK to proceed with the deletion or Cancel if you've had a change of heart. Once you have emptied the Trash, its contents are actually deleted from disk.

N O T E *If you get tired of being asked for confirmation every time you empty the trash, you can disable the warning box by selecting the Trash icon, choosing Get Info from the File menu, clicking the checkbox labeled Warn Before Emptying so that it no longer contains a check, and then closing the Get Info dialog box by clicking its close box.*

Any items that you place in the Trash remain there until you explicitly empty the Trash, even if you turn off your computer. Up until that point, you are free to go through the Trash and rescue any items you've decided to keep. As with any other icon, you examine the contents of the Trash icon by double-clicking it. To remove something from the Trash, either drag it out of the Trash window to another window or icon or to the desktop itself, or click the item once to select it and then choose the Put Away option from the File menu to direct the Finder to put it back where it was right before you dragged it to the Trash.

USING STICKIES

The Stickies desk accessory lets you place the electronic equivalent of Post-It notes directly on your desktop. To create a sticky:

▶ *Select stickies from the Apple menu to start the Stickies application.*

▶ *Select New Note from the File menu (or press N).*

▶ *Type in the text.*

Stickies are yellow by default. If you want to change the color of the currently selected sticky, open the Color menu and choose the shade you want. To change the font of the sticky, open the Note menu and choose Text Style.

You can manipulate stickies just as you would any other window: dragging the size box to resize the window and dragging the title bar to move the window. Clicking the zoom box collapses the sticky to a title bar. Clicking the zoom box again restores it to its previous size.

When you close a sticky by clicking its close box, you're actually deleting it. (By default, the Mac confirms this deletion and lets you save the text of the sticky to a file, although you can turn off this feature using the Preferences menu.) When you're done working with stickies, you can leave the Stickies application by selecting Close from the File menu.

HANDLING FLOPPIES AND CD-ROMS

As mentioned in Chapter 3, to insert a floppy disk on a Mac, you simply push it into the drive. When it's all the way in, it clicks into place. In a moment, an icon representing that disk will appear on the desktop. As with the hard disk, you can view the contents of a floppy disk or CD-ROM by double-clicking its disk icon.

There are several ways to eject a floppy disk or CD-ROM:

▶ *Drag it to the Trash icon.*

▶ *Select the disk or CD-ROM icon and then choose the Put Away option on the File menu. (The keyboard shortcut for this command is ⌘Y.)*

▶ *Select the Eject Disk option from the Special menu. (The keyboard shortcut is ⌘E.)*

Floppy disks are ejected automatically when you shut down the system.

You already know how to copy individual files and folders between disks. You'll also occasionally need to copy the entire contents of a floppy to a different disk—to make backup copies of data or programs or to install new programs.

To copy the entire contents of a floppy disk to another disk, drag its icon to another floppy-disk icon or to the hard-disk icon. If you copy the contents of a floppy onto your hard disk, the Finder automatically stores them in a folder that has the same name as the floppy. You can always rename that folder or move its contents afterwards.

Making a duplicate copy of a floppy disk is easy if you have two floppy-disk drives: Just put the original disk in one drive and the disk you want to use as your duplicate in the other. (Make sure that the duplicate disk is either empty or contains data that you don't mind

EJECTING A FLOPPY DISK

There are several ways to eject a floppy disk or CD-ROM. The easiest way is to drag its icon over to the Trash.

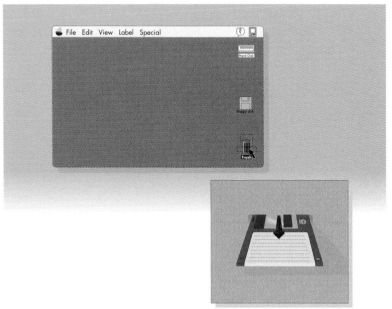

overwriting.) Then move the icon for the first disk (the original) on top of the icon for the second disk (the duplicate). When the Finder asks if you want to replace one disk's contents with those of the other, choose OK.

ABOUT BACKUPS

As on PCs, there are several approaches that you can take to backing up data on a Mac. If most of your work involves creating word processing documents, spreadsheets, and other files that are relatively small, you can simply copy those files to floppy disks whenever you create and change them. If your files are too big to fit on floppies or if you prefer to have one big backup of all your files, however, you will need a different strategy. Either you will need to copy data to a medium other than floppies—such as cassette tape—or you'll need to use a special backup program that's capable of splitting a file or group of files across two or more floppy disks. Like DOS, the Macintosh operating system has its own built-in backup program, which is called HD Backup. See your Macintosh documentation for information on how to use it. You can also buy fancier backup programs at any computer store. Both HD Backup and most other backup programs allow you to perform both full backups (which involve backing up all the files on your hard disk) or incremental ones (which back up only those files that have changed since the last full backup).

In any case, you should decide on *some* method of backing up your data before you accumulate too many files. And whatever strategy you choose, be sure to follow it. Any hard-disk crash is unfortunate. A hard-disk crash when you don't have a backup of your data is a disaster.

If your Mac only has one drive, duplicating a floppy is a bit more complicated. First, insert the disk you plan to use as a backup into the drive. Then choose Eject Disk from the Special menu. The disk will be ejected but its icon will remain on the desktop (even though it's now dimmed). Next write-protect the original disk (the one you want to duplicate) by closing the write-protect notch in its corner. (See Chapter 3 for details.) This will prevent you from accidentally overwriting the original disk rather than the backup. Then insert that disk into the drive and drag its icon to the dimmed icon for the backup disk. When you're asked whether you want to replace the backup disk's contents, select OK to begin the copy operation. You will probably be prompted to switch disks a few times during the process.

A WARNING ABOUT INSTALLING PROGRAMS

Your startup disk (that is, the disk that you boot from, usually your hard disk) must have only one System folder. If you have more than one, your Mac will have trouble deciding which to use; this will almost certainly lead to errors and possibly even data loss. Since the most likely way for you to get extra System folders is by installing old software, whenever you install programs, particularly old programs, you should check to see whether you have copied an extra System folder to your hard disk. If so, drag that folder to the Trash and then choose Empty Trash from the Special menu. (Don't worry. You can't throw out the wrong one at this point because the Mac won't allow you to discard the copy of the System that you are currently running.)

As you learned in Chapter 3, new floppy disks must be formatted or, as they say in Macspeak, *initialized* before you can use them. Whenever you insert an unformatted disk, the Mac assumes you want to initialize it. If you've inserted a double-density rather than high-density disk, you'll be given a choice of one-sided or two-sided formatting. In most cases, you will choose two-sided formatting. The Mac will then warn you that all information already on the disk will be erased. Since the disk is presumably blank anyway, it doesn't matter.

To erase the entire contents of a floppy disk, first select the icon for that disk and then select the Erase Disk option from the Special menu. Since erasing a disk actually initializes it, you will be asked to confirm the operation. If you are erasing a high-density disk, select Initialize to proceed. Otherwise, choose Two-Sided.

LAUNCHING AND SWITCHING PROGRAMS

Starting, or, in Macintosh lingo, *launching*, a program is a simple matter of double-clicking the icon for that program or for any document created within that program. If you double-click a document icon, the Macintosh starts the program and then immediately

WORKING WITH FLOPPY DISKS

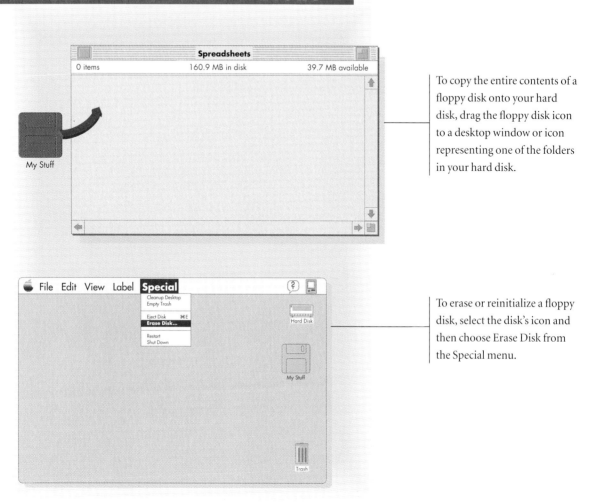

To copy the entire contents of a floppy disk onto your hard disk, drag the floppy disk icon to a desktop window or icon representing one of the folders in your hard disk.

To erase or reinitialize a floppy disk, select the disk's icon and then choose Erase Disk from the Special menu.

opens the specified document. You can also open an application by dragging a document icon on top of it, which is particularly useful in those rare cases when you want to open a document that was created in another application. (This will only work if the data is stored in a format, such as text-only, that is acceptable to the application.)

Starting with System 7.5, there is yet another way to open programs and documents. The Finder maintains two special folders, named Recent Programs and Recent Documents, which contain aliases for all the programs and documents that you've opened recently. Since these folders are directly accessible from the Apple menu, you can reopen a recently used file with only a few mouse clicks. (Open the Apple menu, select Recent Programs or Recent Documents, and then double-click the icon for the program or document you want to use.)

LAUNCHING AN APPLICATION

Launching a program on the Macintosh is a simple matter of double-clicking the icon for the program itself or for any document created within that program.

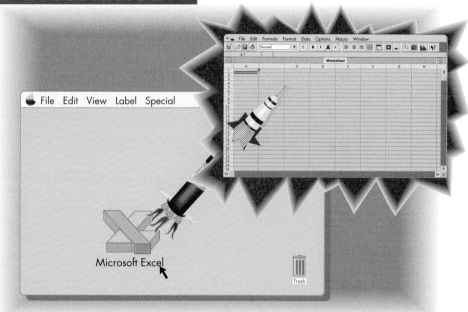

When you launch some applications, the program assumes that you intend to create a brand new document and therefore presents you with an empty document window. In other programs, you will simply see the menu bar change and you'll need to select New from the File menu if you want to create a new document. In contrast, when you launch an application by either double-clicking a document icon or placing the document icon on top of the program icon, you get a document window containing the specified document.

If you want to be able to launch a program or access a document from more than one folder, you can create what's known as an alias. An *alias* is a means of representing a program or document in multiple folders without actually making a copy of the file. You can think of it as a kind of pseudo-icon or duplicate icon that contains information on where the file itself is stored. (You can, for example, make it possible to open a particular letter from any one of three folders by placing the document's icon in one folder and placing aliases for that document in the other two.) See your *Macintosh User's Guide* for details on creating and using aliases.

Once you start launching programs, it can get a little difficult to tell which program is active at any given moment. Regardless of which program is currently active, the last item on the menu bar is the application menu icon. This icon indicates which program is currently active. If it resembles a computer, the Finder is active. If an application program is active, you'll see a logo for that program.

There are three ways to switch from one open application to the next:

▶ *You can click in the window for the application that you want to activate.*

▶ *You can open the application menu (by pointing to its icon and pressing the mouse button) and then select the desired program from the list of programs at the bottom of the menu.*

▶ *You can click the grayed icon for the application itself.*

Clicking the close box in a document window or selecting Close from its File menu does not actually close the application. It merely closes the document window and any document that is currently displayed inside of it. (If you haven't saved all your changes to the document, the Mac will ask if you want to save them before unloading the document from memory.)

The program remains open and active until you activate either another window or the desktop. This can be confusing because in most cases, the screen will be largely empty (as it was before you started the program). The only ways you can tell that the program is still active is that the Application menu icon in the upper-right corner of the screen shows the icon for that program, and the menu bar still shows the choices for that particular program rather than the Finder menu. (Remember that if you see the word "Special" in the menu bar, you know that the Finder is active.) You can tell that an application is running, even if it's not

T H E   L A U N C H E R

System 7.5 includes a feature named the Launcher that was previously available only on Performa model Macs. The Launcher is actually a special type of folder that provides a quick means of launching your favorite applications. To open the Launcher, open the Apple menu, choose Control Panels, and then double-click Launcher. To add applications to the Launcher, just drag their icons from folder windows (or the desktop) into the Launcher window. This creates a button inside the launcher that you can click just once (as opposed to double-clicking) to start the associated program. Once you have placed icons for your favorite programs in the Launcher, you'll probably want to open the Launcher whenever you start up your system. To do this, open the Apple menu, choose Control Panels, double-click General Controls, click on the check box labeled "Show Launcher at system startup," and choose OK. Then, whenever you start up the system, the Launcher window will open automatically and you can click the enclosed buttons to start your favorite programs. If you click the button for a program that is already open, that program will become active.

To remove programs from the Launcher window, open the System folder on your hard disk, and then open the Launcher items folder. Select the items you want to delete and press the Delete key.

currently active, because its program icon will be completely gray and its name will appear in the bottom section of the Application menu. You can activate the program by double-clicking its grayed icon, selecting it from the document window, or clicking inside its document window (if one is open). Even if you activate another window or the desktop, the application remains running and in memory. To switch back to that application, simply select it from the Application menu.

If you actually want to close a program—that is, remove it from memory—select Quit from the File menu. (In most programs, you can also use the keyboard shortcut ⌘Q.) You should close programs when you are done working with them so that they don't take up room in memory and slow down the performance of any other programs you are running.

NOTE *It's quite easy to accidentally click on the desktop while you're working in an application. If you do so, you will inadvertently activate the Finder and the contents of the menu bar will change accordingly. You'll then need to reactivate your application (usually by simply clicking within the document window) before you can use any of its menus.*

VIRTUAL MEMORY

If your computer has limited random access memory or you like to open lots of programs at once, you may need to make use of a feature known as virtual memory. *Virtual memory* allows your system software to treat a hard disk as an extension of RAM, copying programs from memory to your hard disk whenever you run out of room in RAM, and copying them back to memory as needed. See your *Macintosh User's Guide* for details.

THE CLIPBOARD

The Macintosh operating system has a feature, called the Clipboard, that allows you to copy or move data from one place to another. Think of the Clipboard as a tool that you use to transport data. (I sometimes picture it as a tote bag for carrying data from place to place.)

Moving or copying data via the Clipboard involves four steps:

▶ *Select the data that you want to move or copy. In most cases, the easiest way to select data is to simply drag across it with your mouse. (When data is selected, it appears in a different color.) You can also often select a set of data by moving the cursor or insertion point to one end of the data and then holding Shift while you move to the other end. (You can position and move the cursor/insertion point by either clicking with your mouse or using the arrow keys.)*

▶ *Either copy or "cut" (move) that data to the Clipboard, using either the Copy or Cut option on the Edit menu. (You can also use the shortcut ⌘C to copy data or ⌘X to cut it.)*

▶ *Move to the desired location—be it in the same file, a different file, or a file in another application.*

▶ *Paste the data from the Clipboard using the Paste command on the Edit menu (or the ⌘V shortcut).*

Bear in mind that data remains in the Clipboard until you either shut down the system or replace it with something else (by issuing another cut or paste command). This means that you can easily paste the same set of data into several different spots.

If you want to save the contents of the Clipboard so that you can reuse it in future work sessions, you can paste from the Clipboard to the Scrapbook. The Scrapbook is actually a file that consists of multiple "pages" of data which you can easily copy to the Clipboard and then paste wherever you like. Select the Scrapbook option from the Apple menu (the first icon on the menu bar). Then choose Paste from the Edit menu or press ⌘V to paste the contents of the Clipboard into the Scrapbook. It will be added to the Scrapbook as the last "page." Then, anytime you want to paste that data somewhere else, move to that page, and select Copy from the Edit menu (or press ⌘C) to paste it into the Clipboard. (You can move from one page to the next using the scroll bar at the bottom of the Scrapbook window.) Then you can paste from the Clipboard as usual. To remove a page from the Scrapbook, move to that page and then select the Clear option from the Edit menu. To copy a page to the Clipboard while removing it from the Scrapbook, move to that page and select Cut from the Edit menu.

APPLE GUIDE

System 7.5 features a help system called Apple Guide, which you access through the Guide menu (the question mark icon near the right edge of the menu bar). When you open the Guide menu while the Finder is active, you'll see the following options:

▶ *About Apple Guide displays a screen explaining the options on the Guide menu.*

▶ *Show Balloons turns on Balloon Help, which you'll learn about in the next section.*

▶ *Macintosh Tutorial starts an interactive tutorial that guides you through the basics of using the mouse, navigating the menu system, manipulating windows, and so on.*

▶ *Macintosh Guide is the heart of the help system. It provides instructions for a variety of tasks and, whenever possible, guides you through each of the steps involved. It is discussed in a moment.*

▶ *Shortcuts lists keyboard commands and tips that can help you work more efficiently.*

Once you've mastered the basics, perhaps with the help of the Macintosh Tutorial, the option you'll use most often is Macintosh Guide. Selecting Macintosh Guide invokes a dialog box that lets you choose from a broad list of topics, hunt through an indexed list, or search for a particular word or phrase. You use the left side of the dialog box to conduct your search—selecting from the topics list or index, or typing the word for which you want to search. Macintosh Guide responds by displaying a list of topics on the right side. There are usually two types of entries in that list: definitions and entries that start with the words "How Do I." If you select a definition, you'll see one or more screens describing the topic. If you select a "How Do I" entry, you'll see a series of dialog boxes stepping you through the specified process. Whenever the instructions refer to a button, icon, or menu option on the screen, it will be highlighted with a red circle or displayed in red letters. If you make a mistake, the Macintosh Guide either tells you to go back a step or performs the action for you.

In most cases, if you don't understand the instructions, you can click the button labeled Huh? for more detailed information. Once you're done reading about a definition or stepping through a process, click the Topics button to return to the dialog box you saw when you first selected Macintosh Guide.

For more information on using the Macintosh Guide, you can use the Guide itself:

▶ *Select Macintosh Guide from the Guide menu.*

▶ *Click on Index.*

▶ *In the alphabet that appears just above the index, click the H to move to that section in the index itself.*

▶ *Find and click the word "help."*

▶ *Click "Use Macintosh Guide" in the list on the right side of the dialog box.*

▶ *Click OK.*

BALLOON HELP

Another useful tool for learning your way around the desktop is a feature known as Balloon Help. When this feature is on, every time you point to a particular element on the screen—like a menu option, an option in a dialog box, a window, or part of a window such as the title bar or zoom box—a description of that element is displayed. The description always appears inside a little balloon, like the ones used to display dialog in comic books. Hence the name Balloon Help.

To turn on Balloon Help, open the Help menu (represented by a question mark near the right edge of the menu bar) and select Show Balloons. To turn it off again, open the Help menu and choose Hide Balloons.

BALLOON HELP

When Balloon Help is turned on, every time you point to a particular item on the screen, a description of the item appears in a little balloon. (To turn on Balloon Help, select Show Balloons from the Help menu.)

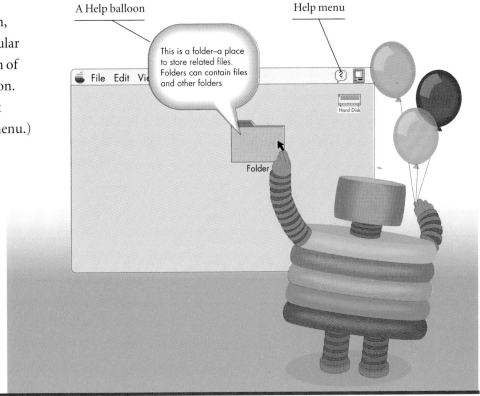

A Help balloon

Help menu

This is a folder–a place to store related files. Folders can contain files and other folders

File Edit Vie

Hard Disk

Folder

CHAPTER 7

APPLICATIONS SOFTWARE

Word Processing

Spreadsheet Programs

Database Management Programs

Installing Programs

Learning an Application Program

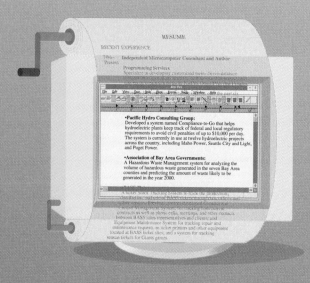

In a sense, application programs are the most important

part of your computer system. They're what enables your computer to actually do something useful, like create documents, perform calculations, or even play games.

There are dozens of types of application programs available. In this chapter, I'll delve into only three of the most commonly used types: word processing programs, spreadsheet programs, and database management programs. In each case, I'll tell you what such programs do, what they look like and how you use them. I'll also provide some pointers on how to choose one of the dozens on the market.

What I won't tell you is the exact series of steps needed to accomplish particular results in particular programs. (You won't learn how to underline a word in the WordPerfect word processing program, or how to copy a set of data in the Lotus 1-2-3 spreadsheet, for example.) Instead, I'll focus on the basic concepts and metaphors used in all word processing, database, and spreadsheet programs, and the range of feats each of those programs can perform. I'll give you the foundation you need before you get to the "which keys to press" or "which items to click on" stage—a foundation that's often overlooked in the manuals.

WILL THE PROGRAM WORK WITH YOUR HARDWARE?

Before you buy a new program, you need to determine whether it will work with your hardware. And if not, what will it cost to replace or upgrade your equipment? Before you go shopping for software, make sure that you know the answers to all of the following questions:

- Which operating system are you running and which version?
- In the case of PCs, what kind of CPU chip does your computer contain. If you're using a Mac, which model do you have?
- How much memory does your computer contain?
- What type of monitor do you have, with what type of graphics display, if any? (You'll learn about various types of graphics display modes, like EGA, VGA, and Super VGA, in Chapter 8.)
- What's the capacity of your computer's hard disk, in megabytes, and how much of that space is currently available?
- What type of printer do you have?

If there is any chance that you'll forget the answer to any of these questions, write down all the answers and bring them with you (or have them handy when you pick up the phone). Then, before you buy, make the salesperson swear that the program will work with your hardware and that you can return the program for a full refund if it doesn't.

WORD PROCESSING

At its simplest, word processing on a computer is just electronic typing. Instead of pressing keys on a typewriter, you press keys on a computer keyboard that looks much like a typewriter. But there is one essential difference. In word processing, the process of composing a document is separate from the process of printing.

This separation of typing from printing, of electronic document from printed copy, makes all the difference in the world. It lets you erase, amend, and rearrange your document without retyping any of the existing text. If you erase characters, the program automatically closes up any gaps left behind. If you insert characters, it pushes existing characters to the right or downward to make room for the new text. If you decide that a particular sentence or paragraph really belongs somewhere else in your document, you simply move it to the desired spot and let your program rearrange the rest of the document (including your page breaks) to accommodate the change. Most word processing programs even let you change your mind about such editorial changes, providing you with an undo and/or an undelete command that reverses the effects of the last deletion or move.

Whenever you are ready to print your document, you simply issue a print command. (This procedure varies from one program to the next, but it's usually quite simple.) If you are less than thrilled with the resulting printout, just return to your electronic document, make additional changes, and print it again.

For many people, the separation between composing a document and printing it takes some of the anxiety out of the writing process itself. Since you can start typing without committing yourself to paper, the move from thinking about writing to actually starting may feel less momentous or intimidating. Knowing that your work is so easy to fix can make it easier to start.

The ability to insert, delete, and rearrange text without retyping is word processing's main selling point, and this alone is worth the price of admission. But word processing programs offer other features that typists never dreamed of. For starters, most word processing programs can perform the following basic tasks:

▶ *Display and print characters in a variety of typefaces and sizes, and with different attributes such as boldfacing, underlining, and italics.*

▶ *Search for and replace a specified set of characters. This feature can prove particularly useful if you find that you've misspelled someone's name throughout a document. You*

W O R D   P R O C E S S I N G   I S   L I K E   E L E C T R O N I C   T Y P I N G

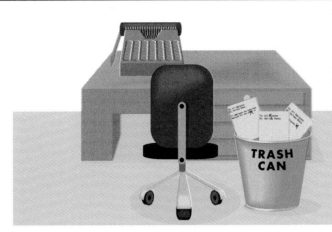

When you type something on a typewriter, the characters are immediately recorded on paper. If you change your mind or notice mistakes, you need to erase characters or retype a page or more of text.

When you type something using a word processing program, the characters you type are simply stored in your computer's memory. You can make any changes you like and print whenever (and as often as) you want.

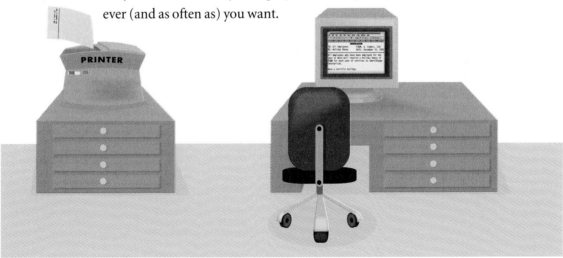

can also use it to save yourself typing. You can, for example, type some obscure character like the ~ every time you want to display your company's name and then later replace every occurrence of ~ with the name itself.

▶ Automatically center text or align it with the right margin.

▶ Right-justify text, so that characters line up at the left as well as the right margin (as they do in books).

▶ *Automatically print page numbers either at the top or bottom of each page. This saves you the trouble of entering page numbers within the text and then moving them around when your editing causes the page breaks to move slightly.*

▶ *Print headers and footers—that is, specified sets of text at the top or bottom of each page. These headers and footers can include the current page number if you like. Some programs let you specify different headers or footers on facing pages.*

▶ *Format and manage footnotes and endnotes. Most word processing programs let you attach footnotes or endnotes to particular spots in your document. If you add additional footnotes or rearrange text, the program automatically moves and renumbers the notes as necessary. If you use footnotes (rather than endnotes), the program automatically figures out how much room is required for notes at the bottom of each page, and correctly prints the footnotes exactly where they belong.*

▶ *Automatically hyphenate words at the end of a line. Most programs use their built-in dictionaries to break words in between syllables and ask you to specify a location for the hyphen in words not found in that dictionary.*

▶ *Arrange text in two or more columns (as it appears in many leaflets and most periodicals).*

▶ *Check your document for misspelled words, a process known as* spell-checking. *Some programs even have an auto-correct feature that can correct typos and misspellings as you make them.*

▶ *Locate synonyms for a selected word. This thesaurus feature can prove invaluable when you find yourself using the same word over and over, or when you can't quite pinpoint the word you want.*

▶ *Enter special characters that you can't generate on most typewriters, including foreign language characters, bullets, and mathematical symbols.*

▶ *Create "personalized" form letters and labels. This feature, commonly known as mail merge, lets you "merge" a set of names and addresses with a letter or other document. The result is a set of letters (or whatever) that includes an individual's name, address, and any other personal information you specify.*

▶ *Incorporate lines, boxes, and even pictures within a document. This capability is particularly useful for producing newsletters or fancy reports.*

▶ *Print envelopes and mailing labels. Some high-end word processing programs can even print envelopes by automatically pulling the name and address from the top of your letter, so that you don't have to retype it.*

Few people actually learn or use all of these features. Within the vast collection of bells and whistles offered by the majority of word processing programs, most people identify a few features that they can't live without and ignore the rest. (I, personally, am hooked on the thesaurus. For you, however, the best thing about word processing may be the spell checker, or the ability to mix and match fonts.)

NOTE Font *means a specific combination of typeface and point size (although a few people use the term to mean typeface, regardless of size). Arial 12-point font means the Arial typeface and a size of 12 points. Helvetica 10-point font means the Helvetica typeface and a size of 10 points. (A point is ¹⁄₇₂ of an inch. The more points, the larger the character.) You'll learn more about fonts in Chapter 8. People frequently use fonts with a larger point size for titles or headings within a document, and sometimes use different typefaces for different elements within the document. In this book, for example, the typeface used in headers at the top of each page is different from that used in the text itself.*

SPELL CHECKERS

Spell checkers can prove invaluable, especially to those who always finished last in spelling bees. (Never send out a resume without using one.) They are, however, no substitute for human proofreading. For one thing, spell checkers only check whether a particular word exists; they don't tell you if it's the right word for a particular context. If you type "here" when you mean "hear," for example, or "major" instead of "mayor," the spell checker will not blink.

Some word processing programs offer even more esoteric features, including

▶ *Special editing tools. Several high-end word processing programs provide a variety of tools that facilitate editing, or writing by committee. These tools allow you to insert or delete text provisionally, subject to the author's approval, or to insert comments into the text, which are visible on screen but skipped over when you print.*

WORD PROCESSING FEATURES

Most word processing programs can automatically check your document for misspelled words and suggest alternatives.

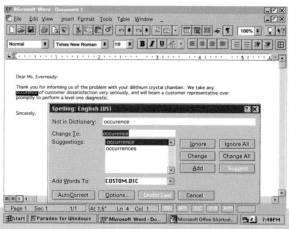

All word processing programs include a search and replace feature that lets you replace each occurrence of one set of characters with another set of characters.

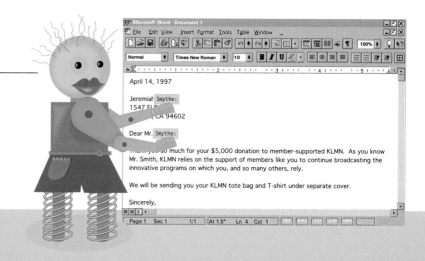

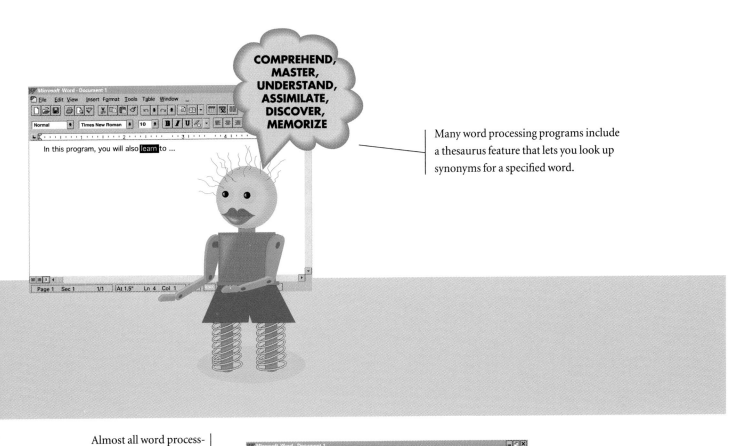

Many word processing programs include a thesaurus feature that lets you look up synonyms for a specified word.

Almost all word processing programs let you generate "personalized" form letters (a feature known as *mail merge*).

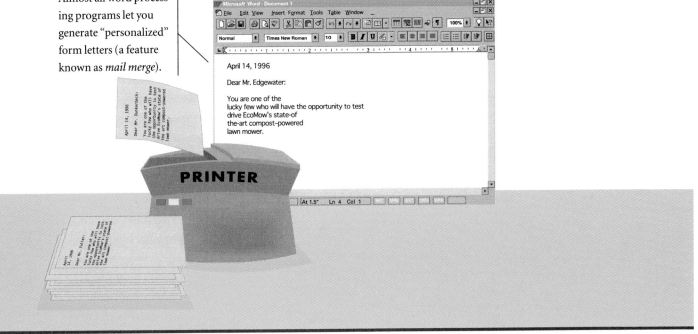

▶ *Tables.* Many word processing programs have tools for creating and managing tables of information (that is, text entered in a grid of rows and columns). Most programs allow you to adjust the width of columns after you enter your text, and some let you apply special formatting—such as shading every other row.

▶ *Create and use styles.* Styles are stored collections of typographic, margin, and line spacing formats. Many high-end word processing programs allow you to create styles for various types of documents. Some include various preset styles—for bibliographies or legal pleadings, for example.

▶ *Outlining features.* Some programs include outliners that help you sketch and then refine the overall structure of a document. Such features let you create a preliminary outline with headings and one or more levels of subheadings, and then rearrange these headings, often simply by dragging with your mouse. Some outliners also let you expand part or all of your outline—to display subheadings and/or descriptions—and collapse them so that you see only the headings themselves.

▶ *Math capabilities.* Some word processing programs have built-in basic math features, allowing you to total or subtotal columns of numbers, for example, or to calculate the difference between an amount charged and amount paid on an invoice.

▶ *Indexes.* Some programs permit you to mark words or phrases that you want included in an index and then create an index of all those words, with their page numbers, on your command.

▶ *Table of contents.* In some programs you can mark section headers in the document and then automatically generate a table of contents, with section names and the page on which they appear.

▶ *Line numbering.* Some programs can automatically number the lines in a document, a feature that can prove particularly useful in producing legal documents.

▶ *Grammar and style checkers.* Some programs let you scan your document for grammatical problems such as incorrect punctuation, double negatives, and split infinitives, and/or for stylistic problems, such as overuse of the passive voice or use of redundant expressions.

▶ *Macros.* Some word processing programs allow you to "record" a set of keystrokes and then play them back whenever you like. The process is analogous to speed dialing a *telephone: When you press one or two keys, the machine responds as if you had pressed a whole sequence of keys. You can use macros to automate any set of steps that you repeat frequently. You might create a macro to enter the closing for business letters. Then every time you pressed the key(s) to play back that macro, the program would automatically type the word "Sincerely" followed by a comma, press Enter/Return three times, and type your name. Some word-processing programs also let you create more sophisticated macros using a macro programming language.*

▶ ***Equation editing capabilities.*** *Some programs let you create, edit, and print complex mathematical equations. Be forewarned that the process is often pretty complicated. You should also be aware that equation editing features help you display and print equations,* not *solve* them.

CHOOSING A WORD PROCESSING PROGRAM

There are three different approaches you can take to selecting a word processing program:

▶ *Talk to friends and colleagues who word process and find out what they like and don't like about the programs they're using. Try to concentrate on people who are producing the type of documents that you plan to create.*

▶ *Make a list of any special requirements you have. Figure out what, exactly, you need the program to do. You may decide that you don't need any fancy features at all, and prefer to focus on finding a program that's simple, streamlined, and easy to learn.*

▶ *If at all possible, take the top contenders for a test drive. Either visit the home or office of an advocate of each program, or spend an hour or two at your local computer store.*

For many people, the real advantage offered by word processing is the luxury of changing your mind—of editing, rearranging, and reformatting the document until it's just about perfect. The ease with which you can accomplish the day-to-day operations therefore outweighs the assortment of fancy features. If you can, make sure that the program makes it easy to accomplish the types of things you'll want to do all the time, like moving a paragraph, deleting and undeleting a block of text, and printing. If you use a lot of bulleted lists or outlines, find out how easy (or hard) it is to create them. If you need to print envelopes, make sure that the program you choose makes it as painless as possible.

WINDOWS SOFTWARE SUITES

Several of the larger software companies now sell "suites" of Windows-based business software: special bundles of software that include at least a word processing program and spreadsheet program. Most suites offer other software as well, such as programs for managing databases, maintaining an electronic personal calendar, designing business presentations, and sending and receiving electronic mail on a network.

The major contenders in this arena include Microsoft Office, Lotus SmartSuite, and Perfect Office from Novell.

If you need both a word processing program and a spreadsheet program—and especially if you need word processing, spreadsheet, and database capabilities—purchasing a suite can prove very economical. Although the programs within each of the suites are designed to work well together and share similar menu structures, this is not reason enough to buy a suite rather than individual programs. (All well-designed Windows programs should be able to share and exchange data easily, and should also have fairly similar user interfaces.) You should only buy a suite if you're happy with all of the programs it contains (or at least the major ones) and with the price. Otherwise, pick and choose programs individually.

USING A WORD PROCESSING PROGRAM

Explaining how to use every word processing program, or even the major few, is beyond the scope of this book. But I can tell you something about what your word processing program will look like. I can also describe the central metaphors and concepts involved in word processing—topics that are often skipped over in manuals and books on the subject. Knowing a bit about the lay of the land will also help if you decide to try out a few word processing programs at your local computer store before you buy.

When you first start up a word processing program, your screen is largely blank. You are, in a sense, confronted with the electronic equivalent of a blank sheet of typing paper. As soon as you start typing, this page becomes filled with the characters that you have pressed on your keyboard.

Most word processing screens also contain a menu at the top of the screen and in some cases a set of icons representing additional choices. (You'll need to refer to your software manual for information on what each of the menu options and icons do.)

Every word processing screen also contains a symbol that serves as a "you are here" marker. (When you first start the program, this symbol appears in the upper-left corner of the typing area.) If you are entering text, this symbol indicates where the next character will appear. If you are deleting text, it tells you which character you are about to erase. If you are using either a Windows-based or a Macintosh word processing program, you will see a vertical line known as the insertion point. If you are using a DOS-based word processing program, you will probably see a cursor (a little blinking line or rectangle).

The insertion point is not the same as the mouse pointer. Most of the time when you're working in a Mac or Windows word processing program, the mouse pointer looks like a vertical line with a wishbone at the top and the bottom. (This symbol is often called a t-bar.) To move the insertion point, just move the mouse pointer to the desired spot and then click. If you have trouble distinguishing the pointer from the insertion point, just remember that the insertion point blinks and the pointer has wishbones. The pointer also moves when you move the mouse itself.

You can move the cursor or insertion point around using cursor-movement keys and, in many cases, the mouse. The cursor/insertion point also moves as you add or erase characters.

One of the first things to understand about word processing programs is that they scroll text. Most documents are too long to display on screen at once. As soon as you fill up the screen with text, the program starts scrolling lines off the top to make room for additional characters.

The best way to get used to this is to start thinking of the work area on your screen (the part below the menu and/or icons) as a window in which you edit and view documents. Since most documents are too long to fit in the window at once, you need to move this window up and down to view different parts of the text. Even though part of your document may disappear from the screen in the process, it's not erased from memory. You can always scroll up or down to bring it back into view.

A central feature of all word processing is a feature known as word-wrap. *Word-wrap* means that as you type, the program automatically "wraps" the text to the next line when you reach the right margin. There's no need to press the Enter or Return key (the electronic equivalent of a carriage return). In a sense, the computer handles your entire document as one long ribbon of characters that wraps from one line to the next. If you erase some characters (removing a section of the ribbon), the program pulls the rest of the ribbon leftward or, if necessary, pulls it up a line to close the gap. If you add characters in the middle (inserting a new section of ribbon), the rest of the ribbon is pushed forward and/or down.

If you learned to type on a typewriter, you may find your old habits hard to break. In particular, you'll have to train yourself not to press the Enter or Return key when you get near the right margin (that is, the right side of the screen). Not only is pressing Enter/Return unnecessary, it can actually create problems.

YOUR SCREEN AS A WINDOW

All word processing programs scroll text. As soon as you fill up the screen with text, lines start disappearing off the top to make room for new lines at the bottom.

When you press Enter/Return, the program inserts what is known as a *hard return*—a code that tells the program "go to the next line here, no matter where you are in relation to the margins." Whenever the program encounters a hard return, it breaks the line at that spot, even if there are only two words on the line. If you inadvertently press Enter/Return at the end of a line and later delete characters from that line, the line break will not change accordingly.

The moral of the story is that you should only press Enter/Return at the end of a paragraph, at the end of a line that you want to be abnormally short (like an address line), or when you want to insert a blank line between paragraphs. The rest of the time, just keep typing and let the program handle the line breaks for you.

Although they are usually invisible, hard returns are characters, just like letters or numbers. Each one occupies a mailbox (byte) in memory. And it can be deleted or moved just like other characters. To get rid of a hard return, place your cursor or insertion point on or to the left of the first character on the subsequent line, and then erase the character right before that spot by pressing the delete key if you're using a Mac or the Backspace key on a PC.

WORD-WRAP

Word processing programs treat documents as a continuous ribbon of text. Whenever you reach the right margin, the program automatically wraps this ribbon around to the next line.

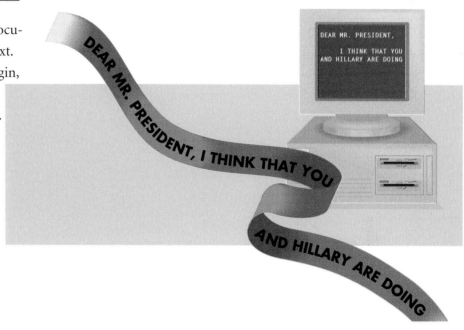

NOTE *In most word processing programs, you can't move the cursor/insertion point past the last character in the document. If you want to start typing three lines down from the top of a blank screen, for example, you can't just move the cursor/insertion point down three lines. You need to press Enter/Return a few times instead, inserting hard returns and thereby pushing the cursor/insertion point downward.*

SPREADSHEET PROGRAMS

In a nutshell, a *spreadsheet* is a grid of rows and columns in which you enter numbers and text. Spreadsheets were actually invented centuries ago as a means of performing and recording calculations. For their first two or three hundred years, the spreadsheet format—a book of pages divided into rows and columns—remained essentially unchanged. Then in the late 1970s, someone got the brilliant idea of automating the spreadsheet—that is, of displaying the same grid of rows and columns on a computer screen and having the computer do the work of performing the calculations. The result was an extremely successful program known as VisiCalc. Since then, spreadsheet programs such as Lotus 1-2-3, Quattro Pro, and Excel have become some of the most widely used types of computer software (second only to word processing programs).

HARD RETURNS

Whenever you press Enter/Return in a word processing program, you are inserting a special code called a *hard return* that directs the program to move to the next line.

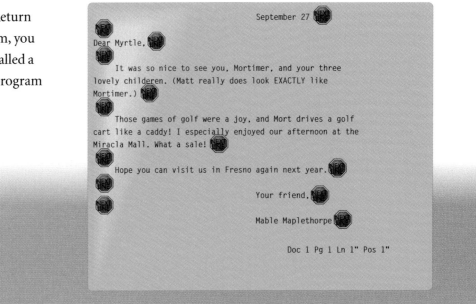

Spreadsheet programs are the number crunchers of the computer world, although they can be used to manipulate text as well. Think of them as powerful, multi-purpose calculators, capable of everything from adding two plus two to calculating a loan amortization schedule to projecting the likely impact of an increase of an energy tax on your cost of goods sold. Spreadsheets excel at performing both calculations on given numbers (what's the total of these 439 expense items?) and at what-if computations (how much will my monthly mortgage payment increase if I change the term from 30 years to 15 years?).

Although the appearance of spreadsheet programs varies a bit from one program to the next, they all have features in common. In almost all cases, the screen is largely occupied by a grid of rows and columns, frequently known as the *work area* or worksheet area. The columns are identified by letters shown at the top of the work area. The rows are identified by numbers (shown at the left side of the work area). The boxes formed by the intersection of individual rows and columns are known as *cells*. Cells are identified by the combination of their column letter and row number. The fifth cell in the second column is known as cell B5, for example. (The letter always comes first.) This is known as the cell's address or cell coordinates.

At any given moment, you are positioned in a single cell, generally known as the *current cell*. You can always tell which cell you are in at the moment by looking at the position of the cell pointer—a highlight that you can move from one cell to the next. (You can move the cell pointer from one cell to another using the cursor movement keys or your mouse.) The address of the current cell is usually displayed on a line just above the work area, in an area usually known as the cell address indicator.

When you create a new spreadsheet, the grid of rows and columns is empty. You start with the equivalent of a blank sheet of ledger paper—a *tabula rasa* waiting for your data.

The size of this "piece of paper" is actually quite huge. Most spreadsheets contain at least 256 columns and 8192 rows (about 2 million cells). What appears on the screen, however, is a small portion of that "page," usually about 8 columns and 20 rows. In order to find your way around the spreadsheet, you need to imagine the work area as a movable window, just as you do in a word processing program. But in this case, you can move the window sideways (to view additional columns) as well as up and down (to view additional rows).

In addition to the work area, most spreadsheets contain a menu bar at the top of the screen. This menu bar is either visible all the time or is invoked by pressing a key (usually the slash key) when you want to use it. We're not going to cover the use of the menu system, since the menus vary from program to program. But in general, you use menu commands to do things like moving, copying, and erasing blocks of data, inserting or deleting columns and rows, printing, saving, and changing the appearance of the data in various ways.

N O T E *In some spreadsheet programs, individual files are referred to as worksheets or spreadsheet notebooks rather than spreadsheets.*

HOW SPREADSHEETS WORK

Although spreadsheets are capable of calculating almost anything you can imagine, they're not set up in advance to perform any particular calculations. It's your job to fill in the grid by entering text, numbers, and instructions (formulas) that direct the computer to perform particular calculations.

Let's take a simple example. Suppose that you wanted to calculate the net income for a company. You might start by entering the numbers for total revenue in one cell and for total expenses in another. (You might also enter text identifying these numbers in two adjacent cells.) Then you would need to enter a formula telling the program to subtract the expenses from the revenue and display the result. You do this by moving to a blank cell and typing in

ANATOMY OF A SPREADSHEET SCREEN

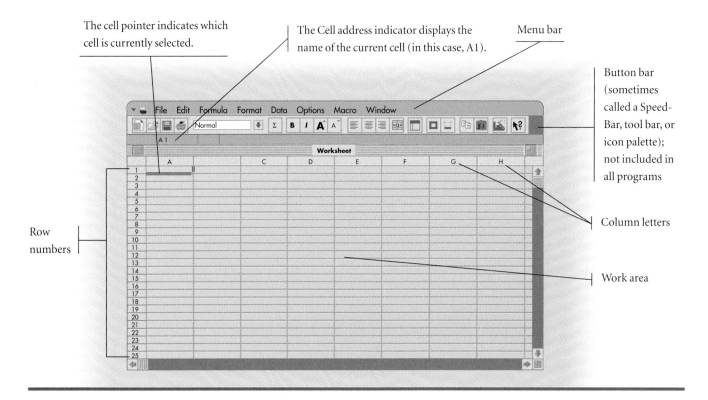

The cell pointer indicates which cell is currently selected.

The Cell address indicator displays the name of the current cell (in this case, A1).

Menu bar

Button bar (sometimes called a Speed-Bar, tool bar, or icon palette); not included in all programs

Column letters

Row numbers

Work area

an instruction describing the desired calculation in terms of cells. If cell B3 contains the figure for revenue and cell B4 contains your expenses, for example, you would enter a formula such as +B3-B4 or (B3-B4) or =B3-B4. (The exact syntax for formulas varies from one spreadsheet program to the next.) You can think of this formula as "take whatever value currently appears in cell B3, subtract the value that currently appears in cell B4, and then display the result in this cell." Then, whenever you change the value in cell B3 or B4, the result of the formula will be automatically—and, in most cases, instantly—updated.

This feature is known as automatic recalculation, and it is one of the main advantages that spreadsheets offer over calculators. Once you tell the spreadsheet what you want it to do, you are free to change the raw data as much and as often as you like, and the program does the work of recalculating the results.

Automatic recalculation actually offers two benefits. First, it lets you change a few of your numbers and have the program recalculate the results. You don't have to reiterate your instructions or reenter any data that didn't change.

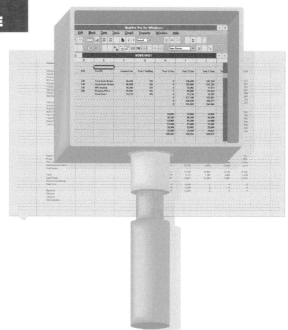

YOUR SCREEN IS A WINDOW ONTO THE SPREADSHEET PAGE

Think of the work area section as a movable window through which you can view different sections of a spreadsheet.

The advantages grow even more obvious when you have more formulas, and when some of those formulas "piggy back" on top of others. The "Stuffed Animal Sales Spreadsheet" figure illustrates this concept. If you changed the dollar amount of dinosaurs sold in January, the total for January at the bottom of that column would automatically be recalculated, as would the total dinosaur sales at the right edge of the row. (Both of those totals are based on formulas that add up all the other values in that row or column.) Then because the total dinosaur sales figure changed, the grand total in the lower-right corner would be recalculated as well, because that number is the result of a formula that adds up all the other values in the column (that is, the total for each type of stuffed animal). If there happened to be another formula based on the grand total, that formula would be recalculated as well.

To put this in more general terms: Every time you change the value in a cell, any formulas that refer to that cell are updated. As those formulas are updated, any formulas that refer to their results are updated as well. In this way, a single change in value may set off a chain reaction, instigating changes in several cells throughout the spreadsheet.

The other advantage of automatic recalculation is that it lets you "play" with numbers. If the Stuffed Animal Sales spreadsheet represented budgeted rather than actual sales

STUFFED ANIMAL SALES SPREADSHEET

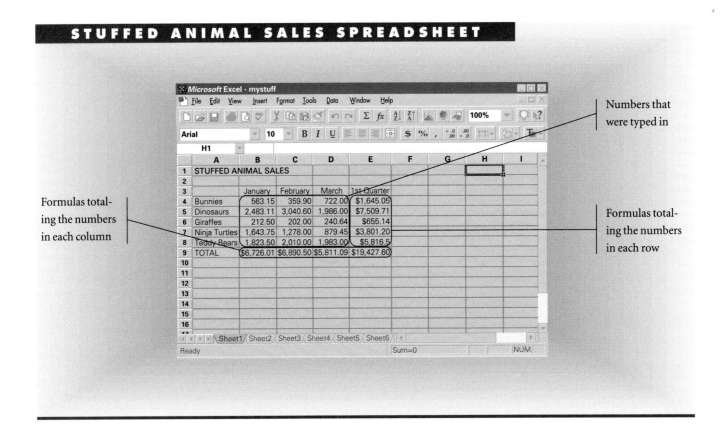

Numbers that were typed in

Formulas totaling the numbers in each column

Formulas totaling the numbers in each row

amounts, and you wanted to get your total sales up to 20,000, you could try adjusting various numbers to see exactly what it would take to get the desired total.

As mentioned, automatic recalculation is only one of the main advantages that spreadsheets offer over calculators. The others include:

▶ *Functions. All spreadsheet programs feature something known as* functions—*built-in tools for performing calculations other than simple arithmetic (addition, subtraction, multiplication, or division). Most major spreadsheet programs offer around 100 different functions, which allow you to calculate averages, square roots, depreciation, payments or earnings on annuities, and standard deviation (to name just a few).*

▶ *Database management capabilities. Most spreadsheet programs offer at least a few tools for managing lists. At a minimum, they allow you to sort a set of rows alphabetically or numerically, and to select items that match specified selection criteria. Bear in mind that if your list exceeds a hundred items or if you need to produce formatted reports or mailing labels, you are better off calling in an expert—namely, a database management program—rather than testing the limits of your spreadsheet program.*

▶ *Formatting tools. Many spreadsheet programs offer desktop publishing tools, enabling you to mix and match fonts within a single spreadsheet, to print spreadsheets sideways, and dress up your spreadsheets with lines, boxes, shading, and graphic elements like pictures and logos.*

▶ *Macros. As described earlier in this chapter, macros are a means of automating an entire series of steps and then "playing them back" with one or two keystrokes. Some spreadsheet programs allow you to record macros—that is, to "memorize" a series of actions as you perform them and then repeat them on demand. Others require you to construct macros by typing commands into cells of the spreadsheet, much as a programmer would type in the lines of a computer program. (In fact, many spreadsheet macro languages are really programming languages in themselves—with all the implied power and potential difficulty.)*

▶ *Three-dimensionality and linking. Many spreadsheet programs offer tools for linking multiple spreadsheet files, so that a formula in one file can refer to cells in another file. Others let you store multiple sets of information—almost like individual spreadsheets—within a single file. (This is called a* three-dimensional spreadsheet *or* spreadsheet notebook.*) Such features can prove extremely useful if you need to consolidate information from several departments or time periods, or want a way to organize several distinct but related sets of information.*

▶ *Graphing tools. Most spreadsheet programs offer some means of representing the numbers within your spreadsheets in graphical form as a bar chart, line chart, or pie chart (among others). Some offer sophisticated graphing features that let you create dozens of different types of graphs, and also allow you to dress up your graphs with lines, boxes, ellipses, text, and other design elements.*

CHOOSING A SPREADSHEET PROGRAM

When comparing two or more spreadsheet programs, start with the basics. See how you like the menu structure. (You may find some more intuitive than others.) Find out the procedure for doing simple things, like entering dates, or copying an entry from one cell to another, or inserting a row. For many people, the ease with which you can accomplish mundane tasks—like entering and formatting data—is at least as important as the high-powered extras.

The first step in choosing a spreadsheet program is determining which special features you need, if any. For example, if you plan to use your spreadsheet to perform crosstabs (that is, to summarize data by two sets of variables, like age and ethnicity, or color and size), make sure that the program supports that type of calculation. (Not all do.) If graphs are critical to your work, check out the graphing talents of various programs: what types of graphs can they generate, what tools do they offer for customizing or annotating graphs, how easy is it to print graphs, can you produce graph slide shows?

Another area to explore is how easily you can exchange data with other programs. Can you easily move data from a spreadsheet into a word processing document? If you also plan on using a database program, how well can the spreadsheet program "talk to" various database programs? As always, data exchange tends to be less of a problem with Mac and Windows programs because they can usually exchange data via the Clipboard feature.

If you want your spreadsheets to look desktop published—with various fonts and accoutrements such as lines and boxes—see how such features are implemented in the program.

DATABASE MANAGEMENT PROGRAMS

Most offices are teeming with files and filing systems, not to mention stacks of paper waiting to be filed. Database management programs are designed to help you manage such masses of data. Their purpose is to turn the names, notes, facts, and figures involved in running a business, a nonprofit organization, or a research project into manageable and, one hopes, useful information. You can think of database programs as a cross between filing clerk and research assistant: They help you both store and retrieve information, and make some sense of it all.

To put it more mundanely, database management programs help you manage and use databases. A *database* is simply a structured collection of information about people (like customers, vendors, members, or employees), things (such as products on hand, documents on file, or properties to rent), or events (orders received, services provided, sales calls made, or student course registrations).

You've probably dealt with many databases already, even if you've never touched a computer. Library card catalogs, inventory systems, rolodex files, and collections of customer ledger cards are all databases. Managing such databases involves the same basic

A SPREADSHEET WITH A GRAPH

Some spreadsheet programs let you display graphs as part of your spreadsheet.

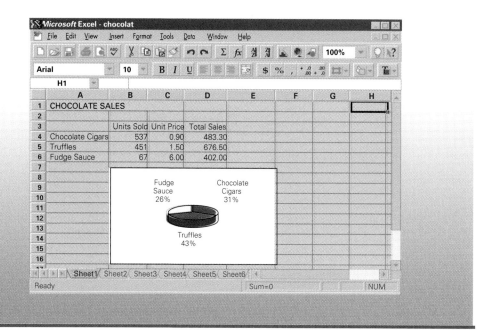

processes, regardless of whether you perform them with the aid of a computer. Those operations include:

▶ *Entering new data*

▶ *Locating previously entered data*

▶ *Changing and deleting existing data*

▶ *Selecting portions of your data, such as all the customers in San Francisco or all the orders that are past due*

▶ *Arranging the data into different sequences, such as in alphabetical order by last name, or by zip code, or by state and within state by city*

▶ *Producing reports and other printed output, including form letters and mailing labels*

▶ *Generating statistics—for example, counting the number of orders for a particular item, or determining the average dollar amount of all orders placed in the last year*

Notice that all of these operations can be accomplished without a computer. In this sense, maintaining a shoe box full of index cards can be called database management. The main advantages of computerizing are

▶ *Speed. In general, putting a database on computer won't save you much time on the input side of things. (It takes about the same amount of time to type a customer's name and address on the keyboard as it does to scribble it on a rolodex card, maybe even a bit more.) Where the time savings occur is on the output side of the equation— once you've got the information in there, you can "massage" the data in any way you like with relatively little time or effort: sorting it into 12 different orders, printing it in a variety of formats, selecting all the customers that live in Cincinnati and like to order red plaid hiking shorts.*

▶ *Increased accuracy in calculations. Assuming they receive the right instructions, computers are generally more reliable at performing calculations than people are.*

▶ *Fewer errors and greater consistency in the data. If you have a lot of data, you want some way to ensure its accuracy. Many database programs let you prevent simple data entry errors by defining rules for what data is acceptable in a field by specifying an allowable numeric range for a field, or a list of valid entries. Some programs also let you define particular items as mandatory, or fill in default values whenever an item is left blank. And some let you set up automatic formatting rules, so that all letters entered in an entry are automatically capitalized, for example.*

Before you get too enthusiastic about how a database management program is going to change your life, there's one limitation you should know about. Database management programs do not turn you into an organized person (or your office into an organized office). If you can't keep your desk in order, you're not likely to fare much better with a database program. On the other hand, if you're serious about the process of setting up a database, the transition to computers can force you to standardize the way you structure and manage information. Since most database programs require you to define in advance exactly which items of information you are going to enter, you'll need to think through exactly what you want to know. Similarly, since computers can't make value judgments, you need to define clear-cut rules about issues like when old customers should be deleted from your mailing list, whether you want to allow the entry of overpayments, or what codes you will use for departments in your personnel list. (If you don't standardize, it will be difficult to find everyone in a

INPUT AND OUTPUT

When you use a database management program, you can input (enter) data once and then output it in a variety of forms—generating lists, labels, form letters, and statistical reports.

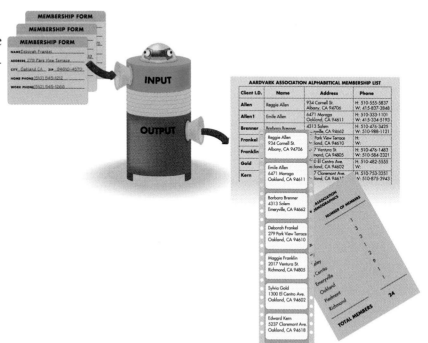

department later.) In other words, computerizing a database can force you to be more thoughtful and systematic than you'd otherwise be, at least during the design phase.

Most database programs are not free-form. They don't allow you to just jot down whatever information you want on each customer or inventory item. Instead, they make you decide, in advance, exactly which items of information you're going to collect. (You can change your mind about this structure, but it takes a little time and effort.) Note: There are exceptions to this rule. Some database programs—known as *free-form database programs*—are more open-ended, allowing you to enter data in whatever format you like.

To take a simple example, suppose that you have decided to use a database program to manage a personnel database. The first step is to set up a structure for your data, specifying what categories of information you intend to include for each employee. (You can think of this as making a mold into which you plan to pour your data.) Only after you have defined this structure can you start entering data.

In database terminology, these individual categories of information are known as *fields* and the entire set of information related to each person, thing, or event is known as a *record*.

When the data is laid out in a tabular or spreadsheet-like form, as it is in the figure "Database Terminology," fields occupy columns and records occupy rows.

In the case of the personnel database, the fields might include first name, last name, address, phone extension, home phone number, department, supervisor, date hired, social security number, department, position, and salary. The entire collection of data for each employee—that is, the full set of fields—is one record. You may leave one or more of these fields empty in some records, but every record has the same set of fields. You also cannot have one or two records with extra fields that don't exist in the other records.

NOTE *In many database programs, besides specifying the number of fields and their names, you need to specify the type of data you will enter (numbers, text, dates, or pictures) and, in some cases, the amount of space you want to reserve for each field.*

Some people refer to a collection of records with the same structure as a *database file*, and others call it a *table*. I'll use the latter term. Many databases consist of a single table; others consist of two tables or more.

Unlike word processing and spreadsheet programs, database programs do not share a common metaphor or a similar look. All they have in common is a comparable set of standard features. Specifically, most database programs have tools for:

▶ *Designing new tables. All database programs have a feature for creating and structuring new tables. Usually, when you issue the command for creating a table, you see a screen with columns for field name, type of data, and in some cases the field size.*

▶ *Viewing and updating data. Most database programs offer one or two standard forms for entering data—often a tabular form and a one-record-at-a-time form. Most also include commands for searching for, changing, and deleting individual records.*

▶ *Creating custom data entry forms. If your database is fairly small and includes relatively few fields, you may find the standard data entry forms sufficient. If you're going to be entering a lot of data, you may prefer to design a customized form. Most high-end programs let you design your own forms—placing fields wherever you like, including descriptive text or instructions, and adding window dressing like lines or boxes to make the data easier to read.*

DATABASE TERMINOLOGY

A table is a collection of records that share the same structure—that is, include the same set of fields. This is a table of data on animals in a wildlife refuge.

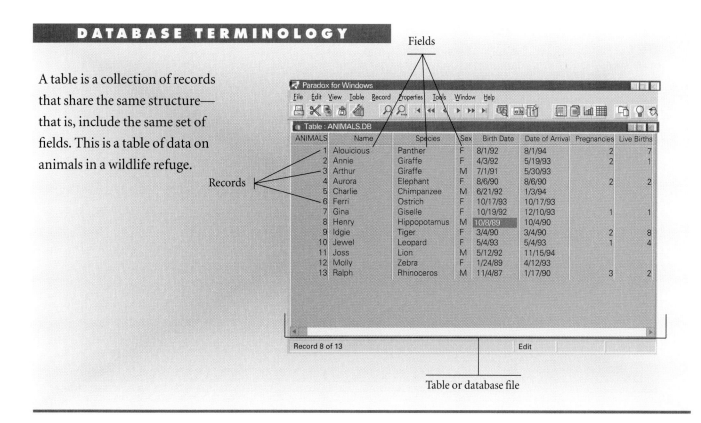

Fields

Records

Table or database file

A CUSTOM DATA ENTRY FORM FOR ENTERING DATA

Most database programs let you design customized data entry forms.

▶ *Designing reports. All database programs have tools for producing reports. Most have features known as report designers that allow you to select and arrange the fields that you want to include, to perform calculations like totals or averages, and, in most cases, to group records into some meaningful order. You might, for example, print a list in which employees are grouped by department, including a count of the number of employees in each department and the average salary at the end of each departmental group.*

▶ *Selecting data. Most database programs provide some tools to help you select subsets of your data. Probably the most common selection tool is something called* query-by-example *(QBE). (As the name implies, you use query-by-example to pose questions about your database—questions like what are the name of all the customers with a past due balance, or how many clients are there in each city.)*

▶ *Macro features or programming languages. Some database programs include macro features or even full-fledged programming languages that allow you (or a professional programmer) to automate repetitive tasks.*

CHOOSING A DATABASE PROGRAM

One of the first questions you need to answer when choosing a database program is whether your database is likely to include one table or many. Sometimes all the information related to a particular business problem is stored in a single table. If your database is a list of customers, for example, and you just need to maintain their names and addresses so that you can periodically send out product or sales announcements, a single customer table is all you need. However, many business applications are not this simple. If you are running a mail order business, for example, and many of your customers place multiple orders, you might have one table for customers and a second one for the individual orders they place. The customer table would include name, address, phone numbers, and other information that is the same for each order. The order table would include the date of the order, the amount, the quantity, product code, price, and so on—the items that vary from one order to the next.

In most cases, if you are dealing with any kinds of events or transactions, your database should include at least two tables: one for the people or things involved in the

MULTIPLE-TABLE DATABASES

Most orders databases contain at least two tables: one for customers and another for orders. For each Customer record, there may be one or more Order records.

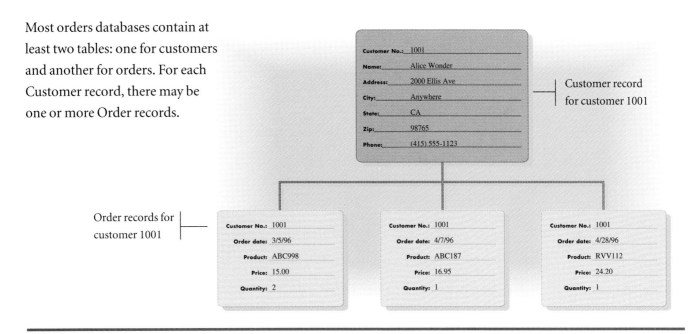

Customer record for customer 1001

Order records for customer 1001

transaction/event, and a second for the transactions/events themselves. Typical examples of such two-table databases include Patients and Visits, Donors and Donations, Clients and Services Provided.

Not all database management programs are designed to manage multiple-table databases. Those programs that let you work with two or more tables at once—and to find and display matches between tables—are known as *relational database management programs.* Relational database programs let you:

▶ *Match up data in two or more tables*

▶ *Transfer data between tables (posting data from an orders table to a balance due field in a customer record, for example)*

▶ *Ask questions related to multiple tables (such as what is the name and address of each customer who placed an order for x)*

▶ *Display related data from two or more tables in reports and data entry forms*

The better relational database programs also help you maintain consistency between tables, preventing deletion of a customer who has orders on file, for example, or making sure that if you change a customer's I.D. number, the I.D. number in all related orders records is changed as well.

Database programs that only let you work with one table at a time are known as *flat file managers*. In general, flat file managers tend to be a little easier to learn and use and a bit less expensive.

Once you have decided you need a relational database program, there are several other factors to consider.

▶ *If you have very specific reporting needs—like reports that include lots of text that you need to word wrap in a column, or reports that must include graphics such as a company logo—make sure the program can handle them.*

▶ *Make sure that the program supports the type of data you have. Almost all database programs let you enter text, numbers, and dates. Some but not all databases can handle graphics (pictures), free-form text fields (fields capable of accommodating any amount of text), and other types of data as well.*

▶ *If you have a relatively small database—say, 2,000 records or fewer—speed is not likely to be much of a problem. Any database program should be sufficient. But if you have a database of 20,000 or 60,000 or 200,000 records, it will be. You may want to see results of performance tests (often called* benchmarks*) or have someone demonstrate the program on a large database. Also, many programs have a limit on the number of records you can enter, or on the size of each record. Make sure these limits are high enough for your needs.*

▶ *Decide whether you need to move data back and forth between your database program and another program—like your spreadsheet or word processing program. If so, make sure that either your database program can export data in a form the other program can read, or that your other program can read data in your database program's own file format. In many cases, you can move data from one Windows program to another via the Clipboard.*

▶ *Check whether it has a query-by-example (QBE) feature or something comparable that makes it fairly easy to select subsets of your data and generate statistics.*

▶ *Determine how easy it is to design data entry forms, reports, and labels.*

▶ *Find out if it includes tools for automating operations, such as macros/scripts, application generators, or a programming language.*

Learning to use a database management program is usually more demanding than learning a word processing or even a spreadsheet program—unless someone has already set it up for you and tailored it to your needs. If you're starting from scratch, expect to spend at least a few days getting started, much more if your needs or your program are particularly complex. If you find the process to be more work and more of a challenge than you're ready for, you have two choices.

▶ *Find a customized database package. If it's likely that many other people are trying to do exactly the same thing as you, you can try looking for a customized database package—that is, a program designed to do exactly what you need. There are, for example, customized database programs designed to manage medical offices, track and solicit donations to various types of nonprofits, and help schools keep track of teacher and student schedules. Finding such programs is not always easy. If there is a magazine or journal devoted to your particular line of business, you may want to scan its ads. Even better, if you can manage it, talk to people who are already using such packages to find out what they like and dislike about them. (If you belong to a professional organization, try asking around at a meeting.)*

If you are going to buy a customized package, make sure that the company that distributes it has been around for a while and is likely to last a while longer. If you have any doubts about the company's longevity, make sure that the program is written in a widely used language and that you have the source code (the original form in which the program was written—a form that other programmers can read and modify). Otherwise, if the company folds next week and you discover a very troublesome bug the week after, you're out of luck.

▶ *Hire a programmer/consultant. There are lots of people who design small databases for a living. Some can help you find a custom package or simply guide you through the creation of a particularly sticky report. You can also hire consultants to develop a completely customized "turn key" system—that is, a system that is built to your specifications and requires no special knowledge of computers or your database program to use. Again, be sure to get the source code.*

There are two potential advantages to buying a customized package rather than having someone write one from scratch. It will usually (although not always) cost less, and you can presume it has been tested by previous users and therefore will have fewer bugs. The disadvantage is that you may have more trouble getting support should problems arise, and the system may never fit your needs exactly. Unless you are lucky enough to find a package that does exactly what you need, you'll have to decide how much you're willing to change the way you do things to fit the system.

If you think you may need expert help, don't buy an obscure package. You'll have a lot more trouble finding someone to help you out with Joe Blow's Database Manager than with a major database program. (The major ones include FoxPro, Paradox, Access, dBASE, Q&A, and Approach for PCs, FileMaker Pro, 4th Dimension, and FoxBase Mac for Macs.)

INSTALLING PROGRAMS

The process of installing a program can take anywhere from a few minutes to half an hour, depending on the size of the program, the speed of your computer, and whether you're installing from floppies or a CD-ROM. (Installing from a CD-ROM is faster and easier because you don't need to keep removing one disk and inserting another.) Most programs come with their own installation program—that is, a program designed solely to copy the main program onto your hard disk and, in most cases, acquire some information about your hardware. With luck, your manual will explain, in fairly coherent terms, how to use the installation program. Look for an installation section in the manual or, in some cases, a separate manual labeled something like Installation or Getting Started. Occasionally, the program's installation instructions will be printed on the box the program is sold in or the envelope containing the disks or CD-ROM.

The first step in installing a program is locating the installation disk. Look for a disk labeled Install or Installation Disk or something similar. If no such disk exists, try looking for one labeled Disk 1. Insert that disk into your floppy-disk drive. The next step varies from one operating system to the next.

In Windows 95, open the Start menu and select Run. Then type **d:SETUP** in the box labeled Command Line where d: is the name of the floppy drive or CD-ROM drive you're installing from. (If you're installing from a floppy disk drive named a:, for example, you'd enter **a:setup**.) Then press Enter or click OK. If this doesn't work, try **d:INSTALL**.

On a Macintosh, look for an icon labeled Installer in the floppy disk's or CD-ROM drive's window and double-click it.

N O T E *Some programs that come on CD-ROM are not meant to be copied to your hard disk in their entirety. (This is especially common in the case of multimedia programs, which tend to consume a huge amount of storage space; often more space than you'll have or be willing to use up on your hard disk.) When you install such programs, you may be asked whether you want to copy all or just some of the program to your hard disk. (The more of the program you copy, the faster it will run, but the more space it will consume.) In other cases, you're not given a choice: A small portion of the program is copied to your hard disk and the rest remains on CD-ROM. If you copy less than the entire program from a CD-ROM to your hard disk, you'll need to insert the CD-ROM whenever you want to run the program.*

Once you have started the installation program, that program takes over, asking questions as necessary and periodically prompting you to insert additional disks (if you're installing from floppies rather than CD-ROM). With luck, the questions will be at least somewhat comprehensible. In general, you should just accept the program's suggestions on where to place the program files or what to call things. If you are offered a choice between a standard or quick installation and a custom installation, pick the standard/quick one. Sometimes installation programs make you use a key other than the Enter key—like Tab or F2— to move from one question to the next. If you press Enter and nothing happens, scan the screen for information on which keys do what.

Most programs are shipped with a file named README or README.DOC which contains late-breaking news about the program. Sometimes it contains information on anomalies in the program. (In most cases, "anomaly" is a code word for bug, used because no manufacturer wants to admit that their program isn't perfect.) Sometimes it contains minor corrections to the manual. If you are using a Mac, you can read the README file by

MODIFYING CONFIGURATION FILES

The installation programs for many DOS programs and some Windows programs like to modify various configuration files on your hard disk. Polite programs will ask whether this is OK with you before proceeding. (Others will make the changes without your permission.) If you do see a message asking if it's OK to modify AUTOEXEC.BAT, CONFIG.SYS, or WIN.INI, select Yes.

double-clicking the ReadMe icon. If you are using Windows, you can launch the Windows Notepad and then use the File Open command to read the file.

LEARNING AN APPLICATION PROGRAM

Once you've chosen and installed a new program, you still need to go about learning it. There are several approaches that you can take toward this process:

▶ *Use the tools that come with the software—namely the manuals, the online tutorial (if there is one), and the built-in help system (if any).*

▶ *Buy a book on the subject at your local bookstore or computer store. Many bookstores carry several different books on the major software packages. My strategy for finding the right one is simple. Start by looking in the index for any operation that you know you'll need to perform. If you can't find your topic in the index, choose another book. (Since much of the time you'll be using the book as a reference, the index may be its most critical feature.) Assuming you can find your topic, go ahead and read what the book says about it. If the explanation seems clear and complete, place the book in your stack of "books under consideration" and try out a few others. When you're done, buy the book with the explanation you liked best.*

▶ *Take a class at a computer school or a community college. (Check local computer magazines, computer stores, and your local yellow pages for computer school locations.)*

▶ *Find a friend who is willing to help you get started. (Since most programs take more than an hour or two to master, don't expect your friend to hold your hand the whole time.)*

Which of these approaches will work depends on your own learning style—some people learn best on their own; others need the enforced discipline or camaraderie of a class. Once you've read through this book, you should know enough buzzwords and have enough understanding of computers to manage either a book or a basic class. (If you have trouble with either, you can probably assume there's something amiss with the author or teacher.)

The one general piece of advice I would offer on learning a new program is to take some time to get your bearings. As you've seen throughout this chapter, most programs work with some kind of metaphor—that is, they treat your screen "as if" it were something more familiar, like a piece of typing paper or an accountant's ledger. One way or another, they present you with a little world. Your first step should therefore involve discovering what kinds of objects populate that world, how you move around in it, and what tools—like menus or sets of icons or function keys—you can use to make your mark. In other words, when you first approach a new program, don't get immediately caught up in accomplishing a specific task. Instead, picture yourself as Alice stepping through the looking glass. Your first task should be exploring the new world. (You can worry about how to get to the next square later.)

COMPUTER USERS GROUPS

If you're at all partial to clubs or other social gatherings, and you live in a metropolitan area, you may also want to hunt for a local computer user's group. User's groups are membership organizations of people who use or are learning to use computers. Most user's groups have members that range from absolute beginners to professional programmers and computer consultants, although some groups lean more toward one end than the other. Such groups can be a tremendous source of free advice and technical support. The larger user's groups usually have several special interest groups (commonly known as SIGs) on various types of software or computer-related topics. The larger computer groups—like the Boston Computer Society and the Bay Area Macintosh User's Group (BMUG)—have dozens of SIGs on almost anything you can imagine doing with a computer. Many computer user's groups also feature a question and answer period where confused or frustrated members can pose questions to the membership at large. With any luck, someone in the audience will know exactly where the problem lies and how to solve it. If you are in the market for a new computer, user's groups are also an excellent source for tips and warnings about local vendors. Finally, many user's groups receive discounts on both hardware and software.

CHAPTER

8

HARDWARE

Monitors

▪

Printers

▪

Storage Devices

▪

Installing New Hardware in Windows 95

▪

Networks

Back in Chapter 2, you were introduced to the basics of computer hardware. In this chapter, you'll go a little further, learning some of the finer points about peripherals (namely monitors, printers, and storage devices) that I didn't want to overwhelm you with earlier in the book. You'll also learn a bit about networks: what they are, what they're for, and how you use them.

MONITORS

The monitor is your computer's primary output device—its tool for displaying information, soliciting information, and responding to your requests. It's also likely to be the center of your attention most of the time you are using the computer. As a result, it's hard to overestimate the importance of a good monitor, meaning one that's clear, easy to read, and free of glare and flicker. A good monitor can make staring at the screen for eight hours bearable. A bad one can cause headaches, fatigue, and eye strain (not to mention grumpiness).

Computer monitors come in three main types: monochrome, grayscale, and color. Monochrome monitors display images in a single color against a contrasting background. The combinations you'll encounter most often are green, amber, or white characters against a black background. Grayscale monitors are monitors capable of displaying various shades of gray as well as black and white. In general, grayscale and color monitors are more expensive than monochrome ones. They are also more likely to be capable of displaying graphics. (You'll learn more about displaying graphics in the next section.)

Just because grayscale and color monitors are generally more expensive than monochrome ones doesn't mean that they're better. If all you want to do with your computer is write the great American novel using a DOS-based word processing program, a monochrome monitor is probably the best tool for the job. Not only will it cost a lot less, it will also be easier on your eyes.

All three types of monitors come in a wide range of sizes. (Monitor size is almost always measured diagonally across the screen.) At the small end are the 9-inch screens on Mac Classics, which are actually not separate monitors at all, but are built into the system unit. At the large end are full-page and two-page screens designed for desktop publishing. These let you display either one or two full pages of text at once, rather than the half page of text typical of other monitors. The majority of monitors range from 14 inches to 20 inches in size.

VARIETIES OF MONITORS

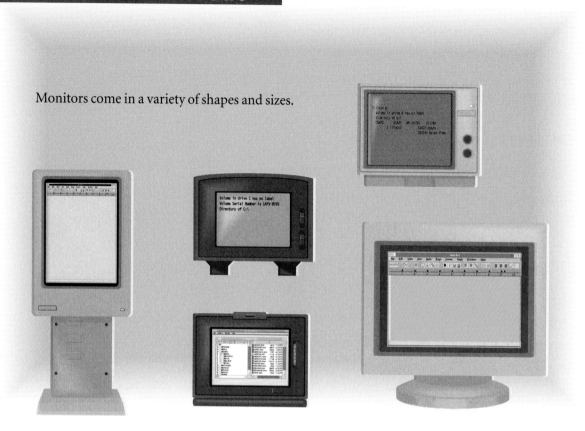

Monitors come in a variety of shapes and sizes.

NOTE *Never buy a monitor until you see it running the applications software that you plan to use. Some monitors are great at displaying color photographs and horrible at displaying text, and vice versa. Make sure that your monitor is well-suited to the particular task you have in mind.*

The monitor itself is only one of the pieces of equipment involved in displaying images on your screen. The other is something known as a *video adapter,* a set of circuitry that translates instructions from your computer into a form your monitor can use.

In most personal computers, the video adapter is an expansion board that fits into a slot on your computer's motherboard. On some Macs, however, video circuitry is built into the motherboard itself and you only need a separate video card for special monitors or for increased speed. You may hear video adapters called things like display adapter card, video card, or video hardware. You might also hear the acronyms for various types of video cards, like EGA and VGA. (You'll learn about those shortly.)

VIDEO STANDARDS AND SCREEN RESOLUTIONS

Some monitors and video adapters are capable of displaying images at various resolutions by using different numbers of dots per inch. When you use a lower resolution, the image expands: You see less on the screen but everything you do see is larger, as if you were looking through a magnifying glass. When you use a higher resolution, everything on the screen shrinks, allowing you to see more information at once. Using a higher resolution may therefore make it possible for you to compose your annual report in one window while viewing a spreadsheet with this year's income statement in another window, for example, or to view a dozen more columns and/or rows of spreadsheet data at one time. The only reason to switch to a lower than normal resolution is if you have trouble seeing and want to display larger characters or images on the screen.

Screen resolution depends on three things: your monitor, your video adapter, and your software. As you already know, the monitor determines whether you can display images in color. It also sets the upper limit of the screen resolution—that is, how many dots per inch you can display on screen. Some monitors are designed to display images at only one resolution. Others, known as *multisync monitors*, can display images at various resolutions.

Resolution is described in terms of number of pixels. A *pixel*, which is short for *picture element*, means a dot used to construct screen images. In the Mac world, resolution is usually described in terms of number of dots (pixels) per inch (dpi), with 72 dpi as the norm. (This

---

TEXT MODE VERSUS GRAPHICS MODE

There are basically two methods of displaying characters and other objects on a computer screen: text mode and graphics mode.

- Text mode uses the computer's built-in character set and a preset grid of rows and columns. Usually text mode uses a grid of 25 rows and 80 columns to display data, but some use 40 or 50 rows and as many as 132 columns.

- In graphics mode, each element on the screen—be it a character, a picture, or a box—is composed of dozens or even hundreds of individual dots. Although drawing images dot by dot is time-consuming, graphics mode offers tremendous flexibility because the results are not limited to a predefined set of characters or a fixed set of locations on the screen. You can draw just about anything, anywhere you like.

Most DOS-based programs display images in text mode, although some give you a choice. Both Windows and Mac programs use graphics mode, which is why their screens tend to be more picture-oriented and visually interesting.

The video adapter you are using determines whether you can display graphics. If you have what's known as a *graphics adapter* and either a color or grayscale monitor, you'll be able to display images in graphics mode.

---

means 72 dots horizontally and 72 dots vertically.) In the PC world, resolution is usually described in terms of the number of pixels displayed horizontally by the number of pixels displayed vertically across the entire screen (rather than within an inch). The most common resolution in graphics mode is 640×480 (640 pixels horizontally and 480 vertically).

N O T E *There is one fundamental difference in the way that Macs and PCs handle screen resolution. On Macs, images are normally displayed at 72 dots per inch (dpi), regardless of the size of the monitor. This means that, by default, you will see more information on a larger screen than on a smaller one. On PCs, the default resolution is usually 640×480 pixels, regardless of the size of the monitor. This means that you will normally see the same amount of information on a 20-inch monitor as you do on a 14-inch monitor, but on the 20-inch monitor, the image will be larger. (Every menu, picture, or character on the screen will be almost one-and-one-half times as big.) If you want to take advantage of the larger monitor to display more information, you need to change to a different resolution, as you'll learn to do shortly.*

As mentioned, the video adapter you are using determines whether you can display graphics and, if so, which of several video standards and resolutions you can use. Among PC graphics adapters, there are several standards for video cards. Currently, the most widely used standard is something called VGA, which stands for Video Graphics Array. A regular VGA adapter displays images at 640×480 resolution (meaning 640 dots horizontally by 480 vertically) and either 16 colors, or, if you have a special video driver, 256 colors. (You'll learn about video drivers shortly.) Super VGA is an enhancement of the VGA standard. It allows for higher resolutions (800×600, 1024×768, and in some cases 1280×1024) and for more colors. If you are buying a monitor tomorrow, be sure to get a Super VGA adapter and a monitor capable of taking advantage of it.

N O T E *You don't need to have a color monitor in order to use VGA. Most grayscale monitors are designed to display images in what's known as grayscale VGA, using various shades of gray rather than different colors to display graphic images. Many laptop and notebook computers feature grayscale VGA displays since they're both less expensive and less demanding on batteries than color displays.*

Some of the older video standards are CGA (for Color/Graphics Adapter) and EGA (Enhanced Graphics Adapter), both of which are now all but obsolete. A few others you may encounter are MCGA (MultiColor Graphics Array), which is a subset of the VGA standard

AN IMAGE AT DIFFERENT RESOLUTIONS

A spreadsheet in 640 × 480 resolution   The same spreadsheet in 800 × 600 resolution

that is used on some low-end IBM PS/2 computers; and PGA and XGA, which are used primarily in high-end drafting and design applications.

Finally, there's the question of software. There are actually two types of software involved in displaying images on your screen. First, there's your operating system and/or applications software and the types of display modes it's capable of using. The other type of software that affects your screen display are *video drivers*—programs that allow your operating system or application programs to converse with your video board. In many cases, you select a video driver when you install a program, by answering questions about the type of monitor you are using. After that, you'll only need to be dealing with video drivers when you change to a different screen resolution.

CHANGING YOUR SCREEN DISPLAY IN WINDOWS 95

By default, Windows displays information in 640 × 480 resolution (640 pixels horizontally, 480 pixels vertically) and uses a palette of 16 colors. As the figure entitled "An Image at Different Resolutions" shows, increasing the resolution can dramatically increase the amount of information you can see at one time. Using a higher resolution also makes it easier to view multiple windows at once. There is a downside to higher resolutions, however: Because more pixels means more work for your computer, you may notice a corresponding decrease in performance, particularly on slower systems. The other potential problem, of course, is that the higher the resolution, the smaller the individual characters and pictures on the screen. Unless you have a large monitor and good eyesight, you may find characters shrinking down to little unreadable smudges at higher resolutions.

There is a similar trade-off with colors. As mentioned, Windows normally displays images using a 16-color palette by default. You can increase the number of colors (sometimes called the *color density*) to 256 colors or, if your display adapter allows, to as many as 16.8 million colors (referred to as "true color"). The greater the number of colors, the clearer your graphic images will be. Note that the number of colors affects the clarity of black and white images as well as color ones, because it determines the number of shades of gray that can be displayed. The downside, again, is speed. The more colors your computer has to display, the longer it will take it to display images on the screen. If you are displaying pictures, photographs, or videos, you'll probably want to use at least 256 colors. But if all you're doing is word processing, manipulating a database, or creating spreadsheets, 16 colors may be adequate and may give you better performance.

To change the resolution of your screen display:

▶ *Right-click the desktop and choose Properties from the context menu to open the Display Properties dialog box.*

▶ *Click the Settings tab.*

▶ *Drag the slider labeled Desktop area to the right for higher resolution (more pixels per inch) or to the left for lower resolution (fewer pixels per inch). The precise resolution setting (640 × 480 pixels, or whatever) will appear below the slider.*

In some cases, Windows needs to restart your computer in order to put the new settings into effect. In others, it simply resizes your desktop and then displays a dialog box asking if you want to retain the new settings. Unless you click Yes within 15 seconds, the old settings are reinstated automatically.

NOTE *If you like using high resolution in general but find it difficult to read the tiny text, try experimenting with the Font Size setting in the Display Properties dialog box. By default, Windows* *uses Small Fonts. Switching to Large Fonts increases the displayed size of the fonts used for menus, dialog boxes, and messages, as well as for the text in any documents you create or view. Note that this change only affects the size of characters on screen; it has nothing to do with the point size of printed text.*

To adjust the number of colors used in your display, open the Display Properties dialog box (as described above) and use the Color palette drop-down list to select the number of colors. Remember that the more colors you use, the greater the demand on your system.

The range of choices you have for resolution, font size, and color density depends on your monitor, your display adapter, and the video drivers you have available. If you are unable to drag the slider, for example, then either your monitor or display adapter only supports a single resolution, or you only have a video driver for that one resolution. If you think that your monitor and display adapter can support more options than are available to you in the Display Properties dialog box, try contacting the manufacturer of the display adapter to see if it has video drivers to support the combination of resolution, font size, and color density that you're after.

MAC On a Mac, you can change to a nonstandard resolution if you have a multisynch monitor and a relatively fancy video card. See your video card manual for the details.

HOW MONITORS WORK

The monitors for most desktop computers work just like television sets: They use something called a *cathode ray tube* (CRT) to project images onto a screen. A CRT is essentially a vacuum tube with an electron gun at one end and a flat screen at the other. The electron gun "shoots" a single stream of electrons at the screen. The inside of the screen is coated with special particles, known as *phosphors*, that glow when struck by the electrons.

In monochrome monitors, there is one electron gun and each phosphor dot results in one dot on the screen. In color monitors, there are three phosphor guns and each screen dot consists of three phosphor dots: one red, one green, and one blue. The color of the dot on screen depends on the intensities of the various electron streams. If a particularly high-intensity beam is directed at the red phosphor dot, for example, the screen dot is very reddish. If the green dot is hit with a high-intensity beam, you get a very greenish dot on the screen.

In both types of monitors, each of the electron beams is directed at one spot at a time, but the beams themselves move, scanning horizontally across a single line of the screen, then dropping down a line and scanning across that one, dropping down another line, and so on. Think of these beams as moving search lights that continually and repeatedly pan across the screen. As various phosphors are struck by the electron beam(s), they glow for a fraction of a second and then fade again. To keep the image from fading or flickering, the monitor must hit the same phosphors with electrons dozens of times in one second. The term *refresh rate* means the amount of time it takes the monitor to scan across and down the entire screen, "re-zapping" all the phosphors.

HOW CRTS WORK

Inside a CRT, one or more electron guns at the back of the monitor shoot electrons toward the screen. When the electrons hit phosphors on the inside of the screen, the phosphors glow, creating patterns of dots on your screen.

TAKING CARE OF YOUR MONITOR

If you leave your monitor on for a long period of time with the same image displayed on the screen, the phosphors responsible for displaying the image can become worn out. Once this happens, you'll see a shadow of that image superimposed on anything else you display on the screen, kind of like a permanent ghost image. This problem, often called *phosphor burn-in*, is generally an issue only on monochrome monitors. You can prevent phosphor burn-in by using a special program, known as a screen saver, that either blanks out the screen or displays a moving image (like changing geometric shapes or fish swimming in an aquarium or a set of flying toasters) whenever you haven't touched the keyboard or mouse for a certain amount of time. As soon as you press any key or move your mouse, the previous screen image is restored. (Windows comes with its own screen-saver programs. You can also buy screen savers from just about any store or mail order company that sells software.)

Since phosphor burn-in is rarely an issue on color monitors (unless you leave your screen displaying the same image for days on end), using screen savers on such monitors is generally unnecessary. Many people like to use them anyway, for their esthetic or entertainment value (there are some mesmerizing screen-saver programs out there).

Energy-saving on monitors is a separate issue. Some monitors feature an energy-saving mode, which both reduces the monitor's power consumption and minimizes wear and tear on the monitor itself. If you have a "green" monitor—that is, a monitor that features an energy-saving mode—whenever you haven't touched the keyboard or mouse for a while, the screen goes blank and only a bare minimum of electricity continues to flow to the monitor. As soon as you touch your keyboard or mouse, the monitor returns to normal mode (and the normal amount of energy consumption).

Another way to pamper your monitor (and your own eyes) is to clean the screen periodically. Most monitors pick up an inordinate amount of dust, not to mention fingerprints. You can often get rid of both by wiping the screen with a soft, dry cloth. You can also safely clean most monitors with a glass cleaner such as Windex, provided that you spray the cleaner on a cleaning cloth rather than directly on the screen. (If you spray it on the screen itself, you run the risk of soaking some of your monitor's circuitry.) A few monitors have special coatings designed to cut down on glare, which may not take kindly to cleaners. If you have an expensive monitor, be sure to check the monitor manual for warnings and advice before you apply anything but a dry cloth to the screen.

Then there's the issue of taking care of yourself while you use a monitor. Most monitors have contrast and brightness controls, usually on the front of the monitor but sometimes on the side or back. Use these to adjust the image so that it's clearest and easiest on your eyes. And remember that a badly positioned monitor can be, literally, a pain in the neck. As mentioned in Chapter 4, you can minimize neck strain by positioning the monitor so that its upper edge is at or just below eye level. Most monitors also have swivel stands that you can use to adjust the angle of the screen to eliminate glare and/or neck strain.

COMPUTER MONITORS MAY (OR MAY NOT) BE HAZARDOUS TO YOUR HEALTH

Virtually all desktop computer monitors emit some amount of electromagnetic radiation (EMR). So do many household appliances, including microwaves, electric blankets, radios, and TVs. Now before you panic, bear in mind that the type of radiation that all these devices emit is something called nonionizing radiation, which is quite different from the ionizing radiation emitted by nuclear reactors and weapons.

There is evidence that, at high levels, electromagnetic radiation is harmful to health. Some studies have found an increased incidence of certain types of cancer among children living right next to power plants, which emit very large amounts of EMR. But as yet there is no definitive answer on whether the amount of EMR emitted by computer monitors is dangerous. Although a few studies have shown a link between extensive computer use and increased rates of miscarriage, others have found no link at all.

If you use a computer only occasionally, the issue is probably not worth worrying about at all. However, if you plan to spend most of your workday in front of a CRT and you like to err on the side of safety, here are a few precautions you can take to minimize your risk.

▶ *Turn off your monitor when you are not using it. (Don't just dim the screen or use a screen-saver program, as this has no effect on EMR emissions.)*

▶ *Sit at least 20 inches away from the monitor, or more if possible. (The amount of radiation is inversely proportional to the square root of your distance from the screen. In other words, if you're twice as far from the monitor, you receive one quarter the radiation. If you're three times as far, you receive one-ninth the dose.)*

▶ *Avoid sitting near the sides or back of CRT monitors, since they emit more EMR than the front.*

▶ *Buy a monitor shield designed to block EMR.*

▶ *Buy a low-emission monitor. The Swedish government has developed a standard, called MPR II, defining acceptable levels of EMR. You can now buy many monitors in the U.S. that meet these standards. In general, smaller monitors have lower emissions than larger ones, and monochrome monitors have lower emissions than color ones.*

Whatever the risks of extensive monitor use turn out to be (if any), they're likely to be greatest for fetuses, particularly in the first trimester. Until more research is done, you may therefore want to be especially careful if you are pregnant.

N O T E *The screens on laptop and notebook computers use a completely different type of technology than that used in desktop computer monitors, and do not emit EMR.*

LAPTOP AND NOTEBOOK DISPLAYS

The screens on most laptop and notebook computers use a technology known as liquid crystal display (LCD). Briefly, LCD screens work as follows: Liquid crystals (a fluid that reflects light) are sandwiched between two polarized pieces of glass or plastic. These polarized sheets shut out all light waves except for those that are parallel to their particular plane. Inside the display, tiny electrodes pass current through the crystals, causing them to form spirals that bend the light to a greater or lesser degree. The amount of current determines the amount of spiraling, which in turn determines how much of the light actually makes it through the front of the screen. (In areas where the light is not bent at all, the beam is completely blocked and the screen remains dark.) In the case of color LCD screens, the light passes through various color filters.

LCD screens are often characterized as either passive or active matrix displays. In passive matrix displays, groups of pixels (screen dots) share the same electrodes. In active matrix displays, which are considerably more expensive, each pixel gets a transistor of its own. The resulting images are much clearer and easier to read. Active matrix displays also drain batteries much faster than passive matrix displays, making them less appropriate for long airplane flights and other work sessions conducted without the benefit of an electrical outlet.

PRINTERS

For years people have predicted that computers would make paper obsolete. While this may be true in the long run, in the short run they seem to be having the opposite effect. By giving people the power to endlessly manipulate and analyze their data, computers have facilitated the production of mountains of reports and memos that we had somehow previously managed to live without.

For most of us, printing is still the final step in any project we undertake on the computer. When you finish the letter, you print and send it. When you get done calculating how much money you could make if only you did x, you print out the spreadsheet and show it to your spouse, boss, or coworkers. Sooner or later, you'll want a hard copy, if for no other reason than that it's easy to carry around and show to others.

There are several different types of printers used with personal computers; by far the most common types are dot-matrix, laser, and ink jet printers.

DOT-MATRIX PRINTERS

Dot-matrix printers work by striking a cloth, nylon, or mylar ribbon with a set of small wires. The resulting characters are composed of a pattern of dots, just like characters displayed on a monitor. There are two types of dot-matrix printers, characterized by the number of wires (or pins) they use. 9-pin printers are less expensive (costing as little as $150) but produce poorer quality output. 24-pin printers cost a bit more but are capable of generating "near letter-quality" print, meaning print that looks almost typewriter quality.

THE MAIN TYPES OF PRINTERS

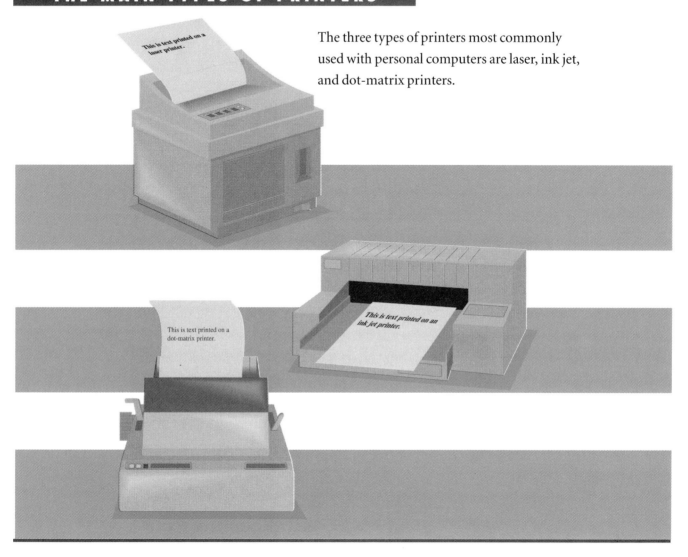

The three types of printers most commonly used with personal computers are laser, ink jet, and dot-matrix printers.

Because dot-matrix printers are impact printers—that is, they have components (the wires) that actually strike the page through an ink-laden ribbon—they are perfect for printing on multipart business forms. They can print labels, checks, and other continuous forms designed to be fed through a printer in a single stream. (Such forms have little holes on the edges that fit over sprockets in the printer's tractor feed mechanism so they can be pulled through the printer.)

Some but not all dot-matrix printers can also print on single sheets of paper. (If you are buying a dot-matrix printer and need to print on single sheets, find out whether the printer can do so and with how much effort on your part.)

Fonts are complete collections of upper- and lowercase letters, numbers, and punctuation in a particular type style and, in most cases, a particular size. Fonts are available in two forms: hard and soft. *Hard fonts* are hardware-based, meaning they are built into either the printer itself or font cartridges that you install in your printer. *Soft fonts* are software generated. In most cases, the instructions for soft fonts reside on your computer's hard disk and are "downloaded" (sent) to your printer memory as part of the printing process. Soft fonts are sometimes called downloadable fonts.

One of the nice things about Windows is that it comes with a slew of soft fonts that you can use in any of your Windows-based application programs. In addition, Windows has its own set of screen fonts to match its printer fonts, so that you can see exactly what your output will look like before you print. The Mac also comes with matching sets of screen fonts and soft printer fonts.

Fonts are also distinguished by whether they can be adjusted to different sizes. Fonts that come in specific sizes are known as *bitmapped fonts* (sometimes called fixed-sized fonts on Macs). In bitmapped fonts, each character is composed of a fixed pattern of dots. In contrast, fonts that can be reduced or enlarged to any size are known as *scalable fonts* (or sometimes as variable-sized fonts in the Mac world). Scalable fonts consist of mathematical descriptions of each letter, number, and punctuation mark in a typeface. When you use such fonts, either the printer or your application program calculates the pattern of dots necessary to create each character in the point size you request.

The downside of impact printing is noise. Most dot-matrix printers will drive all but the hearing-impaired crazy after 15 minutes at most. If you tend to print long reports, either install the printer in a closet or another room, or purchase a sound enclosure to dampen the noise. (You can buy such enclosures for $100 to $200, depending on the size of your printer.)

LASER PRINTERS

Laser printers print better, faster, and more quietly than dot-matrix printers, producing output that looks close to typeset. Laser printers are also more expensive, ranging from about $650 all the way up to $10,000 (with most falling in the $1,000 to $3,000 range).

N O T E   *Although most laser printers cannot begin to challenge typesetting machines in the realm of printing complex graphics or photographs, the better ones do come close in the case of text.*

Like dot-matrix printers, laser printers build images, including individual characters, out of dozens or hundreds of tiny dots. Technologically, however, laser printers bear far more resemblance to photocopiers. Like photocopiers, they produce images by electrically charging a metal drum that then attracts particles of toner in a specific pattern. The drum then rolls across a piece of paper that has an even greater electrical charge, causing the toner to jump from drum to page.

The fact that this process involves no impact—that is, there are no wires or other moving parts that strike the paper—has two implications. First, laser printers are extremely quiet. Second, they are useless on multipart forms (since there is no impact to carry the image through a piece of carbon paper). Laser printers also cannot print on continuous forms of any kind, including sticky mailing labels. (You can, however, buy sheets of laser printer labels for a rather steep price.)

The advertised speeds for laser printers typically range from 4 to 10 pages per minute (as compared to the 1 to 3 pages per minute typical of dot-matrix printers). Take these ratings with a grain of salt, however, since they measure the speed it takes to print a single page of text (sans graphics) over and over. When you're printing different pages, and especially when you're printing graphics, you can expect less speed.

The quality of laser printer output is typically measured in terms of *resolution*. (In discussions of printing, resolution refers to the density of dots used to construct characters or symbols on the page.) Laser printers typically print at a resolution of somewhere between 300 and 1200 dots per inch (dpi), as compared to a range of 72 to 240 dpi for dot-matrix printers. (Typesetting machines typically print at 1270 dpi and up.)

Bear in mind that 300 dpi means 300 dots per inch horizontally by 300 dots per inch vertically, for a maximum of 90,000 dots in any square inch of a page. This is more than adequate for most business correspondence. You may want a higher resolution for desktop publishing or printing graphics.

INK JET PRINTERS

Ink jet printers occupy a middle ground between dot-matrix and laser printers in both price and quality of output, but they use a technology all their own. Like dot-matrix printers, they have print heads that move horizontally across the page, applying ink one line at a time. But while dot-matrix printers use wires that strike an inked ribbon, ink jets spray streams of ink through tiny holes in the print head. Again, since no impact is involved, these printers are relatively quiet and incapable of printing on multipart forms.

Although the resolution offered by ink jet printers is similar to that of laser printers, the output is not quite as good. This is because the ink tends to spread through the fiber of the paper as it dries, giving characters a slightly fuzzy quality.

OTHER TYPES OF PRINTERS

The less commonly used types of printers include

▶ *Label printers, which are small specialized printers designed solely to print labels— directly from the screen, from a mailing list file, or from the printer program's own built-in database. If you use a laser printer for most of your work, you might consider buying a label printer as a relatively low-cost means of printing labels. (Printing labels on laser printers not only requires expensive labels, it involves wasting labels whenever you want to print less than a full sheet's worth.)*

▶ *Color printers, which used to be prohibitively expensive but the price has dropped considerably in the last few years. There are a few color dot-matrix printers and laser printers, but most color printers are either ink jet or thermal wax printers. Thermal wax printers produce brighter, clearer colors than most other types of color printers. They are on the expensive side, however, in terms of both initial purchase price (typically $5,000 and up) and supplies (which generally run 45 to 75 cents per page). (Color ink jets can now be purchased for around $700. Color laser printers run between $10,000 and $65,000.)*

▶ *Plotters, which use pens to draw very detailed designs on paper. They are used primarily for generating blueprints and engineering drawings, but can be used for printing graphics as well.*

USING A PRINTER

The first step in actually using a printer is turning it on. With luck, you should need to do very little fiddling aside from that. Most printers have a series of buttons, often known as a *control panel*, on their top or front edge. At a minimum, you will have buttons labeled On-Line and Form Feed, or FF for short. (I'll talk about the On-Line button in a moment. The Form Feed button ejects a page from the printer.) Most dot-matrix printers also have a button labeled Line Feed, or LF for short, designed to move the page up one line at a time. Most laser and ink jet printers and some dot-matrix printers also have extra buttons that let you control things like page sizes and fonts. For information on these buttons, refer to your printer manual.

PAGE DESCRIPTION LANGUAGES

All laser printers, and some nonlasers as well, have built-in page description languages. A *page description language* is a programming language that lets you define exactly how ink will be applied to a page. The most sophisticated page description language is something called PostScript and printers capable of reading this language are known as PostScript printers. Not only does PostScript allow you to print text in a wide variety of fonts, scaled to any size that you like, it also lets you achieve special effects such as rotated, shadowed, or twisted characters.

PostScript is also used by most typesetting machines, making PostScript printers ideal for desktop publishing if you plan to have the final copy produced by a typesetter. Since PostScript commands are "device independent," they produce very similar results on different equipment. Aside from its higher resolution, the version produced by a professional printer will be identical to that produced on a PostScript laser printer in your office.

PostScript printers tend to be more expensive and slower than other laser printers. But if much of your work involves either desktop publishing or generating graphics, they're worth the price.

The other page description language commonly used on PC printers is called PCL. PCL, which stands for Printer Control Language, is the page description language used on Hewlett-Packard laser printers. It has gone through several revisions, with PCL 5 being the latest and most powerful (although not nearly as powerful as PostScript).

The page description languages used in the Mac world include PostScript and QuickDraw (a page description language used to display images on the screen as well as on the printed page.)

The On-Line button lets you temporarily wrest control of the printer from your computer. When you first turn on your printer, you should be "on line," meaning ready to accept data and/or commands from your computer. (On most printers, a little light on or next to the On-Line button is on whenever you are on line.) On many printers, when you want your printer to listen to you instead of your computer for a moment, you must take it "off line" by pressing the On-Line button. Then you are free to use any of the other buttons on the control panel. (On other printers, you can use the Form Feed or Line Feed buttons without taking the printer off line.) When you're done using the control panel, remember to press the On-Line button again to turn control back over to your computer. (The On-Line button is like a toggle key on your keyboard—you use it to reverse the printer's current on-line status.)

N O T E   *On most printers, the On-Line light will go off automatically whenever you run out of paper or encounter a printer jam or other problem. This lets you know that the printer cannot accept any new input from the computer until you fix the problem. (Don't worry. You won't lose any data in the meantime.) You might also want to take a dot-matrix printer off line temporarily if the paper is starting to jam up. This gives you the chance to realign the paper. When you're ready, you can press On-Line again to resume printing.*

If you have a dot-matrix printer, it's usually better for you to eject and scroll paper using the Form Feed and Line Feed buttons rather than to scroll the paper manually. This also allows your printer to keep track of where it is on the page. If you are using continuous forms, make sure that the print head is just below the perforation between pages when you turn on the printer. Then use the Form Feed button any time you need to eject a page. If your printer starts printing in the middle of each page rather than at the top, use the Line Feed button to move the print head to the top of a page, and then turn the printer off and on again.

In most cases, your application program will automatically eject the last page from the printer when it's done printing. Occasionally, however, a program may not eject the last page. If you're waiting and waiting for a page, check whether the light on or right next to the Form Feed light button is on. If so, there's a page in the printer waiting to be ejected. To eject that page, take the printer offline by pressing the On-Line button, press the Form Feed button to eject the page, and then press On-Line again.

PRINTING IN WINDOWS

As you might expect, there are several ways to print a document in Windows 95. If the document is already open, just open the application's File menu and choose Print. You can also click the Print button on your application's toolbar, if it has one. If the document is not already open, you may find it faster to drag and drop the document icon onto the printer icon. To do this, start by getting to the desktop, and finding and opening the folder that contains the document. Next, double-click the My Computer icon and then double-click the Printers

PRINTER BUFFERS AND SPOOLERS

In general, printers are far slower than computers. Your computer can send data to a printer much faster than the printer can print it. Most printers have some built-in memory that serves as a *printer buffer*—that is, a kind of holding pen for data that is waiting to be printed. This is why if you interrupt printing, your printer keeps going for a while. In this case, you can often stop the printer more quickly by turning it off and then on again. This effectively erases the printer's memory.

In most cases, the printer buffer will be quite small—enough to hold a few lines of data in the case of dot-matrix printers, a few pages on laser printers. As soon as the printer buffer fills, the computer needs to stop and wait before sending the next chunk of data. If you are printing a very long report, this could effectively tie up your computer for several minutes or even hours.

By default, both Windows and the Mac operating system solve this problem by sidetracking data en route from your computer to your printer and storing it on disk until your printer is ready for it. In the meantime, you're free to get back to work in your application program. This process is known as *print spooling* or *background printing*.

icon. Once both the document icon and the printer icon are visible on your desktop, drag the document icon over to the printer icon and release the mouse button.

If you frequently print documents without opening them first, you may want to streamline the process by creating a shortcut for your printer on the desktop. Then you can just drag your document icon to the printer shortcut. To create a shortcut for your printer:

▶ *Get to the desktop and double-click the My Computer icon.*

▶ *Double-click the Printers icon.*

▶ *Right-click the icon for the printer you want to add to the Send To menu and select Create Shortcut from the context menu.*

▶ *When Windows displays a dialog box asking if you want the shortcut to be placed on the desktop, choose Yes.*

You can simplify printing unopened documents even further by adding an item for your printer to the Send To menu that appears whenever you right-click a document icon and choose Send To. The contents of the Send To menu are stored in a folder named SendTo, which is located inside the Windows folder. To add a printer (or any new destination) to the Send To menu, you need to place a shortcut for it inside the SendTo folder. You can do this as follows:

▶ *Open the SendTo folder by double-clicking the icon for your hard disk in the My Computer window, double-clicking the icon for the Windows folder, and then double-clicking the icon for the SendTo folder. Make sure that the window does not already contain an icon for your printer. (If it does, you can skip the rest of these steps.)*

▶ *If you already have a printer shortcut on your desktop, right-drag it from the desktop to the SendTo folder and, when asked whether you want to copy or move, select Copy. If you don't have a printer shortcut, double-click My Computer, double-click Printers, and then right-drag the icon for your printer from the Printers folder window to the SendTo folder window. Choose Create Shortcut(s) here from the context menu.*

▶ *Because the name of the shortcut you use becomes the name of the item on the Send To menu, you might want to start by renaming the shortcut, removing the words "Shortcut To" and leaving just the name of your printer. (Remember that to rename an item, you just click twice inside the item's label and start typing or, in this case, deleting.)*

NOTE *If you are using user profiles on your computer, each user will have his or her own SendTo folder. To find yours, use the Find command and look for a folder with the name that you use when logging in to Windows.*

When you initiate printing by selecting Print from your application's File menu, you'll usually see a Print dialog box like the one in the figure, The standard Windows 95 Print dialog box. You can use this dialog box to customize printing, printing only the current page, for example, or printing specified pages, or printing multiple copies. For information on using this dialog box, use the ? button in its upper-right corner, or look up Printing in the application's Help system.

NOTE *If you want to leave the Print dialog box without actually printing, click the Close button rather than the OK button.*

When you initiate printing using a Print button on an application toolbar, Windows usually prints a single copy of your document, without awaiting any further instructions. When you initiate printing by dragging a document icon to a printer icon or shortcut, or by selecting your printer from the Send To menu, you may or may not see a Print dialog before printing begins; it depends on the application you used to create the document.

MANAGING THE PRINT QUEUE

When you print a document, Windows usually creates a temporary file, called a spool file, on your hard disk. During the few moments when this file is being created, you can't do anything else with your computer. As soon as the spool file is complete, however, you can return to your application and continue working. In the meantime, the spool file has taken up residence in a temporary holding pen known as the *print queue*. If there are no other print jobs already waiting in the print queue, the new spool file is routed directly to the printer. Otherwise, it has to wait its turn. In either case, the actual printing occurs in the background, and you are free to do other work.

You can check the status of a printer's print queue by double-clicking the printer's icon in the Printers folder or, if you have a shortcut for the printer on your desktop, by double-clicking the shortcut. Windows displays a list of all the documents in the queue, in the order in which they'll be printed, and the amount still left to print. To remove a single document from the queue, select it and then choose Cancel Printing from the Document menu. (If

THE STANDARD WINDOWS 95 PRINT DIALOG BOX

Windows was in the midst of printing the canceled document, this will effectively stop it in its tracks. If there are other documents in the queue, Windows will move on to printing them.) To remove all documents from the queue, choose the Purge Print Jobs option from the Printer menu. You can also purge all print jobs from a local printer (that is, one that's attached to your computer rather than accessed through a network) without opening the print queue, by right-clicking the printer's icon and choosing Purge Print Jobs from the context menu.

While a document is printing, there's a second way to access the print queue. Whenever a document is printing, a printer button appears near the right edge of the taskbar. (If you have the clock displayed, the button appears just to the left of the clock.) If you point to this button, Windows will tell you the number of documents in the print queue. If you right-click the button, you'll see a menu with an option titled Open Active Printers and an option for each individual active printer. Select your printer to display its print queue.

SELECTING PRINTERS

Unless you're on a network, chances are you only have one printer attached to your computer. If you have a fax modem, you'll still need to deal with selecting printers, however, because Windows "thinks" of your fax modem as a printer as well. (You'll learn more about sending faxes from your computer in Chapter 10.) If your computer is part of a network, you may also need to switch back and forth between your local printer and the network printer, or between different printers on the network.

The first thing to know about selecting printers in Windows is that there's always one device designated as the default printer: This is the device to which Windows directs print output unless you specifically request otherwise. To direct print output somewhere else, you select Print from the File menu inside your application and then, in the Print dialog box, select a different printer in the Name drop-down list. The printer you select will become the default for the current work session only—meaning that Windows assumes that you want to print to this printer unless you specify otherwise, up until you leave the application. As soon as you load or switch to another program, or close the application and then open it again, Windows resumes printing to the designated default printer.

To designate a different printer as the default printer, right-click the icon for that printer in the Printers folder, and choose Set As Default. The specified printer becomes the default printer for all your Windows applications.

Printing on a Mac

When you issue the command to print in a Mac application—either by selecting Print from the File menu or by clicking a Print button on a toolbar—you see a dialog box in which you can specify which pages to print, print quality, paper source, and so on. As soon as you click Print, the printing process begins.

By default, the Mac operating system spools print jobs, meaning that whenever you print, the Mac normally creates a temporary file on disk that contains the data you want to print. While this file is being created, you see a message like "Spooling page #1 for background printing." Once spooling is complete, you are free to return to work while printing occurs in the background. The advantage of this method of printing is that it quickly frees your computer up for other activities. The disadvantage is that it may take a little longer for the document to be printed because your computer has to divide its attention between printing and whatever other work you're doing on your computer. If you'd rather have the printing happen as quickly as possible, even if it means you have to stop work in the meantime, open the Apple menu and select Chooser. Then double-click the icon for your printer. You'll see a dialog box with option buttons labeled On and Off under the heading Background Printing. Click Off to turn off print spooling. Click On if you want to turn it back on again.

Assuming that you leave spooling (aka background printing) turned on, your print jobs are automatically placed in a print queue. To view this queue, pull down the Application menu and select PrintMonitor. The document that is currently printing will appear near the top of the Print Monitor dialog box, under the label Printing. To cancel that print job, click the Cancel Printing button. Below the current print job, you'll see a list of any documents that are waiting to be printed. To remove a document from this waiting list, select and click Remove from List. You can also temporarily halt all printing by opening the File menu and choosing Stop Printing. To continue printing where you left off, open the File menu again and choose Resume Printing.

If you have more than one printer attached to your computer or available to you on a network, you can select a different printer by opening the Apple menu, selecting Chooser, and then clicking the icon for the printer you wish to use. To define paper size, orientation, and other printing options, choose Page Setup from the File menu from within your application.

STORAGE DEVICES

Most computer hard disks contain too much data to back up onto floppies easily. (A modest 300MB hard disk would require several dozen floppies to back up in its entirety, even if you use a back-up program that compresses data as it goes.) If you're going to make regular backups of your data and programs (and you definitely should), you'll need some other mechanism for storing data long term. Here are some of the possibilities.

▶ *Tape drives can record up to 8 gigabytes (approximately 8,000 megabytes) or more on a single cassette tape. Just like more conventional tape recorders, however, they access data sequentially, and are therefore suited for backup rather than regular data storage.*

▶ *Removable-media drives combine the best features of floppy and hard drives. Like floppy drives, they use disks that are removable. Like hard drives, they store dozens of megabytes (usually somewhere between 20 and 250 megabytes) on a single disk. This makes them perfect for backing up data and transferring large amounts of data from one computer to another. In addition, removable-media drives allow you to keep expanding your computer's storage capacity indefinitely at a relatively low cost. Every time you run out of space, you just buy another cartridge. There are two basic types of removable-media drives: Bernoulli (pronounced Ber-new-lee) drives, which use cartridges containing a flexible, floppy-like disk; and Syquest drives, which use rigid disks more like the platters used in hard drives.*

▶ *A new technology called **CD-Recordable (CD-R for short)** lets you create CDs in a format that can be read by a regular CD-ROM drive (as well as by a CD-R drive). CD-R drives cost more than regular CD-ROM drives, although their prices have been dropping rapidly. While most CD-R drives only let you record data once on a CD, some let you add additional data in separate sessions, adding to what's been previously recorded. One of the main attractions of this type of drive is that discs you record on using a CD-R drive can be read in any regular CD-ROM drive. As the price of CD-R drives continues to drop, they are starting to become a viable mode of backing up data. Since CD-R drives are much slower than hard disks, however, they're likely to be used primarily for back up and long-term storage rather than for storing data or programs that will be used regularly. A newer type of drive, called **CD-Erasable (CD-E for short)** lets you erase discs and reuse them. Since most people use CD-R drives to archive data long-term and since the discs themselves are cheap (in the $10 range), this isn't that much of an advantage.*

▶ ***WORM (Write Once/Read Many) drives*** *contain disks that you can record on only once. Whatever you record on the disk remains there permanently, as if written in indelible ink, that you can neither erase nor overwrite. For this reason, WORM drives are perfect for archiving large amounts of data, and are frequently used by banks and accounting firms as a means of maintaining a permanent, unalterable audit trail. WORM disks typically hold 1 to 1.5 gigabytes (approximately 1,000 to 1,500 megabytes) of data.*

▶ ***Magneto-optical (MO) drives*** *use both a laser and an electromagnet to record information on a cartridge, the surface of which contains tiny embedded magnets. These cartridges can be written to, erased, and then written to again. They are more expensive than CD-R drives, but hold more data (typically in the 1–1.5 gigabyte range).*

INSTALLING NEW HARDWARE IN WINDOWS 95

One of the big selling points of Windows 95 is a feature known as *plug and play*. Plug and play is a standard developed by Microsoft and various computer hardware manufacturers that's aimed at taking the pain out of installing new hardware devices on PCs. Prior to plug and play, installing new hardware meant finding and installing special drivers (programs designed to let your computer talk to your peripherals) and making sure that the new device didn't try to use various communication channels and memory locations already claimed by another device. Plug and play was designed to eliminate such problems. Theoretically, if you have a computer designed for plug and play and are using a plug and play operating system (like Windows 95), installing a plug and play printer, sound card, modem, CD-ROM drive, or other peripheral should be a simple matter of plugging in the device.

It's not always quite this simple. Assuming that you are using a plug and play computer, when you attach a plug and play device, you may see a message indicating that Windows has recognized the new device—either immediately or the next time you start up your system. If Windows needs a driver that is not currently installed, you may at that point be asked to insert a disk or the Windows CD-ROM. If you don't see a message but the device appears to be working, you can assume that everything is fine. If the device is not working properly, try using the Add New Hardware wizard. (A *wizard* is a series of dialog boxes designed to step you through a process.) To run this wizard, open the Start menu, choose Settings, select Control Panel, and then double-click the icon for Add New Hardware. Then follow the instructions on your screen.

When you install what Microsoft calls a *legacy* peripheral (that is, an older device that is not Plug and Play compatible), you'll need to use the Add Hardware wizard, as described above, to let Windows know about the new device. (Computer people use the term *legacy* to refer to anything that's leftover, that's no longer on the cutting edge.)

NOTE *When you get to the point where you're asked to choose the manufacturer and model number of your device from lists, and your particular device is not listed, try contacting the manufacturer of the device to see if they've developed a Windows 95 driver. (A* driver *is a program that allows your computer and your operating system to communicate with a specific type of peripheral.) If not, look in your manual to see if the device emulates another type of device. Many*

PLUG AND PLAY BIOSES

Technically, a computer designed for plug and play is one that uses a plug and play BIOS. The BIOS, which stands for Basic Input/Output System, is a part of your operating system that is stored in a ROM chip inside your computer. (It's the BIOS that performs some of the initial hardware tests when you turn on your computer and that loads the rest of the operating system.) Most PCs created during and after 1996 use a plug and play BIOS, most built before 1995 do not. PCs built during 1995 are a toss-up: you'll need to check your system documentation.

printers can emulate Epson printers or Hewlett Packard LaserJet printers, for example. If so, se-lect the manufacturer and model of the device that your own device can emulate from the lists.

Whenever you remove a legacy peripheral from your system, you need to let Windows know that the device is gone. This enables Windows to reuse the resources (places in memory and internal communications channels) that it previously allocated to that device. To tell Windows that you've removed a legacy device:

▶ *Right-click the My Computer icon and choose Properties from the context menu.*

▶ *Click the Device Manager tab.*

▶ *Click the View devices by type option button. The Device Manager displays a list of your hardware devices organized by type.*

▶ *Select the name of the item you have removed from your system. (If you don't see the item, look for a category heading that describes the type of device you removed, and click the plus sign to its left to display a list of items in that category.)*

▶ *Click the Remove button.*

▶ *Click the Close button to close the Systems Properties dialog box.*

ABOUT PORTS

Computers usually pass information to and from peripherals using two types of ports: parallel and serial. (Recall that a port is a connector, usually at the back of the system unit, where you can "dock" peripherals.) Parallel ports transmit units of data simultaneously, like a set of soldiers marching abreast. Serial ports pass information on a single wire, one unit of data at a time. If you look at the back of your PC, the parallel ports are the ones with 25 holes in them. Serial ports have pins sticking out—either 9 pins or 25 pins. (There's a third type of port known as a SCSI port which is sometimes used to connect devices like external CD-ROM drives, tape backup units, or external hard disks. It contains holes, like a parallel port.)

Most PC printers are parallel printers, meaning that they are designed to be connected to a parallel port. But a few are serial printers, meaning that they need to be connected to a serial port. You can tell which type you need to plug the printer into by looking at the connector at the end of the printer cable: If it has holes rather than pins, you need to plug it into a serial port.

When you install a legacy device, you may be asked the name of the port to which it is connected. In most cases, your printer will be connected to LPT1, which is the name of the first parallel port (or, more precisely, the name of the internal communications channel which is connected to that parallel port). If you have two printers connected to your computer, the second one will probably be connected to LPT2. Your mouse will probably be connected to the first serial port, which is usually referred to as COM1. (Again, technically speaking, COM1 is the name of a communication channel inside your computer rather than the name of the port itself.) Your modem, if you have one, will probably be connected to COM2. A serial printer will probably be connected to COM2 as well.

NOTE   *If you have trouble getting a legacy device to work, look up "hardware conflict troubleshooter" in the Windows Help index. This will take you to a wizard that will step you through the process of resolving conflicts among peripherals.*

NETWORKS

Networks are groups of computers that are linked together. There are three reasons to network computers:

▶ *To enable multiple computers to share peripherals, such as expensive printers, scanners, and fax equipment.*

▶ *To allow people to exchange messages via computer (a process known as electronic mail) and to easily transfer files from one computer to another.*

▶ *To allow computers to share data and/or programs—so that, for example, three people in a department can write a report together, or work with the same spreadsheets. This capability is particularly useful in the case of databases, which may need to be accessed and changed by many different people in an organization.*

The term *Local Area Network* (LAN for short) means a network in which the computers are all connected with wire cables. (This generally means that they're in the same part of a single building.) LANS are contrasted with Wide Area Networks, aka WANs, in which some of the links in the chain are connected by modems and phone wires or satellites.

The details of setting up a network are best left to experts. But to make a long story fairly short, there are three essential steps in the process:

▶ *Special expansion boards, generally known as* network cards, *must be installed in each of the computers.*

▶ *The computers must be physically connected in some way, usually via wire cables.*

▶ *Network software designed to control the flow of information across the network must be installed on each of the computers.*

The business of running a network can also be fairly complicated. For this reason, most networks of any size are assigned a full- or at least part-time network administrator. (If your report won't print or your computer starts displaying error messages, the network administrator is the person to see.) Nonetheless, there are a few pieces of information that everyone on the network should know, if for no other reason than to help you communicate with the network administrator.

Most networks include one or more computers that are designated as file servers. A *file server* is a computer whose hard disk is accessible to other computers on the network. Its job is to "serve" data and program files to these other machines via cables or other network connections. On some smaller networks, each computer can access the hard disk of any of the other computers, and there is no one computer (or more) dedicated to the task of delivering goods to the others. Such networks are known as *peer-to-peer networks*, because all the computers in the chain are on roughly equal footing.

When there is a dedicated file server—that is, a computer that's used for nothing other than serving the other computers on the network—the other computers are usually called either *nodes* or *workstations*.

Even if your computer is part of a network, you need to explicitly "log in" to the network in order to use it. The procedure for logging in varies from one type of network to another. In most cases, you'll either start by typing LOGIN (pronounced log in) or your computer will be set up to type it for you. Next, you'll be asked for your user name (that is, the name you're known by on the network) and then a password. Assuming that the network recognizes both your name and password, it goes ahead and gives you access to other computers and resources on the network.

In most cases, you will be able to access the file server's hard disk just as you would any other disk. On a PC, the server's hard disk is usually assigned one or more drive letters (just as your own hard disk is usually labeled C). On a Mac, network drives are represented by icons at the right side of the desktop, just like other drives.

NOTE   *Most networks have built-in security features that allow the network administrator to limit access to sensitive data (such as personnel or financial data). In such cases, your user name determines which data files and programs you can use.*

When you're done using the network, you should "log out," meaning disconnect from the network.

ELECTRONIC MAIL

Most networks have electronic mail (e-mail) programs that enable people on the network to send messages to other people on the network via computer. Once you get used to it, you may well find this mode of communicating superior to both answering machines/voice mail

A NETWORK CONFIGURATION

Networks are groups of computers that are linked together in order to share data, programs, or peripherals, and/or to facilitate communication and file exchange within an organization.

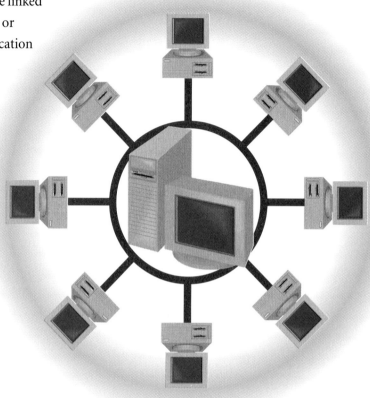

and interoffice memos. It can eliminate the need for "phone tag" and make it easy to convey information that's too involved to leave on voice mail. (E-mail also has the advantage of being easier to store and review later.) In addition, e-mail is easier and faster than printing and then delivering memos. In some organizations, it's the preferred vehicle for sharing ideas, making announcements, scheduling meetings, and so on.

When you want to send a message to someone using electronic mail, you type in the message and then request that it be sent to a particular person's electronic "mailbox." (Many e-mail programs let you send the same message to several mailboxes at once.) In most cases, this means that the message is stored, as a small file, in a subdirectory of the file server's hard disk that has been reserved for a particular person's "mail." In some e-mail programs, as

A FILE SERVER SERVING FILES

A file server is a computer that "serves" data and program files to other computers on a network.

soon as your message has been sent, a window appears on the recipient's screen indicating that a message is waiting. He or she can then read and/or print the message whenever it's convenient. In other programs, the recipient only finds out about your communiqué when explicitly asking for messages.

MULTIUSER SOFTWARE

By allowing multiple users to access files on the same disk, networks open a potential Pandora's box. What happens when more than one person tries to change the same spreadsheet or decides to edit the same report?

Suppose, for example, that a company's customer list resides in a database file on the network's file server. This makes it possible for more than one person to access and update the same list. Whenever someone looks up a particular customer, a copy of the data for that customer is copied into memory on that person's computer and displayed on his or her screen. Now suppose that two people look up the same customer, and then both decide to edit the data. (Say one person wants to update the customer's address and the other wants to revise the credit limit.) If the database program allowed both people to change the record simultaneously, one person's changes would cancel out the other one's. If the person making the address change saved the record first (by moving to another record or leaving the database), the revised copy of the customer record that exists in their computer's RAM would be

SHARING DATA

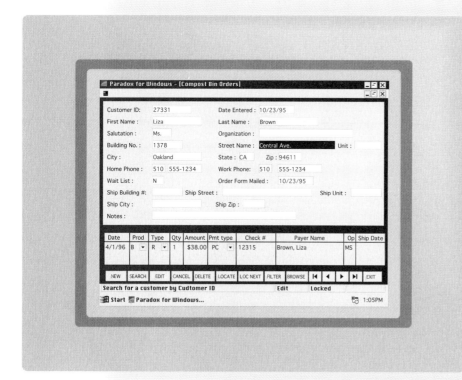

Multiuser application programs prevent two (or more) users from updating the same file or, in the case of databases, the same record simultaneously. Otherwise, whoever saves the data last will overwrite changes just made by another user.

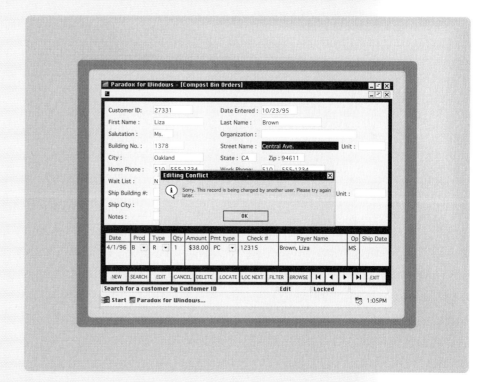

copied back to the file server. Then, as soon as the person changing the credit limit saved his or her version of the record, their version of the data—which includes the old address—would replace the version on the file server.

Most major application programs come in multiuser as well as single-user versions and the multiuser versions are designed to prevent exactly this type of mishap. Different application programs handle the problem of simultaneous editing in different ways.

▶ *Some won't allow anyone to use a file that is in use by someone else.*

▶ *Some let other users view a file that is being used by someone else, but not change it.*

▶ *Still others let multiple people view the same data, but only allow one person at a time to change it. In the case of word processing, spreadsheet, or graphics programs, this generally means only one person at a time can change a file. In the case of database programs, it usually means that only one person at a time can change a particular record within a file.*

NETWORK ETIQUETTE

Following are some guidelines on how to use a network without aggravating your coworkers.

▶ *Don't run programs from the server if you don't have to. Whenever you run a program that resides on the file server's disk, you are tying up some of the server's brain power. In certain cases, this is unavoidable, but if you simply want to create a spreadsheet for your own use and you have a copy of the spreadsheet software on your own hard disk, there's no need to tie up the server.*

▶ *Don't run single-user software from the server. If someone else tries to use it at the same time, you're likely to bring down the entire network (and possibly ruin a dozen people's day).*

▶ *Don't hog the printer. If you are sharing a printer with several other people on a network, try to avoid printing huge reports in the middle of the work day. Since the printer will handle various people's print jobs one at a time, you will prevent everyone else from printing until your report is completed.*

▶ *Don't delete files that you don't recognize. If you get an irrepressible urge to clear space on the file server, make sure you don't delete anyone else's files, at least not until you've determined how important they are.*

CHAPTER 9

MULTIMEDIA COMPUTING

GROWL

In the last few years, multimedia has become one of the biggest buzzwords in the computer industry. Computer systems are regularly advertised as "multimedia PC," games are touted as being multimedia, and so on. And like most buzzwords, the term multimedia is probably used more often than it's understood. Here, then, are some simple definitions.

A *multimedia program* is a program that communicates in more than one medium. In practical terms, this means any program that employs any combination of text, pictures, sound, and full motion video. The first multimedia computer programs were encyclopedias, which mixed text and graphics. Today's multimedia applications often feature full-motion video and sound, and range from elaborate and visually stunning games to sophisticated interactive training programs.

A *multimedia computer* is any computer that can take full advantage of multimedia programs—that is, it can generate sounds and display pictures, and store large quantities of data. (Both sounds and pictures consume a great deal of disk space.) In terms of hardware requirements, this means a computer with a reasonably fast processor, a graphics monitor (usually color), plenty of memory, a sound card, speakers or headphones, and a CD-ROM drive.

This chapter will introduce you to the world of multimedia computing, examine the hardware you need and how it works, and explore the basics of playing with sound, video, and photographs in the Windows 95 and Macintosh environments.

MPC AND MPC 2 STANDARDS

PC In the early 1990s, a consortium of multimedia hardware manufacturers developed a set of standards for multimedia computing. These standards, known as MPC and MPC 2, are aimed at bringing some consistency to the multimedia marketplace. (As of this writing, a new standard called MPC 3 is in the works.) If you see a computer in a store with an MPC logo, you know that the computer meets certain basic requirements for multimedia computing and is therefore guaranteed to work with multimedia PC software.

A computer with any MPC logo contains a CD-ROM drive, a sound card, a set of speakers or headphones, and either Windows or OS/2. (Although the standard only calls for Windows 3.x, Windows 95 offers much better support for multimedia.) A computer with a logo that says just MPC, without a number, contains a 386SX processor or better, at least 2MB of RAM, a hard disk that holds at least 30MB, a CD-ROM drive of any speed, and a VGA or SVGA display. A computer with an MPC 2 logo contains at least a 486SX processor, 4MB of RAM, 160MB of hard-disk space, a double-speed CD-ROM drive, and a monitor that can display 65,536 colors at 640×480 resolution. These days, this is the minimum you'll need to run most multimedia applications. If you're using multimedia applications more than occasionally, you'll probably want at least 8MB of RAM and a quad-speed CD-ROM drive. Multimedia applications tend to demand more power than most other applications, and the more memory, hard-disk space, and CD-ROM speed you have, the better.

MULTIMEDIA COMPUTING

Macintosh computers have always been strong in the multimedia arena, with PCs only recently starting to catch up. All Macs have graphics capabilities built in and most of the newer Macs have sound capabilities—including speakers and microphones—built in as well. As a result, virtually any relatively new Mac with a CD-ROM drive can be considered a multimedia computer, although you can always add fancier graphics adapters and speakers if you're a multimedia aficionado.

UPGRADING TO MULTIMEDIA

PC　If your PC has a 486SX or better processor and at least 200MB of disk space, you should consider upgrading your computer to multimedia rather than replacing the whole system. If you plan on handling the upgrade yourself, the easiest way to go is to buy a multimedia upgrade kit. These kits include a CD-ROM drive, a sound card, and speakers, all of which are already set up to work together.

If you already have one of the components, or if you prefer to mix and match them yourself, be sure to buy a CD-ROM drive and sound card that can work together. Unless you're comfortable fiddling around inside a computer and are good at making sense of the kind of poor instructions that often come with the computer equipment, you may want to bring in an expert to help you. Either find an experienced, technically minded friend to rope into the job, or find a local computer store that will do it all for a fee.

MAKING NOISE WITH A COMPUTER

PC By themselves, most PCs are only capable of beeps and a few whirring sounds. If you have a PC and want to be able to hear the music, speech, or sound effects in multimedia software, you either need to buy and install a device called a sound card, or buy a PC that already includes one. (Any multimedia PC should come with a sound card installed.)

A *sound card* (aka sound board) is a circuit board that is capable of translating program instructions into sounds. When you hear sound from a CD-ROM program (such as a game) on a PC, the sounds are actually being generated by the computer's sound card. The CD-ROM is simply delivering instructions to the sound card about what sounds to produce and when.

A sound card fits into an expansion slot inside your computer's system unit. If your computer doesn't already have a sound card, you can add one (assuming that you're not afraid to open up your computer and assuming that your system unit has an available expansion slot). Sound cards range in price from about $70 to several hundred dollars. As you might guess, the more expensive boards can produce richer, more complex tones. For good sound, you'll want a board that supports stereo and uses 16-bit rather than 8-bit technology. You should also make sure the board meets MPC 2 standards (most new ones will). After that, it's a matter of how good you want your CD-ROMs to sound and which features you want. You may also want to stick with brand names, to ensure that all your current and future software will work with the board. SoundBlaster boards, made by Creative Labs, are always safe since they're more or less the standard. Pro Audio Spectrum boards are also popular and well respected.

If you want your computer to communicate in sound, you'll probably want speakers as well. Although it is possible to hook up the sound card to your stereo system, for most people a pair of inexpensive computer speakers is adequate and more convenient. If you want to record your own sounds, plan on buying a microphone as well.

A pair of computer-compatible speakers will cost you anywhere from $20 to several hundred dollars. Any pair of speakers should work with any sound board, so choosing speakers is simply a matter of deciding how much you care about sound quality and how much you're willing to pay for it. Even $20 speakers will allow you to distinguish and understand voices; they just won't sound that great when you're playing music. To set them up, you

SOUND CARDS

just plug them into a jack at the back of your computer, which is, in turn, attached to your sound card. (Look for a jack labeled something like Speaker In or Spk In.)

NOTE *Speakers contain magnets that can destroy the data stored on floppy disks. Unless your speakers are designated as "magnetically shielded," keep them at least a few inches from your floppies. You don't have to worry about CD-ROMs since information on CD-ROMs is recorded with lasers rather than magnets.*

MAC There is no need to add sound cards to Mac computers because all Macs have sound capabilities built into their motherboards. Most have built-in speakers as well, although you can get better sound by using higher-quality external speakers.

PLAYING AUDIO CDS

All CD-ROM drives can play audio CDs (that is, the music CDs you usually play in your stereo system) as well as CD-ROMs. Playing CDs on a computer lets you listen to your favorite music at work without installing a stereo in your office. Once you start playing an audio CD, it keeps playing while you do your other work. If you're worried about disturbing co-workers, you can always listen through headphones. (Just be wary of humming along too loudly.)

If you don't have a set of speakers, or if your speakers are not connected to your CD-ROM drive, headphones are actually your only option for listening to audio CDs. You can use regular stereo headphones, which you can purchase at most stores that sell stereos or home electronics, and just plug them into the headphone jack on the front of the drive. If your CD-ROM drive has a volume control knob on the front, you can use it to control the headphone volume. If you do have speakers but they don't make a peep when you play an audio CD, see the sidebar on Listening to CDs Through Speakers on a PC.

PC If you're using Windows 95, as soon as you insert an audio CD into the drive, Windows starts playing the disc. It also launches a utility program named CD Player that allows you to jump from track to track, create "play lists" that determine which tracks are played and in what sequence, or direct the drive to play tracks in random order. When you first insert a CD, the CD Player application starts up in a minimized state: All you'll see on your screen is a task button on the taskbar that says CD Player and displays the number of the track that's being played and the length of time that track has been playing. If you want to move around on the CD or create a play list, click the task button to open the CD Player window. For information on using the CD Player, open the Help option in the CD Player window and select Help Topics.

NOTE *If you close the CD Player application (by selecting Exit from the Disc menu or clicking the window's close box), the CD will stop playing. You can start it up again by opening the Start menu, selecting Programs, picking Accessories, and then choosing CD Player. When you see the CD Player window, click the Play button (the one with the single right-pointing arrow).*

MAC If you have a Mac, as soon as you insert an audio CD, an icon labeled Audio CD will appear on your desktop. To play the CD, you have two options. You can double-click the CD icon and then double-click the icon for the track you wish to hear. You can also open the Apple menu and choose CD Remote or AppleCD Audio Player (only one of the two will appear on the menu) and then click the Play button. In either case, you'll be launching an applet that allows you to select tracks and specify the order of tracks. For information on using this applet, see the manual that came with your CD-ROM drive. If you have an external CD-ROM drive, you'll either have to listen to the CD through headphones or to plug your speakers into the audio output jack on the CD-ROM drive.

LISTENING TO CDS THROUGH SPEAKERS ON A PC

PC On a PC, you can only hear an audio CD through your speakers if your CD-ROM drive is properly connected to your sound card. This connection from the CD-ROM drive to the sound card isn't necessary when you play CD-ROMs because in that case the CD-ROM knows to send instructions to the sound card and it's the sound card itself that actually generates the sounds. In contrast, when you play music CDs, the CD contains the actual sounds (not a set of instructions for generating sounds). In order to hear these sounds through speakers, you need to explicitly route the sounds to the sound card, which then amplifies the sounds and directs them out through the speakers.

If you have an internal CD-ROM drive, a sound card, and speakers, but you can't get the sound to come out of the speakers, either you or a technician will need to connect the sound card to the CD-ROM drive using an audio cable. Most internal CD-ROM drives come with audio cables that you can use to connect to sound cards, although not all of them work with all sound cards. Many sound cards come with cables as well. Check your CD-ROM drive and sound board manuals for details about exactly what to plug in where. If you have trouble with the cable, try contacting the CD-ROM drive manufacturer and/or the sound card manufacturer for suggestions.

If you have an external drive, you can plug headphones directly into the drive's audio output jack. If the drive is self-amplifying, you can also plug speakers directly into this port.

TURNING UP THE VOLUME

As mentioned earlier, if your CD-ROM drive has a volume control on the front, you can use this control to adjust the volume of headphones plugged into the headphone jack on the CD-ROM itself. Most speakers also have volume controls of their own, which you can use to adjust the loudness of any sounds that travel their way.

PC On PCs, you can often adjust the volume of the sound card itself. The easiest way to do this in Windows 95 is by using the Volume button that appears near the right edge of your status bar (assuming the status bar is positioned at the bottom of your screen). The Volume button looks like a little speaker. (If you point to the button, a ToolTip with the word Volume appears.) When you click the Volume button, Windows displays a little Volume Control window with a slider that you can use to adjust the sound card volume: Drag the slider upward to increase the volume and downward to decrease it. It also offers you a Mute check box that you can use to turn the sound off altogether. When you're done adjusting the volume, click anywhere else on the screen to close the Volume Control window.

MAC If you're using a Mac, you can adjust the volume for audio CDs using the CD Remote or AppleCD Audio Player application (whichever is installed on your system). To adjust the volume for alerts and CD-ROMs, open the Apple menu, double-click Control Panels, and then double-click Sounds. (*Alerts* are the sounds your computer makes when it wants to get your attention.) Then use the slider to adjust the volume.

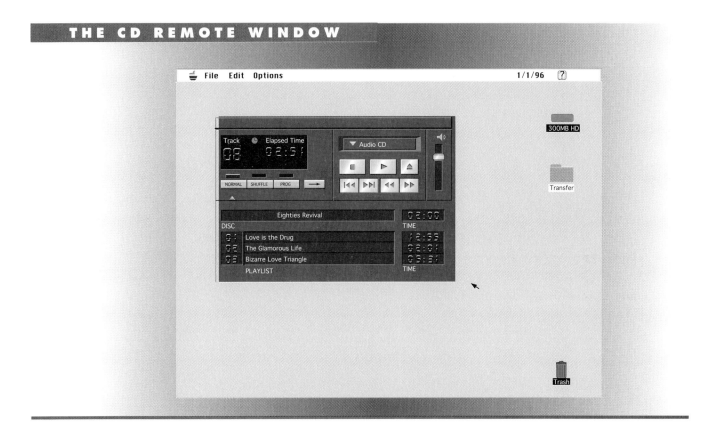

CONTROLLING WINDOWS AND MAC SOUNDS

PC Windows 95 is a fairly vocal program. If you have a sound card and speakers and are running Windows, you'll no doubt notice sounds occurring when you perform certain actions—such as attempting to close a document window without saving your changes first, or attempting to move past the end of a document, or exiting Windows. You can customize the sounds associated with such events, assign sounds to other events, or opt for total silence using the Sounds Properties dialog box. To get to this dialog box, open the Start menu, choose Settings, and then pick Control Panel. When you see the Control Panel folder window, double-click the icon labeled Sounds to display a Sounds Properties dialog box. Near the top of the dialog box, you'll see a list of Windows events. Any event that is preceded by a little speaker symbol has a sound file associated with it. To assign a sound to an event or to change the sound associated with an event, select the event and then click the arrow at the right edge of the Name dropdown list to open a list of .WAV files in the Media subfolder of the Windows folder. (A .WAV file, pronounced "wave" file, is a Windows sound file. It has an extension of .WAV and can be played on any computer that has Windows and a sound card.) To select a

THE WINDOWS 95 SOUNDS PROPERTIES DIALOG BOX

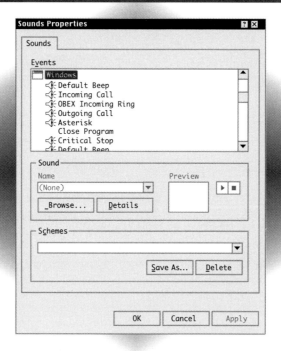

sound file in a different directory, use the Browse button. Once you've selected a sound file that intrigues you, you can hear what it sounds like by clicking the arrow button to the right of the box labeled Preview. If you want no sound played for a particular event, select <none>.

N O T E *Most of the items in the events list pertain to Windows as a whole and Windows-based applications. If you scroll down to the bottom of the list, however, you'll see a few events associated with the Windows Explorer and possibly some other Windows applications (depending on which applications you have installed on your computer).*

When choosing sound files, you are not limited to using the sound files that come with Windows itself. You can use any .WAV file you can find or create. There are probably thousands of .WAV files available on Bulletin Board Systems, online services, and the Internet. (You'll learn more about these resources and about downloading files in Chapter 10.) If you have a microphone, you can also make your own .WAV files using the Windows sound recorder utility. You'll learn to do this in the section entitled "Recording Your Own Sounds." Many sound cards also come with a program for recording and editing .WAV files.

To use a .WAV file from a directory other than your Windows directory, simply select the appropriate drive letter and/or directory name from the Files list to display a list of .WAV files in that location.

To change the sounds associated with a whole range of system events, select a sound "scheme" from the Schemes dropdown list. You can also create your own schemes by assigning sounds to specific events and then clicking the Save As button and assigning a name to that collection of sounds.

NOTE *To turn off all the sounds associated with Windows events, open the Schemes list and choose "No sounds."*

The Apply button saves your changes without closing the dialog box. The OK button saves your changes and closes the dialog box. The Cancel button cancels your changes and closes the dialog box.

Some of the Windows events to which you can attach sounds include:

Event Name	Occurs When...
Asterisk	A dialog box appears offering more information about your current situation.
Critical Stop	An urgent dialog box appears displaying a warning, but allowing you to proceed anyway by clicking OK.
Default Beep	You've clicked outside a dialog box, tried to move past the end of a document, or something equally harmless.
Exclamation	A dialog box appears, urging caution.
Question	A dialog box appears, asking you a question.
Windows Exit	You are leaving Windows.
Windows Start	You are loading Windows.

MAC The sound a Mac makes when it wants to get your attention is known as an *alert*. (You'll hear this sound whenever you click outside an active dialog box, for example.) If you don't like the sound, you can pick another one using the Sounds Control Panel. To get there, open the Apple menu, double-click Control Panels, and then double-click Sounds. To both hear and select a different sound, just choose it from the sounds list. You can adjust the volume of the sound using the slider to the left of the list. To record your own sound, click the Add button and start recording. If you have a microphone built into your monitor, just speak into that. If you have an external microphone, make sure it's hooked up and turned on before you start recording. There are also hundreds, if not thousands, of Mac-compatible sound files available for free on computer bulletin boards. If you want to use one of these files as your alert sound, just put it in your system folder. Then, when you open the Sounds Control Panel, the new sound file should be part of your sounds list.

To associate sounds with other operating system events—such as turning on or shutting off your computer, or emptying the trash—you'll need to purchase a sound manager program or download one from a computer bulletin board service.

RECORDING YOUR OWN SOUNDS

Perhaps you'd like to hear a bit of Miles Davis when you turn on your computer, or R.E.M., or the sound of your two-year-old saying hello. Or maybe you'd like to attach verbal instructions to a complicated spreadsheet file, explaining the logic of the calculations or telling the user which cells to fill in. There are two main reasons to record your own sounds: You can associate the sounds with particular operating system events and you can attach them to particular documents.

PC If you want to record your own sounds in Windows 95, you'll need a microphone (which you should be able to pick up at any music or home electronics store) and a sound recorder program. Windows 95 includes a Sound Recorder application that you can use for this purpose. To launch it, open the Start menu, select Programs, choose Accessories, select Multimedia, and then pick Sound Recorder. When you reach the Sound Recorder dialog box, open the File menu and choose New. Make sure your microphone is turned on and then click on the Record button (the button that contains a circle) to start recording. As you talk (or sing or whatever) into the microphone, you should see some activity in the box above the buttons. You'll also see the slider above the buttons that indicates how much time you have left move from left to right. To stop the recording before you run out of time, click the Stop button (the one that contains a square). To play back the recording, click the Play button (the one with a single right-pointing arrow). To adjust the volume, open the Effects menu and select either Increase Volume or Decrease Volume.

When you're satisfied with the recording, open the File menu and choose Save. In the Save As dialog box, use the dropdown list labeled Save In to specify the folder where you want to save the file. (If you plan to assign the sound to a Windows event, you may want to put it in with the other event sound files in the Media subfolder of the Windows folder.) Then click in the File Name text box, type in the file name, and select OK.

If you're not happy with the recording, just open the File menu and select New again and, when asked if you want to save your changes, select No. Then click the Record button to start recording again. (If you just record again without selecting File and then New, your new recording will be added onto the old one.)

To record from an audio CD, you'll need a more sophisticated recording program. Most sound cards come with mixer programs that allow you to choose which device you're recording from—microphone, CD-ROM drive, stereo system, MIDI synthesizer, or even several different sources simultaneously. If you plan to record from an audio CD, make sure that your sound card is properly connected to your CD-ROM drive. (If you can hear the CD through your computer's speakers, you're probably fine.) See the manual that came with your recording software for recording instructions.

N O T E   *Although it's usually legal to record sound and music from an audio CD, LP (does anyone still have them?), or a radio or TV program for your own use in your own home, it's illegal to distribute such recordings, even to your best friend, or to play them in public.*

MAC   If you're using a Mac, you can, as mentioned, record your own alert sound using the Add button in the Sounds Control Panel. If you have a sound manager program, you can also record sounds to associate with other operating system events.

Many recording programs give you a choice between recording in 16-bit or 8-bit mode. If you have an old 8-bit card, you don't really have a choice. If you have a 16-bit card, you can use either mode. (If you're not sure which you have, try checking the documentation that came with the card. Most new cards are 16-bit.) Recording in 16-bit mode will create larger files but give you better sound quality than 8-bit mode. You will sometimes also have a choice of recording sampling rate—11, 22, or 44KHz. The higher the setting, the better the sound quality and the larger the sound file. Finally, if your sound card has two microphone jacks and you have two microphones, you can choose between recording in mono or stereo. As you'd expect, stereo sounds better but makes for bigger files.

Once you've finished recording your sounds or music, you can use your sound recording program to edit the resulting sound file—trimming off unwanted portions, and, in some programs, amplifying sections or inserting silences.

WATCHING VIDEO CLIPS ON YOUR COMPUTER

Explaining how to make and edit movies on a computer is well beyond the scope of this book. But watching full-motion video on a computer is a snap. There are thousands of short video clips on the Internet, bulletin board services, and online services like Compu-Serve and America Online, waiting for your perusal. They range from little movies of your favorite TV stars to great moments in sports to footage of a short airplane ride over the Himalayas. You'll learn how to find and download these clips in Chapter 10.

PC If you have Windows 95, be sure to get an .AVI version of the video clip. (AVI stands for Audio Visual Interface and is the standard file format for Windows video files.) To view it, you can just locate the file—either in a folder window or an Explorer window—and double-click on it. If you'd like a little more control, you can use the Windows Media Player. To launch the Media Player application, open the Start menu, select Accessories, choose Multimedia, and then pick Media Player. Once you see the Media Player window, open the File menu and choose Open to open your video file. Then you can click the play button to start it up. You can use other buttons to stop, or to move forward or backward. For more details, open the Help menu in the Media Player window and select Help Topics.

MAC If you have a Mac, you'll want to collect video clips in QuickTime format. Quick-Time is the software that allows the Mac to create, display, edit, and compress video. You won't actually use QuickTime directly at all, but you will be able to play any QuickTime "movie" on your Mac by simply double-clicking the icon for the video file or by embedding the video file in a document. (You'll learn to do the latter in the next section.) This launches an applet called Movie Player, which lets you stop the action, fast forward, rewind, and so on.

EMBEDDING SOUNDS AND VIDEOS IN DOCUMENTS

Both Windows and the Mac Operating System let you embed sound files and video files inside documents. This allows you to do things like insert a set of spoken instructions in a word processing document or spreadsheet, or include a short video clip in a written presentation (assuming you either have the software and skills to create the video clip, or have paid someone to produce one for you).

PC If you're using Windows 95, you can include a sound or video file in a document by opening the document and then issuing the command for inserting an OLE object. (OLE stands for Object Linking and Embedding, which is the technology within Windows that lets programs communicate and exchange data.) When asked for a file name, specify the .WAV (sound) file or .AVI (video) file you want to use. The exact command will depend on the application you're using. If you're inserting a file in a Word for Windows document, for example, you would select the Object command from the Insert menu, and then select Create from File. If you insert a sound file, you will see an icon that looks like a megaphone. (You might want to type in directions next to the sound file icon, such as double-click here for instructions.) If you insert a video file, you'll see the first frame of the video. To play the file, just double-click the sound icon or picture.

MAC If you're using a Mac, the procedure is almost identical. Just locate the command for inserting an object in your application and then specify the sound or video file you want to use.

WHAT IS MIDI?

The term MIDI stands for Musical Instrument Digital Interface. MIDI is a communications standard that was developed by the manufacturers of electronic musical equipment. It defines how computer music software, synthesizers, and other electronic equipment can exchange both information and electrical signals.

A MIDI file is a file that contains information on the order, volume, pitch and duration of notes, as well as the instrument used to create them. You can think of it rather like a set of electronic sheet music—a set of data that allows a computer to reconstruct a set of sounds—as opposed to .WAV files that store the sounds themselves. When you play a MIDI file, your sound card's built-in synthesizer reads the file and, in essence, re-creates the music. One of the big advantages of MIDI files is that they occupy a fraction of the space occupied by files like .WAV files, which store actual sounds.

If you're using Windows 95, you can play MIDI files with the Windows Media Player. Your sound card may well have a program for playing MIDI files too. If you're using a Mac, you need to purchase a separate program to play MIDI files. If you want to record your own MIDI files, make sure you buy a sound card that has a MIDI interface, meaning a place to plug in your synthesizer or electric piano.

NOTE *MIDI files are really designed to be played using an external synthesizer rather than the little synthesizer that's built into your sound card. Playing them through a sound card gives you a hint of what they sound like, but if you want to hear them in their full glory, you'll need more sophisticated (and expensive) equipment.*

USING PHOTO CDS

Assuming you have a monitor that can display graphics, there's one more thing you can do with your CD-ROM drive. You can display and manipulate photographs. A photo CD (brand name Kodak CD) is a compact disc that contains digitized photographs—that is, photographs in a form that can be stored and manipulated on a computer. Assuming you have the right type of drive, you simply take your finished roll of 35-millimeter film or slides to any photofinisher who has a photo CD system. The photofinisher develops your film, digitizes the photographs, and stores them on a photo CD for you.

There are several reasons to do this:

▶ *You can view the images on your computer—either one at a time or in a series, much like a slide show.*

▶ *You can use the images as wallpaper in Windows and on the Mac. (Wallpaper is a graphic that is repeated across the desktop, in place of the usual gray or other solid color background.)*

▶ *You can embed the images in documents. This can be a great way to get images for a newsletter or flyer. (See the manual for your word processing or desktop publishing program for details on working with graphics.) Many of the newer database programs let you store and display graphic images too. You could take photographs of all the employees of your company and store them in the company personnel database for example.*

▶ *If you have a photo manipulation program, such as Adobe PhotoShop, you can touch up and manipulate the images—fine-tuning colors, changing the contrast, and so on—and then print the final version.*

A single photo CD can hold approximately 100 images. If your photo CD isn't full and your CD-ROM drive is multisession compatible, you can take the disc back to the photofinisher and have more photos added. (A *multisession compatible CD-ROM drive* is one that can read CDs that were created in more than one session.) Most newer CD-ROM drives, and all drives with the MPC 2 logo, are multisession compatible.

When photo CDs are created, each photograph is recorded in five different sizes or, more specifically, with five different numbers of pixels, and you get to choose which version you want to use. The number of pixels determines the amount of information the image contains. In this case, however, more does not necessarily mean better. A lot of information also means a lot of space on disk: An image with a greater number of pixels can consume as much as 18MB of disk space. In addition, very few monitors can display all of an image using 2048 × 3072 pixels (the largest size) even at their highest resolution. In general, it makes sense to use images with a number of pixels that suits your monitor and/or printer. If all you want to do with the image is display it on your screen, pick an image with close to the same number of pixels as your monitor's resolution if you want to fill the screen. If you plan on printing the image, experiment until you find the image that prints at the desired size on your printer.

PC If you have a PC, you can purchase photo CD software from Kodak, which will allow you to view the images in all five sizes, and to save them in common graphics formats such as .PCX and .TIF. Once you've saved an image in one of these formats, you'll be able to insert it into documents, as described shortly. If you want to be able to change the images— enhancing the contrast or penciling in a mustache—you'll need a higher-end photo manipulation program like Adobe PhotoShop. For instructions on using these programs, see the software documentation.

MAC If you have a Mac, the only requirements for viewing the images on a photo CD are that you have both QuickTime 1.6.1 or later and Apple Photo Access stored in your system folder. Both of these programs are part of the Macintosh operating system and chances are they are already properly installed. You don't actually work directly with either of these programs, but they work behind the scenes to allow you to view and manipulate images.(As mentioned, QuickTime is a program that allows other programs to integrate graphics, video, sound, and animation into documents. Apple Photo Access is specifically designed to let you work with photo CDs.)

When you insert the photo CD, a photo CD icon appears on the desktop. (The icon's label will start with the letters PCD followed by a number supplied by the photofinisher.) When you double-click the icon to open the photo CD window, you'll see icons labeled Slide Show, Slide Show Viewer, Photos, and PHOTO_CD. Double-click the Photos folder to open it and you'll see five folders, one for each size. Open the folder for the size you want and you'll see a window full of folders, each with a small image of one of your photographs. To see a larger image, click the desired folder.

By default, the image appears in a window opened by TeachText or SimpleText. (If you're using System 7.5, the first time you open a photo CD file you'll be asked which

VIEWING PHOTOS ON A COMPUTER

program you wish to use for viewing photos.) If you want images displayed in another program, open the File menu, select Preferences, and then select a different program in the Using dropdown list. If the program you want to use does not appear in the list, you can add it using the Add button. Once the image is displayed, you can view and print the image, copy and paste it into your Scrapbook, or copy and paste it into other documents or graphics programs. You cannot rename the images on your photo CD because the disc is read-only. You can, however, copy the images to your hard disk or a floppy and then rename and change them at will.

NOTE *If you intend to view photographs using TeachText or SimpleText, you will probably need to increase the amount of memory assigned to the application. To do this, in the Finder, find and click the icon for the application (TeachText or SimpleText). Then open the File menu, choose Get Info and assign a larger amount of RAM.*

To view several images in sequence, double-click the Slide Show icon in the photo CD window. You can then use the Slide Show Viewer controls to stop or start the slide show, scroll to a particular image, or move forward or backward through the images. You can control how the images are displayed by choosing Preferences from the File menu, choosing your options, clicking OK, and then restarting your computer.

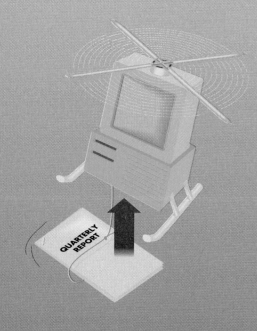

A modem is your computer's link to the outside world. It's been estimated that over 12 million computers in the U.S. alone are equipped with a modem. The number worldwide is probably two or three times that. Once you install or attach a modem, the people behind all those computers become potential teachers, clients, collaborators, or even friends.

The list of things you can do with a modem includes

▶ *Exchanging data with friends and colleagues. You could use a modem to obtain a report or spreadsheet from an associate in another city, for example, or to send a coworker a file of orders received while you're on the road.*

▶ *Accessing your office computer from a computer at home or a laptop in a hotel room, making use of the same programs and data that you would have if you were actually sitting in your office.*

▶ *Using the Internet and online information services such as CompuServe, Prodigy, and America Online to obtain technical support on computer programs, look up stock prices, make plane reservations, read the latest news from the wire services, go shopping, pay your bills, participate in a college seminar, solicit advice on when and how to prune your roses, or send electronic mail to clients, coworkers, or friends.*

▶ *Using bulletin board systems to carry on electronic conversations on everything from politics to gardening to science fiction.*

N O T E   *We'll get more into the specifics later, but for now, just know that the main difference between online information services and bulletin board services is that online services cost money and provide a wealth of services, like up-to-the-minute news and weather, stock quotes, and access to reference literature. Bulletin board services are generally free (although you will pay for the phone call, which can get expensive if the service is across the country). They also tend to offer fewer services and often focus on specific topics. There are bulletin boards specifically geared toward mathematicians, real estate agents, and people interested in 12-step recovery programs, to name just a few. The Internet offers many of the same services as the online information services, plus access to millions of articles and academic papers, thousands of free computer programs, the library card catalogs of thousands of universities, a huge and growing matrix of* *interlinked, interactive, multimedia documents known as the World Wide Web, and a "global community" of millions of users.*

This chapter covers all the basics of telecommunications—that is, of transmitting information between two computers via modems and phone lines. It starts with an overview of the hardware and software involved, and a description of what the process is like. Then you learn about different types of modems and communications programs: the programs that provide the interface between you and your modem, and that guide the transmission of data from one system to the other. Next, you delve into some of the complexities involved in getting computers to "talk" and exchange files. The chapter ends with a brief description of online information services, bulletin boards, and the Internet (a kind of global computer network for distributing information).

HOW COMPUTERS COMMUNICATE

There are two prerequisites to telecommunication. On the hardware side, you need a modem. On the software side, you need a communications program that can tell the modem what to do and handle the technical details of transmitting and receiving data.

N O T E *Once your modem has successfully established a connection to another modem, you are said to be "online." When no such connection exists, you are "offline."*

The main purpose of the modem is to translate data from a form palatable to a computer into a form palatable to a telephone and vice versa. Most computers are digital devices. They store and manipulate information by turning on and off sets of tiny electronic switches. (When turned on, a switch represents the number 1; when off, it represents the number 0.) Transmitting digital data is therefore a bit like sending morse code: At any given instant, the signal must represent either a dot or a dash. There are no gradations. Telephones, in contrast, transmit data as an analog signal (sound wave) that varies in frequency and strength, rather like the line drawn by an electrocardiograph machine.

The primary function of a modem is to translate digital signals into analog ones and vice versa. When you send data, the modem converts the digital information from the computer into analog signals that can be transmitted over phone wires: a process known as *modulation*. When you receive data, the modem converts the analog signals received from the phone into digital codes that your computer can manage (a process known as *demodulation*). The term modem is a hybrid of the terms modulate and demodulate.

COMPUTERS ONLINE

In order for two computers to communicate, they must both have modems and be running communications programs.

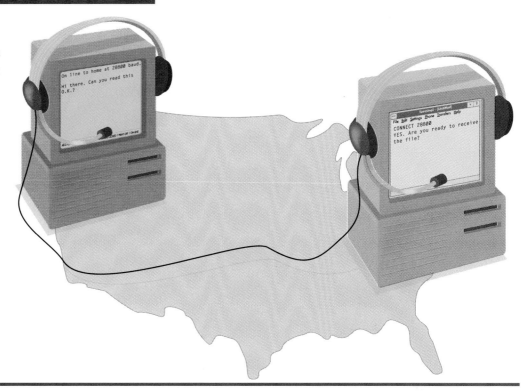

ON BITS AND BYTES

As mentioned in Chapter 1, computers store and manipulate information as numbers, regardless of whether the information in question consists of numbers, letters, pictures, or any other type of data. Internally, computers represent all numbers using base 2, a numbering system that employs only two digits—0 and 1. (Humans, in contrast, like to think in base 10, which involves ten digits: 0 through 9.) Base 2 is often referred to as binary notation or a binary numbering system. The reason computers "think" in base 2 is that they represent information in terms of the presence or absence of an electrical or magnetic charge. The number 1 is used as the numeric equivalent of on, or charged. Zero is used to mean off, or uncharged.

In computer terminology, the electronic representation of a 0 or a 1 is known as a *bit* (short for binary digit) and there are eight bits to each byte of information. (That is, it takes eight 0s and/or 1s to represent a single character.) For example, the pattern used to represent a lowercase "a" on a personal computer is 01100001. As mentioned, when bits are stored inside a computer, they are stored as electrical or magnetic charges. When information is transmitted from one part of the computer to another or from a computer to a modem, bits are represented by small bursts of electricity—where a single burst represents an *on* bit (a number 1) and a pause between bursts represents an *off* bit (a number 0). A lowercase "a," for example, is represented by a pause, two bursts of electricity, four pauses, and another burst of electricity.

You won't actually have to think about bits very much. People always describe the capacity of a disk or the size of a program in terms of numbers of bytes rather than bits, for instance. As you will see later in this chapter, however, you will encounter the term in discussions of modem speed, since modems transmit data one bit at a time.

DIGITAL AND ANALOG SIGNALS

The purpose of modems is to transform digital information generated by a computer into an analog form that can be transmitted over phone lines (a process called *modulation*) and to transform analog signals received over the phone line into digital codes that your computer knows how to use (*demodulation*).

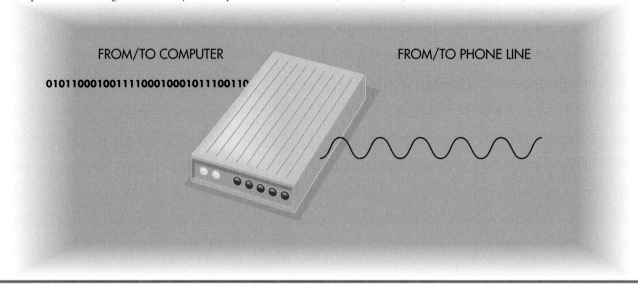

FROM/TO COMPUTER

0101100010011110001000101110011

FROM/TO PHONE LINE

There are basically two types of modems:

▶ *Internal modems, which are expansion boards that are installed inside your system unit*

▶ *External modems, which look like flat plastic or metal boxes (about the size of a rather thin hardback book) that usually plug into the back of your computer*

Internal modems are often cheaper and consume none of your precious desk space. External modems offer the advantage of visible status lights—little lights on the front end of the device that can help you (or the expert you get on the phone) figure out where the problem lies if you have trouble establishing a connection with another computer. External modems are also easily transferred from one computer to another. This can save you the expense of buying two modems if you have both a desktop computer and a laptop, for example.

Aside from living quarters, what distinguishes one modem from the next is the speed at which it can transmit data. The speed at which modems send and receive data is typically measured in bits per second (bps), with 1200 being the low end these days and 28800 being the high end. Most modems now in use transmit data at a maximum of either 9600 bps or 14400 bps.

You may also hear the term baud rate used to describe modem speeds. These days, baud rate is actually an outdated term. In slower modems, baud rate (which measures the number

INTERNAL AND EXTERNAL MODEMS

Internal modems are circuit boards that fit into expansion slots inside your computer.

External modems are little boxes with lights on the front that you connect to your computer with a cable.

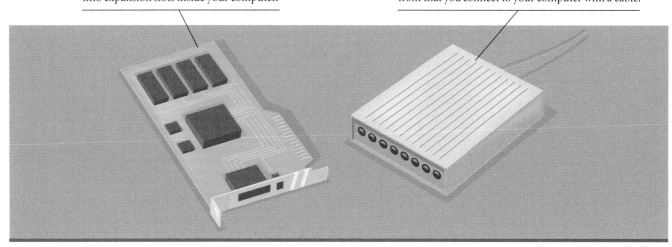

of times the frequency of the analog signal changes per second) was equivalent to the number of bits transmitted per second. In faster modems, however, two or three bits may be transmitted for every frequency change—making bps a different and more useful measurement. Nonetheless, if someone says they have a 9600 baud modem, they probably mean a modem that can transmit data at 9600 bps.

Modem speed doesn't matter that much if you are using your modem strictly to send short messages via electronic mail or carry on online conversations with friends or colleagues. Speed does matter, however, when you are sending or receiving files. It takes almost twice as long to transmit a file at 14400 bps as it does at 28800 bps, and three times as long at 9600 bps. Try transmitting a file that's 50K or more and the difference will be very noticeable. Modem speed also makes a big difference when you're accessing the Internet, particularly if you're using the graphics-intensive World Wide Web.

MAKING SENSE OF BPS

As a rule of thumb, you can divide the bps rate by 10 to determine the number of characters (bytes) transferred per second. A 60K (60,000-character) file will take approximately 20 seconds to transmit at 28800 bps (60,000 divided by 2880) and approximately 40 seconds at 14400 bps (60,000 divided by 1440). This rule of thumb is only approximate because the actual transmission rate varies slightly depending on the amount of interference on the phone line (if any) and the protocols you use to transmit the data. (You will learn about communications and file transfer protocols under "Using a General Communications Program" later in this chapter.)

Another factor to consider when purchasing a modem is compatibility. One of the earliest and most popular modem manufacturers is a company named Hayes. Hayes modems use a set of commands—a simple language really—that has become a standard for modems in general. The phrase "Hayes-compatible modem" means a modem that understands the Hayes commands for dialing, checking to see whether a modem has answered the phone, hanging up the line, and the like. Most modems currently manufactured are Hayes compatible. Make sure yours is one of them.

A final factor to consider when choosing a modem is whether it has fax capabilities. See the upcoming section on fax modems for details.

PLUGGING IN YOUR MODEM

External modems come with an intimidating number of connectors. There are at least three connections to be made:

▶ *From your modem to a power source*

▶ *From your modem to your computer*

▶ *From your modem to the telephone line*

If you are using a single phone line for both the modem and voice communications (that is, if you plan to talk on the same line that you use to telecommunicate), you may want to connect your modem into your telephone as well.

To connect your modem to a power source, you simply plug its power cord into a wall outlet or power strip. (The power cord features a little transformer box and a standard electrical plug.)

To connect an external modem to your computer, you plug a cable running from the modem into a serial port at the back of your system unit. As explained in Chapters 2 and 8, ports are data channels designed to carry data and instructions between your computer's memory and an I/O (input/output) device. Most computers feature two types of ports: serial ports, which are generally used for modems and mice and occasionally for printers, and parallel ports, which are always used for printers. At the back of the system unit, you will usually find one or two serial ports that serve as gateways into the computer's internal communication channels.

PC On PCs, serial ports are always "male" (that is, have pins sticking out) and have either 9 or 25 pins. Most PCs have either one or two serial ports, but it's possible to have neither. (If you don't have a serial port, you either need to buy a circuit board that includes a serial port or use an internal modem.)

9 TO 25 PIN ADAPTERS

If the connector on the end of your modem cable has the wrong number of holes for your particular serial port (say your modem cable has 25 holes and your serial port has only 9 pins), you'll need to get a special 9 to 25 pin adapter from your computer store. This is rather like buying an adapter that lets you plug a three-prong plug into a two-prong electrical outlet.

MAC Most Macs come with two serial ports: one identified by a telephone symbol and another by a printer symbol. Although you can actually plug your modem into either one, it's best to use the telephone port since this is the one that communications programs will assume you are using.

PC The internal communications channels inside PCs are known as *COM ports*. (Although many people use the term serial port and COM port interchangeably, technically a COM port is an internal data channel and a serial port is the connector at the back of your computer that lets you connect an external device, like a modem, into that data channel.) All COM ports start with the letters COM. If you have only one serial port, it's connected to the COM port named COM1. If you have two serial ports, they're connected to COM1 and COM2.

If you have an internal modem, it's still configured for a particular COM port (usually COM1 or COM2), but the connection into that communication channel is made entirely inside your computer. When you set up your communications software, you need to tell it the name of the COM port your modem is connected to. If you don't know, try telling your software that you're using COM2 if you have a mouse and COM1 if you don't. If this doesn't work, try the other setting. The actual command for telling your software which port you're using will, of course, vary from one program to the next. Look for commands named setup, settings, or configuration, or, better yet, read your manual.

Some communications programs will ask which port your modem is connected to during the installation process, but all of them let you change the port setting later if necessary. A few communications programs let you select an "autodetect" option during the installation process, directing the program to test the various serial ports to determine which has a modem attached.

MAC The serial ports on Macs are called simply the modem port and the printer port.

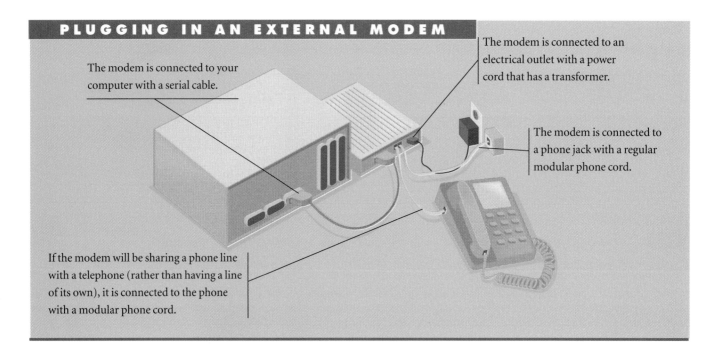

PLUGGING IN AN EXTERNAL MODEM

The modem is connected to your computer with a serial cable.

The modem is connected to an electrical outlet with a power cord that has a transformer.

The modem is connected to a phone jack with a regular modular phone cord.

If the modem will be sharing a phone line with a telephone (rather than having a line of its own), it is connected to the phone with a modular phone cord.

Finally, all modems—both external and internal—need to be connected to phone lines. If you have a separate phone line for your modem, you will generally run a modular phone cord from a phone jack on your wall to the back of your external modem, or to the piece of your internal modem card that protrudes from the back of your computer. If you don't have a phone line just for this purpose, you run one cord from the modem into the phone and another from the modem into the phone jack. This way, you and your modem can share the same line. (In most cases, there are specific spots on the modem for plugging in cables to the phone line and to the telephone itself. Check your modem documentation to determine which is which.)

N O T E   *Try not to attach a modem to a phone line that has call interrupt. Otherwise, an incoming call may either break the connection between modems or introduce a signal that your modem will not know how to interpret. (If you happen to be in the middle of transmitting a file, such errant signals can ruin the file transfer or make it necessary for you to retransmit the file from scratch.) In most cases, you can disable call waiting by dialing *70.*

FAX MODEMS

Many of the modems currently being sold are fax modems—meaning they not only let you send and receive data, they also let your computer double as a fax machine. Like regular modems, fax modems come in both internal and external varieties. They also have advantages and disadvantages relative to regular fax machines, both in terms of sending and receiving faxes.

In terms of sending, fax modems are particularly useful for sending documents and graphics created on your computer because they eliminate the need to print the data first. On the other hand, if you want to use a fax modem to transmit data that you have only in "hard copy" (that is, on paper), you need to first scan it into your computer using a scanner.

In terms of receiving faxes, fax modems let you read incoming faxes on your computer before deciding whether they're worth printing. And if you do decide to print, you can print on regular paper rather than fax paper. On the other hand, it usually takes a little longer to print a fax on a printer than on a fax machine. If you have a page printer (laser or ink jet as opposed to dot-matrix), you'll also need a fair amount of memory. In addition, you can only receive faxes when your computer is turned on and your fax software is running, which means that you either have to tell your associates only to send faxes during your regular hours or leave your computer on during off hours. (Some companies, such as Delrina, the makers of WinFaxPro, are responding to this problem by offering fax mailbox services that store incoming faxes until you're ready to view them.)

To send and receive faxes from your computer, you need a communications program with fax capabilities. Windows 95 includes a built-in fax program named Microsoft Fax. (To use this program, you need to install both Microsoft Exchange and Microsoft Fax, either when you first install Windows 95 or later. See your Windows 95 documentation for details.) If you're using an operating environment other than Windows 95, you'll need to install a separate fax-capable communications program. Many fax modems come bundled with such programs.

PC In Windows, once you have installed a fax modem and a suitable communications program, sending faxes from your computer is simply a matter of "printing" a document to your fax software. Just open the document you want to fax, select the Print command from the File menu, and then choose your communications program from the drop-down list of printers. As soon as you select OK, your communications program will take over long enough to request information on the intended recipient and the cover page you wish to use, if any. (If you selected Microsoft Fax as your printer, you'll be stepped through a set of dialog boxes by the Compose New Fax Wizard.) Then you'll be returned to your document and the actual faxing will proceed in the background. If you frequently fax existing documents without opening them first, you can add your fax program to the Send To menu that is displayed when you right-click a document icon and choose Send To. For details, see the instructions in Chapter 8 for adding a printer to the Send To menu.

You can also send faxes from within most fax-capable communications programs. You may choose to do this if you just want to fax a quick note and have no need to create it in another application (or to save it to disk). Some programs let you fax documents created in other Windows applications—temporarily loading the application and "printing" the specified file. See your communications program manual for details.

MAC If you're using a Mac, the process of sending a fax varies depending on the fax/communications software you are using. In some cases, the process works just like it does in Windows: You open a document and then "print" it to your fax/communications progam, using the application's Print command. In other cases, the fax progam is loaded when you turn on your computer and, when you're ready to fax, you open the document and then select your fax program from the Application menu. In either case, you'll be asked to supply the name and fax number of the intended recipient and a short time later you'll hear the fax modem dialing the phone number and then transmitting your fax.

The procedure for receiving faxes—on both Macs and PCs—depends on whether you have a separate phone line for your fax modem. If you do have a separate phone line, you can usually leave the fax modem set to auto-answer mode, so that the fax modem will automatically answer any incoming calls on that line. (To do this, look up the procedure for turning on auto-answer mode in your fax program's manual or Help system.) Some fax modems have a feature known as Adaptive Answer or Automatic Fax/Data Detection which allows them to determine whether an incoming call is from a modem or a fax. Some also offer security features, so that you can only accept calls from particular callers or modems. If the fax modem doesn't have a phone line of its own, you'll have to wait until the phone starts ringing and then issue a command in your fax program directing the fax modem to answer. This means that you'll need to have people who want to send you faxes call you ahead of time, so you'll know whether you or your fax/modem should answer the next call.

NOTE *Most fax modems do fine at sending faxes. Receiving faxes is a trickier affair, however, and some fax modems perform the task more reliably than others. If you need to be able to receive faxes regularly, solicit advice from friends or scan computer magazines for reviews of fax modems to see which ones in your price range are most reliable.*

When you receive a fax, it generally goes into something called a *fax queue*. To view it, load your communications program (if it's not already loaded) and issue a command for viewing received faxes. If the fax was received in Binary File Transfer (BFT) format, you will see an icon next to the text of your message. Double-click the icon to edit the file.

Even if a fax consists entirely of text, your fax modem will usually receive it as a graphic image. This means that you usually can't load it into your word processing program and edit it afterwards. There are three exceptions to this rule. First, if your communications program supports BFT and the person you're exchanging a fax with also has a system that supports BFT, the file will be transmitted as an editable e-mail message. (Microsoft Fax supports BFT and the Windows 95 versions of most fax-capable communications programs will as well.) Second, if your computer is part of a network and is using the Windows for Workgroups operating system, you can use the Microsoft At Work fax program to fax editable documents to anyone who is running Microsoft at Work. Finally, some high-end communications programs—such as WinFaxPro—include optical character recognition (OCR) capabilities that allow you to translate some or all of a received fax into a text file that you can import into a word processing program or other application. OCR will not work on all faxes: It does best with sans serif fonts in a fairly large typeface and requires a fax image with good print quality. In most cases, sending a document as a file or sending it in BFT format is a more efficient and reliable way of transmitting editable text than OCR. (You'll learn about transmitting files later in this chapter.)

Making full use of your fax modem may or may not require buying a specialized fax program: It depends on what you want to do. Most general communications programs include at least minimal fax capabilities and, as mentioned, Windows 95 includes a faxing program of its own. If you want to do the fancy stuff—like OCR, scheduling faxes to be sent at a later time (when the phone rates drop, for example), sending faxes to lists of recipients, or retrieving newly received faxes from your laptop or other remote computer—you'll probably need to buy a specialized program like WinFaxPro or a high-end communications program like ProComm Plus. (If you're shopping for a program, make a list of all the features you need and then all the features you'd like, and take it with you to your local computer or software store.)

COMMUNICATIONS SOFTWARE

Hardware (namely a modem) is only half of the telecommunications equation. The other is software or, more specifically, a communications program that serves as the intermediary between you and your modem, and that handles all the technical details of telecommunication. Communications programs provide tools that let you tell your modem what and when to dial or when to answer the phone, that let you send messages to the computer on the other end of the phone line, and that allow you to send and receive files.

There are three basic types of communications programs:

▶ *General communications programs allow you to connect to information services, bulletin board systems, electronic mail services, and regular modem-equipped PCs. Some of the more popular commercial general communications programs are Pro-Comm Plus, Crosstalk, Smartcom, Versaterm, White Knight, and Blast. There are also shareware programs like ProComm, Qmodem, and Telix that you can often get from users' groups or bulletin board systems. (Shareware programs are distributed for free but if you like the program, you are supposed to send a small fee to its creator.) Windows comes with its own general communications program called HyperTerminal. Occasionally you will find general communications programs bundled with modems.*

▶ *Front-end programs are designed to help you access and navigate through informational and electronic mail services. Some services—like America Online, The Microsoft Network, and Prodigy—can only be accessed through a front-end program. Others, like CompuServe, can be accessed through either general communications programs or front-end programs, but the latter can make it easier to find information or explore particular topics (saving you money as well as time). Bear in mind that front-end programs are tailored to a particular service: You can't use Prodigy's software to access CompuServe, or the CompuServe Information Manager program to access America Online. Most online services give you their front-end programs for free when you subscribe to their service. CompuServe is the notable exception.*

▶ *Remote-control programs let you operate one computer from another computer. You can use such programs to access your office computer from home or, if you're a computer whiz, to troubleshoot a client's system without leaving your office. Once you have connected to a computer using a remote-control program, you see on your screen exactly what appears on the other computer's screen, and you can operate the other computer as if you were sitting in front of it—running that computer's programs, creating and saving files, and even printing. In most cases, if there's a person at the remote computer, he or she can use the computer as well, perhaps demonstrating a problem he or she is having so that you can fix it. Some of the more popular remote-control programs are PCAnywhere, ReachOut, Carbon Copy, Blast, and Remote2.*

The difference between using a front-end program and a general communications program is a little like the difference between riding a bus and driving a car. In one case (front-end programs), you don't need to do much work, but you can only go to specified places, namely one information service. In the other case (general communications programs), you can go anywhere you want, but the driving is up to you. Front-end programs already know everything they need to know about CompuServe or America Online or whatever service you're using to properly configure your modem. You don't have to do much of anything until the connection is already made. With general communications programs, you need to understand and deal more with the technical details of connecting to another computer and transferring files. (You'll learn about these details in the next section.) The downside of front-end programs, of course, is that you can't use them for anything but accessing one particular service.

The amount of work involved in using a remote-control program depends on which end you're on. If you're the "remote"—that is, the side that's dialing in—you'll need about the same amount of know-how that you need to run a general communications program. If you're the "host"—that is, the side that's being dialed into—you don't need to do much of anything. In fact, much of the point of remote-control software is that little or nothing needs to happen on the host end of things, allowing someone to call a computer that's completely unattended or attended by someone who knows little or nothing about modems (or computers for that matter).

The type of program that's right for you depends on what you plan to do with your modem.

▶ *If you'll just be calling a particular information service, get a front-end program designed for that service. (As mentioned, most of them are free with a subscription to the service.)*

▶ *If you plan on calling bulletin boards or exchanging files directly with other PCs, and perhaps occasionally using an online service, get a general communications program.*

▶ *If you need to call into your office computer and access files while you're not there, or exchange data with someone who's not very computer literate, get a remote-control program.*

If you want to be able to do some combination of these things, you'll probably want more than one program.

NOTE *If you're planning to subscribe to an online service and the friends or colleagues with whom you plan to exchange files use the same service, you can just send files back and forth via the service. This saves you the trouble of learning and using a general communications program. It also allows you to upload and download files whenever you choose: You can send a file even if the recipient is not at his or her computer at the moment, and you can pick up a file anytime after it's been sent. (You'll find this particularly convenient if the person with whom you're exchanging files is hard to reach or in a different time zone.)*

USING A GENERAL COMMUNICATIONS PROGRAM

Many computer users who are perfectly comfortable building spreadsheets or commandeering databases freeze at the prospect of using a general communications program. Once you understand some of the basics, however, general communications programs are actually easy to manage. Before delving into the details, let's start by examining the steps involved in using a general communications program to establish a connection between your computer and the computer of a friend or colleague (as opposed to an information service or bulletin board). The process works like this:

▶ *You and the person on the other end decide who will call whom and which communication protocols you will use. (You'll learn all about communications protocols in the next section.)*

▶ *You both turn on your computers and, if you have external modems, your modems as well. (You don't need to turn on internal modems.)*

▶ *You both start up your communications programs.*

▶ *One of you issues a command directing your modem to dial the other modem's phone number and the other person issues a command directing his or her modem to answer the phone when it rings.*

▶ *If you're the person who initiates the call and your modem is equipped with a speaker (most are), you'll actually hear a dial tone and then the sound of your modem dialing the phone. Then you'll hear a high-pitched tone—your modem's equivalent of "Hi there. Are you a modem?" (Think of it as a modem mating call.) Meanwhile, the modem on the other end answers the phone and returns a slightly higher-pitched tone to indicate "Yes, I am a modem." The two modems then exchange information about how they intend to exchange data, a process known as a* handshake. *If you're on the receiving end of the call, you'll probably hear the sound emitted by the remote modem and then the answering tone of your own. In most cases, you'll then see a message such as "Connect 9600" or "Connect 14400," indicating that a connection has been established at the specified transmission rate.*

▶ *At this point, you can test the connection by typing a short message. If there's a problem with the connection—maybe the systems are using incompatible communications settings—the person on the other line will either see nonsense characters or nothing at all. If all goes well, however, you'll be able to type a message on your keyboard and have it show up on your friend's screen and vice versa. At this point you're ready to exchange files.*

The procedure is similar when you call up an online service or BBS, except that the modem on the other end is already set up to answer the phone when you call. In addition, as soon as a connection is established you'll usually be asked to "log in," meaning identify yourself and, in most cases, enter a password.

What happens once you are online depends on who you're calling and what you're trying to accomplish. If you are calling or receiving a call from a person at another personal computer, the next step will probably be exchanging files. (You'll learn about file transfers a little later.) If you're calling an information service, you'll probably see a menu of choices and will begin navigating through the system, seeking out information to read, choosing files that you want to copy to your computer, leaving messages for other people, or joining in an electronic conversation with others currently logged into the system.

In any case, when you're done "telecommunicating," you either log out of the online service or bulletin board system or type good-bye to your friend or colleague, and then direct your modem to hang up the phone, severing your electronic connection. Then you exit from your communications program.

THE MODEM HANDSHAKE

As soon as one modem answers a call from another, the modems trade information about how they intend to exchange data. This process is known as a *handshake*.

A similar set of steps occurs when you use a front-end or remote-control program, but many of the technical details are either managed by the program itself or are handled ahead of time when you define settings during the program installation process.

COMMUNICATIONS PROTOCOLS

Modems can only connect over phone lines if both systems send and receive data in similar ways. Both need to transmit data using the same transmission speed, number of data bits, type of parity (if any), and number of stop bits. (You'll learn the meaning of the last three of these terms shortly.)

In most cases, you don't need to worry about any of these things if you are using a front-end program, since the program already knows everything it needs to know about the information service's settings and directs your modem to communicate accordingly. If you are using a general communications program or if you're setting up a remote-control program, however, you need to direct your modem to transmit data in a manner acceptable to the modem on the other end of the line.

Speed is the first thing your modems need to agree upon. In order for modems to communicate, they must both be sending and receiving data at the same rate. This means that if your modem can send and receive data at 14400 bps but the computer on the other end of the line can only send and receive at 9600 bps, the connection must be made at 9600 bps. In some cases, a high-speed modem will sense the slower speed of the remote modem and decelerate accordingly. In others, you'll need to explicitly tell your modem to use the slower speed using your communications software before your modem dials or answers the incoming call.

The meaning of the other settings, commonly known as communications protocols, is a bit more obscure. If you want to know all the details, refer to the sidebar called "Parity, Data Bits, Stop Bits, and Duplex." If you'd prefer being spared the details, all you need to know is that you'll almost always use one of two combinations of settings:

▶ *8 data bits, no parity, and 1 stop bit (referred to as 8N1)*

▶ *7 data bits, even parity, 1 stop bit (referred to as 7E1)*

The most commonly used combination is 8N1, although some online services require 7E1. (If you have trouble establishing a connection to an online service using one combination, try the other.)

PARITY, DATA BITS, STOP BITS, AND DUPLEX

The number of data bits refers to the number of bits used to represent each character. When you connect to another PC, you usually set this to 8. When you connect to online services, you frequently need to change it to 7.

The parity setting determines whether the modems will employ a type of error correction known as parity checking. When you connect directly to another PC, you will usually leave Parity set to None. When you connect to an online information service, you may need to set Parity to Even. (The information service itself will tell you which settings you need to use.)

A stop bit is a signal used to mark the end of a character. In PC communications, you always use a single stop bit.

Some communications programs also ask you to define a duplex setting. The *duplex* setting indicates whether your modems can send and receive data at the same time. When duplex is set to half, both modems can send and receive data, but only one of them can transmit data at any one time. When duplex is set to full, your modem can send and receive data simultaneously. These days, nearly all systems are capable of full-duplex communications.

Most communications programs allow you to define default settings for your transmission speed and communications protocols through some kind of setup command or setup menu option. Some also have a dialing directory feature that lets you store both the

DEFINING COMMUNICATIONS PROTOCOLS

In most communications programs, you define your communications protocols once and then change them only as necessary. This is one of the dialog boxes for defining communications protocols in ProComm Plus for Windows.

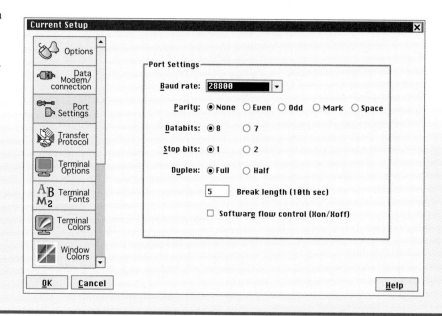

phone numbers of systems that you call regularly and the settings that you want to use when calling those numbers. If your friend Joe has a 9600 baud modem, for example, you can store that speed along with his phone number. Knowing that CompuServe likes the settings 7E1, you can store those settings along with the CompuServe number. Then, whenever you issue the command for dialing a number in your directory, the program automatically uses the appropriate protocols.

TERMINAL EMULATION MODES

When you connect to another computer via modem, your computer is temporarily transformed from a computer in its own right into a "dumb terminal"—a passive input and output device. The other computer, often known as the host computer, calls all the shots. As you enter characters they appear on the other computer's screen (and sometimes are "echoed" to your screen). If you are using an information service or remote-control program, as you enter commands, the host computer carries them out and then sends back output to be displayed on your screen. Sometimes the host computer expects a particular type of terminal at your end of the line. You can tell your computer to act like a particular type of terminal by changing its terminal emulation setting. In most cases, you don't even need to think about this setting: You can just leave it as is. If you are having trouble establishing a connection to a BBS, an information service, or the company mainframe, however, changing the terminal emulation setting is a good place to start. If you are accessing a bulletin board, try setting the terminal emulation mode to ANSI. Otherwise, set it to VT-100. If neither of these settings works, try TTY.

FILE-TRANSFER PROTOCOLS

One of the main reasons for using a modem is to be able to send and receive files (reports, academic papers, spreadsheets, programs, whatever) across phone lines.

When you send a file from your computer to the remote computer, it's called *uploading*. When you receive a file from the remote computer, it's called *downloading*. The easiest way to remember the terms is to imagine the remote computer as hovering above you somewhere, so that sending a file entails moving it up to the "computer in the sky" and receiving a file means bringing it down.

In most cases, when you transfer files via modem, you don't simply send them character by character; you use what's known as a *file-transfer protocol* to control the flow of data and check for errors. Think of a file-transfer protocol as a carefully choreographed strategy that two communications programs use to ensure that the data sent on one end matches the data received on the other. The program sending the data performs a calculation on each block of data it transmits and sends the results along with the data. The program receiving the data performs the same calculation and checks its results against the results transmitted by the other program. If an error is detected in a particular block, that block is retransmitted. (If you see a message on your screen about errors in the transmission, it doesn't mean that the data you got is bad; it just means that it took the modems a few tries to get it right.) In order for this strategy to work, the communications programs on both ends need to be using the same file-transfer protocol.

In some programs, you define your file-transfer protocol ahead of time. (Look for a settings or setup command, and then an option for file transfers or something similar). In other programs, you choose a protocol when you issue the command to send or receive.

ZMODEM is considered by many to be the best file-transfer protocol, but some older communications programs don't support it. One advantage of using ZMODEM is that the person on the receiving end doesn't need to press any keys or click any menu options to receive a file. If ZMODEM isn't available on both ends, try either XMODEM or YMODEM. (YMODEM offers the advantage of letting you transmit a group of files at once.)

If you are using an online service or bulletin board, you will often be asked to specify a file transfer type as well as a file transfer protocol. Your choices will include text files (sometimes called ASCII files) and binary files. (They may include other more specialized file types as well.) The only files that can safely be transmitted as text files are files that only contain

UPLOADING AND DOWNLOADING FILES

Uploading means sending a file to a remote computer and *downloading* means receiving a file. The easiest way to remember the terms is to think of the remote computer as hovering somewhere above you.

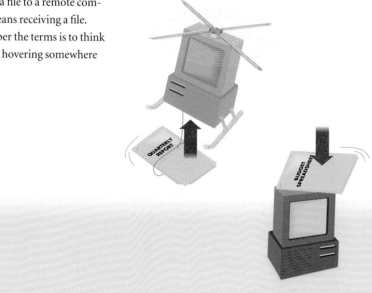

characters with ASCII codes under 128. This includes letters, numbers, and most punctuation. Be sure to transmit all other files—including most word processing files, as well as programs, spreadsheets, databases, and graphic images—as binary files.

FILE COMPRESSION

File compression means translation of a file into a coded format that occupies less space than the original file. The amount of space you'll save by compressing a file depends on the file type, but it's not unusual for compressed files to take up half the space of the originals or less. (Graphic files and database files tend to compress the most.) There are two reasons to compress files:

(1) To save room on disk. If you have files that you use infrequently but still want to keep on your hard disk, for example, you might compress them to free up disk space. You might also compress large files in order to fit them on floppy disks.

(2) To save time when sending data from one computer to another and thereby minimize bills from both the phone company and information services. (The smaller the file, the less time it takes to transmit.)

Bear in mind that you cannot actually use files in their compressed form. Rather, you need to decompress (expand) them to their original size.

If you plan to send files via modem, you may want to investigate compression programs to minimize your phone bills. If you download programs from a computer bulletin board, you may have to learn about compression programs because the files you receive will probably be compressed and will need to be decompressed before you can use them.

The most widely used file compression program is a DOS shareware program named PKZIP. Files that have been compressed with PKZIP have an extension of .ZIP and are often referred to as zipped files. (Anytime you download or are handed a file that has a .ZIP extension, you can assume that it has been zipped and that you need to unzip it before you can use it.) In order to unzip such files, you need to use another DOS program named PKUNZIP.

Many zipped files actually contain compressed versions of multiple files. When you unzip a file you may therefore get several decompressed files, not just one. The easiest way to get copies of PKZIP and PKUNZIP is to download them from a BBS or online information service.

If you are using Windows, the software to use is a shareware program named WinZip. WinZip can unzip (decompress) files that were created with PKZIP and can create compressed files (known as archives) in PKZIP format as well as several other compressed file formats. You can obtain a free review copy of WinZip on the Internet and on some of the online services. (On the Internet, you'll want to access a Web site with the following URL: http://server.winzip.com/winzip. You'll learn about Web sites and URLs later in this chapter.) Once you've downloaded WinZip, you just locate the file (probably called WINZIP95.exe) using My Computer, the Windows Explorer, or the Find command, and then double-click it to start the installation. After installation, open the program's Help menu and select Brief Tutorial for a simple introduction to the program.

The compression program usually used on Macs is called StuffIt. There are also Mac utility programs for decompressing files created with PKZIP.

ONLINE INFORMATION SERVICES

One of the main reasons to buy and use a modem is to gain access to online information services. There are already over a dozen national online services and more are introduced nearly every month. Some, like the Dow Jones News/Retrieval Information Service (which focuses on financial information and services), are quite specialized. Others, like America Online, CompuServe, Prodigy, the Microsoft Network, GEnie, and Delphi, are broader in scope and try to offer at least a little for everyone.

The services that you'll typically find on the general-purpose online services include

▶ *Electronic mail services—that is, the ability to send and receive messages and files via "electronic mailboxes" (folders of files on the information service's hard disk). Whenever you call into the service, you are automatically informed if you have mail waiting and can either read it online or download it to your own computer to read or print later.*

▶ *News, weather, and sports information, including Associated Press clippings and, on some services, more extensive press clips from UPI, Washington Post, and Reuters World and Financial Reports.*

▶ *Travel information and services that let you find out about airline flights, hotels, motels, and car rentals and then make reservations online.*

▶ *Financial information and services, including current stock market price quotes, access to online brokerage firms, and access to home banking services.*

▶ *Online databases including access to encyclopedias, Consumer Reports, dictionaries, and health-related databases that provide up-to-date information on disabilities, and diseases such as AIDS and cancer.*

▶ *Forums (aka special interest groups), which are essentially ongoing electronic conversations on a particular topic. Depending on the topic and the people involved, they resemble an electronic version of a clubhouse, lodge, study group, professional network, café, or singles bar. There are forums on cooking and wine tasting, religion, national politics, working from home, raising various species of pets, and hobbies like photography, gardening, coin and stamp collecting, sailing, and genealogy. CompuServe features a White House forum on which you can debate politics with fellow citizens or download copies of press releases or transcripts of presidential press conferences. Many information services offer professional forums that allow various types of professionals (including doctors and nurses, entrepreneurs, journalists, musicians, lawyers, and computer programmers and consultants) to exchange information and advice, generate ideas, and collaborate on projects. Finally, most information services offer dozens of forums on computer hardware and software.*

▶ *Games, both single player and multiple player. In single-player games, you play against yourself or the computer. In multiple-player games, you play against one or more people currently online.*

▶ *Shopping services for everything from clothes to cameras to computer hardware and software. You can even have gourmet food or flowers delivered anywhere in the country.*

Some online services have monthly fees. Others charge only for time spent online. Most have additional charges for special services and a few offer discount rates for calls before or after prime time (which starts somewhere between 6 and 8 a.m. and ends between 6 and 7 p.m., depending on the service).

NOTE *Most online services can be accessed through local telephone numbers, so that you don't need to pay for long distance charges.*

Although there is plenty of overlap among online services, they each have their own "personalities" and strengths. CompuServe probably has the most extensive research tools

THE AMERICA ONLINE MENU

This is the main menu for America Online, currently the largest online service.

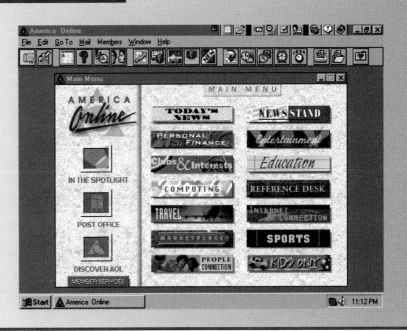

GETTING TECH SUPPORT ONLINE

As mentioned, most general-purpose online services offer forums on various types of hardware and software. Some of these forums are exclusively devoted to technical support and are monitored by the technical support staff of the manufacturer. Others also feature information-sharing, conversation, and exchanging of sample files and utilities. If you post a question in such a forum, you may either get an answer from the manufacturer's tech support staff or from an experienced user who happened to get there first. One advantage of using forums for tech support is that you don't have to limit yourself to regular business hours. If you have a Monday deadline and a problem crops up on Friday, you can post a message and, with luck, some knowledgeable user will dial in over the weekend and offer a solution. Some hardware and software manufacturers also have their own bulletin board systems, on which you can post questions, read product announcements, and download technical information or even program updates. (Bulletin board services are discussed in the next section.) Many software companies now have Web pages on the Internet as well, with answers to frequently asked questions (known as FAQs) and other technical information about their products. (You'll learn about Web pages later in this chapter.) At this point, you can access information through these Internet sites but you can't use them to post questions.

and databases, and the widest range of forums on computer hardware and software. America Online offers an exceptionally smooth, easy-to-use interface and has excellent resources for children. Delphi is known for its friendliness and sense of community. Prodigy is strong on news stories, and on services for children, although many people find the on-screen advertisements distracting and/or annoying.

Depending on your needs and interests, you may pick a service because of the particular services or forum topics it offers. Or it may be a question of ambiance. If your main reason for using an information service is to send files to a particular set of people, your choice may also depend on which services your intended recipients are using.

Another factor to consider when choosing on online service is the access it provides to the Internet. As you'll learn near the end of this chapter, the Internet is a huge and rapidly expanding web of computer networks, which offers some of the same goodies you'll find on online services, plus the opportunity to communicate with users worldwide. Most of the online services now offer some form of access to the Internet, as part of the basic service or for an additional fee. Most of them also offer their own "Web browsers" for navigating the Internet's vast resources. If Internet access is important to you, be sure to investigate what the various online services have to offer in this area.

If you're interested in sampling a service, keep your eyes out for free introductory offers. Many software packages come with a free introductory subscription to CompuServe, for example, in part because the software company wants to encourage you to use CompuServe rather than your telephone to solicit technical support.

As mentioned, if you plan to use an information service regularly, you'll probably want to get a front-end program that makes it easier to navigate through the system and find the information you want. If you use the CompuServe Information Manager program, for example, you can specify services and forums that you're interested in or files that you want to upload or download before you go on line. Once you are on line, the program takes care of as much work as it can automatically—logging you into the forum, sending or retrieving your mail, and so on. It also provides you with menus that you can use to browse through services, forums, and files, sparing you the need to memorize cryptic commands. If you regularly participate in one or more forums, you can automate the process even further with programs like Tapcis or Ozcis, which will dial up CompuServe, download the descriptions of any new messages or files posted to the forum since your last call, and then immediately disconnect. You can then look through the list of messages and files, check off the ones you are interested in, and let the program dial in again to retrieve them for you. One good way to find out about front-end programs is to request opinions on line from other users of the service.

NOTE *Always leave an information service by issuing the proper command for doing so. (In many cases, you can type **bye** or **off**, or select Exit from a File menu.) If you simply disconnect or turn off your modem without explicitly signing off the service first, it may take a while for the* *service to notice that you're no longer on line. In this case, you will be charged for any time that elapses between the moment when you actually disconnected and the moment that the service recognizes your absence.*

HOW TO SIGN UP

Here are contact phone numbers for some of the major online services:

America Online	(800) 227-6364
CompuServe	(800) 848-8199
Delphi	(800) 695-4005
GEnie	(800) 638-9636
Prodigy	(800) 776-3449

ELECTRONIC MAIL SERVICES

There are some services—like MCI Mail and AT&T Mail—that specialize in e-mail. These services generally charge by the number and length of the messages sent rather than by time spent on line. Although they don't offer information services per se, they do offer e-mail services beyond those available on the more general-purpose information services.

Even if the person you want to reach doesn't have a modem or a subscription to your e-mail service, you can save some money on courier or express mail services by sending a letter to MCI mail and having someone print it out locally and deliver it from there.

There are front-end programs for MCI Mail available for both PCs and Macs. PC users can use Lotus Express. Mac users can use Desktop Express.

MICROSOFT EXCHANGE

Windows 95 includes a program called Microsoft Exchange that centralizes the sending and receiving of e-mail. This program is especially handy for people who send and receive mail via more than one program and/or service—the Internet as well as The Microsoft Network, for example, or the Internet and a network e-mail program. Microsoft Exchange provides you with one place from which to compose and send messages to any of the services you use, and to collect mail from all your services. (With one command, you can have Exchange dial up each of your services in turn, collect any mail that's waiting, and log off.) By default, Exchange is set up to send and receive mail via Microsoft Mail (if you're on a network), Microsoft Fax, and the Microsoft Network on-line service. If you install the Microsoft Plus! add-on to Windows 95 and have already used it to set up Internet access, you'll have drivers for sending and receiving Internet mail as well. You access Microsoft Exchange via the Inbox icon on your desktop or by opening the Start menu, choosing Programs, and then selecting Microsoft Exchange.

SENDING MAIL BETWEEN SERVICES AND THE INTERNET

You can send information between the major online services, or between online services and the Internet, using the Internet's mail capabilities. This means that if you have an account on CompuServe and your friend or colleague has an account on America Online, you can still exchange messages.

▶ *To send a message from the Internet to someone on AOL, address it to their AOL screen name, followed by the characters @aol.com.*

▶ *To send a message from CompuServe to someone on the Internet, address it to INTERNET: followed by the recipient's full Internet address.*

▶ *To send a message from CompuServe to someone on AOL, address it to INTERNET:* screenname@aol.com *(where* screenname *is the recipient's AOL screen name).*

▶ *To send a message from AOL to someone on the Internet, just use the recipient's full Internet address.*

▶ *To send a message to someone on CompuServe from AOL or the Internet, use their CompuServe ID followed by the characters @compuserve.com. If the CompuServe ID has a comma in the middle, you must type a period in its place.*

Although sending text files between services is a snap, sending binary files (and this includes files created in word processing programs) is a bit more complicated. In order to send a binary file via the Internet, you must *encode* the file (translate it into a special format using a program called an encoder). The person receiving the file must then decode it, using the same encoder program, before using it. Wincode is a very popular freeware program which you can download on the Internet itself. (Use one of the search engines available in your browser to search for Wincode.)

BULLETIN BOARD SYSTEMS

A bulletin board system (BBS) is a computer with a modem and a reasonably large hard disk that acts as repository for files and messages. In order to serve as a BBS, a computer must also be equipped with a special type of communications software, known as bulletin board software, that logs in users as they call and maintains a database of files and messages. Most BBSs run 24 hours a day so you can call whenever the fancy strikes you, and, unlike information services, most are free to use. The person who administers the bulletin board (and usually owns the computer) is called the *sysop* (sysop is short for system operator and is pronounced SIS-op).

In most cases, you use a bulletin board service to leave mail for other users of the board, to send and receive files, and to participate in ongoing "conferences" (discussions consisting of a series of messages sent in by callers, usually relating to a particular topic). If friendly discussion is what you have in mind, your choice of BBS will be based on what types of conferences it offers.

Some BBSs are open to the general public. Others are available only to people in a particular field, or who belong to a particular organization (like a users' group), or who are friends of the person who set up the bulletin board. Some BBSs are private—run by computer consultants or companies to facilitate the transmission of data to and from clients and/or employees.

You can often find bulletin board listings in computer magazines, especially local ones. Many bulletin boards also have lists of BBSs in their file libraries. Look for a file that starts with the characters USABBS##.ZIP (where ## are digits representing the month).

If you hear about a BBS that seems potentially interesting, try calling up to see what it offers. (Your best bet is to set your communications settings to 8N1 and your terminal emulation to ANSI.) Once you're connected, press **Enter** once or twice. You will then be asked to "log in," meaning identify yourself. Once you enter your name, the BBS will see if you're already a registered user. If so, you'll be asked to enter your password. If not, you'll probably be asked a series of questions and then asked to define a password. After you log in, you'll generally see a menu of choices. If you need help, there's usually a help key or help command available. (Scan the screen for details.)

NOTE *Bulletin boards have traditionally been one of the major sources of computer viruses. See Chapter 3 for information on how to protect your computer from infection.*

THE INTERNET

To its devoted participants, the Internet represents the true promise of telecommunications and indeed of the entire computer age. The Internet (or simply the Net) is a global federation of networks that have agreed to share information and resources across extremely fast information channels. Started as a tool to let scientists and researchers share expensive computer resources, in the last several years the Internet has grown into something far

THE INTERNET

The Internet is a global matrix of computer networks that allows users to access information stored on millions of computers throughout the world.

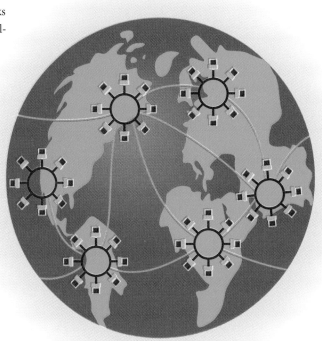

larger, more diverse, and more unpredictable. Between 1983 and 1995, the number of hosts (networks providing information) on the Net has grown from 500 to over 6 million, and the number continues to increase exponentially. Current hosts include networks run by private businesses, nonprofit organizations, and individuals, as well as the original collection of colleges, universities, and governmental agencies. Anyone with a computer network and a little cash can become a "site" on the Net. And unlike the online services, the Net is neither owned nor run by any single organization or company. It is simply a huge, open-ended (some would say anarchic), and rapidly expanding system for communicating and disseminating information.

Until recently, the only way to gain access to the Internet was through one of the participating networks. The Internet was therefore primarily the province of professors, students, and government employees (mostly at the Department of Defense). Now thousands of companies provide public access to the Internet for a fee. In addition, most of the online

A BULLETIN BOARD SYSTEM MAIN MENU

services now offer Internet access, along with tools for exploring and exploiting the Net's vast and sometimes overwhelming resources.

Just about everyone's first question about the Internet is "What can you do with it?" Given the Net's astronomical growth, however, next month's answer is likely to be quite different from this month's. In some ways, the Internet resembles a huge party that's just beginning to reach critical mass: everyone's excited about its prospects, but no one's sure exactly how it will turn out or who will be dancing with whom in a few hours. Given the volume of expansion and change, it's impossible to say what people will be doing on the Net in the future. I'll therefore have to limit myself to a description of some of what's happening on the Net at present: It's anyone's guess what will be happening next month or next year.

THE WORLD WIDE WEB

Much of the Net's growth in recent years can be attributed to something known as the World Wide Web, frequently known simply as "the Web." As its name implies, the Web is a system that connects information, regardless of where it's stored—letting you jump from an article on orchid care stored on a computer in Dubuque, to a related article on plant pruning on a system in Sydney, Australia. Making the leap from one computer's Web *page* (interactive

A WEB PAGE IN NETSCAPE

URL of the current site

Link to another Web page

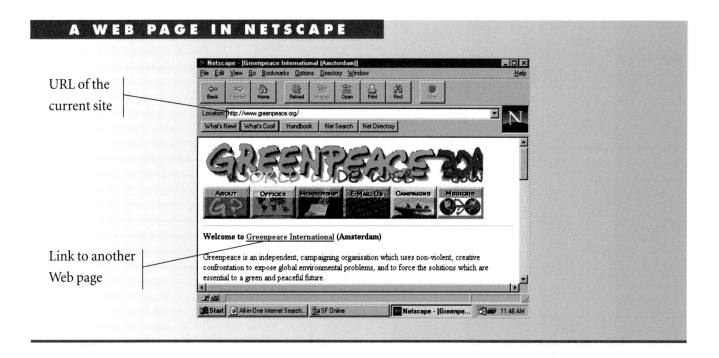

document) to the other's is a simple matter of clicking a picture or piece of text—known as a *link*—on the screen. Such links allow users to interact with documents stored on computers across the Internet as if they were part of a single text.

One of the main reasons for the Web's success is its graphical interface: In place of the text-based interfaces and arcane UNIX commands that used to characterize life on the Net, the Web sports colorful typeset pages, graphics, sounds, video, and sometimes live movie footage. In fact, there is fierce competition among Web sites for the hippest and most innovative pages. (A Web site is a computer that makes Web pages available on the Web.) There are even several Web pages that are nothing but catalogs of the coolest Web sites of the week (with links to each of those sites).

Programs designed to let you access and navigate the Web are known as *Web browsers*. As of this writing, the one considered by many to be the premiere browser is Netscape, created and distributed by Netscape Corporation. Mosaic was one of the first Web browsers, and remains quite popular. America Online, CompuServe, and Prodigy offer built-in browsers as part of their Internet packages. Using links to jump from site to site to site is commonly known as *surfing* the Web.

Although the Web is only one part of the Internet, it's probably the most accessible, user-friendly, and fun part, as well as the fastest growing. The other pieces of the Net include the newsgroups and mailing lists, FTP, Gopher, and Telnet, all of which you'll learn a little about shortly.

WHAT PEOPLE DO ON THE NET

So what *can* you do on the Net, as of the moment? For starters, you can do most of the things you can do on the online services, including chat with people from around the world, plan your trip to Bali, send irate missives to your senator or representative, download stock quotes, and read the latest local, national, and international news. However, because no single entity runs or oversees the Net, its content is a lot more diverse than that of the online services. You'll find more of the avant garde, the innovative, the obscure, and the ridiculous. (You'll find fewer TV personalities, for example, and more deadheads, academics, artists, and computer nerds.) You'll also find resources you won't find anywhere else. Since it doesn't cost much to set up a Web site, any person or institution that wants to make information or ideas available is free to do so, in their own way. In addition, since most academic institutions are Internet hosts, they can and often do open their library doors to the public, which provides you with unparalleled resources for research.

The Net's resources include

▶ *Government and legal documents, including bills currently before Congress, state and federal laws, and U.S. Supreme Court decisions.*

▶ *The entire Library of Congress card catalog.*

▶ *Educational materials from several museums, such as the Smithsonian and the Exploratorium (an interactive science museum in San Francisco).*

▶ *An NPR home page with material meant to supplement programs on PBS.*

▶ *Hundreds of online magazines, or "zines."*

▶ *Huge libraries of shareware and public domain software, available for downloading.*

▶ *Job listings.*

▶ *Millions of sites that are essentially advertisements. About half of the Web consists of cutting edge billboards for companies, small and large, that want to attract attention and customers. Some will take orders online.*

▶ *Information on political organizations, political campaigns, and a broad range of public interest groups.*

▶ *Online courses.*

▶ *The entire text of literary classics like Moby Dick and Alice in Wonderland.*

▶ *Weather satellite photos.*

▶ *Webster's Dictionary and Roget's Thesaurus.*

▶ *A form for looking up a zip code.*

The drawback to this profusion of information is that it's overwhelming. The challenge for new users (and even old hands) is figuring out exactly what's out there and how to extract your needles from the information haystack.

TALKING TO PEOPLE ON THE NET

The millions of Internet hosts and the resources they offer are only one of the big reasons for accessing the Net. The other is person-to-person communication. There are three ways to communicate with individuals and groups of individuals on the Net: e-mail, mailing lists, and newsgroups.

E-mail on the Net works just like it does on online services and e-mail services: you send a message directly to someone's electronic address and it's stored in their electronic mailbox, awaiting retrieval. To send mail to me, for example, you'd address it to lisabiow@sfo.com. To pick up your mail, you issue a command (usually by clicking a button or selecting a menu option). You then usually have the option of either reading and replying to the mail online, or saving it to disk so you can deal with it later.

NOTE   *As described in the discussion of online services, you don't need to be on the Internet to send and receive Internet mail: you can exchange mail with people on the Internet via most of the online services.*

The Internet features thousands of electronic mailing lists ("lists" for short) covering a huge range of interests: from bluegrass music to yoga, AIDS research to woodworking, home schooling to Elvis memorabilia. Once you "subscribe to" (ask and receive permission to join) one of these lists, you receive copies of all the mail sent to the list and can send mail to all the subscribers. It's rather like finding a group of electronic pen pals. Given the huge number of people on the Net, everyone can find others with whom they have common ground, in terms of intellectual interests, professional goals, and lifestyle. Although there may not be anybody in your home town or even your state who shares your interest in Chinese word processing, for example, you can be sure there are several people on the Net who do (even if most of them are in other countries). The free-form nature of lists is both part of their charm and one of their drawbacks: Because every piece of mail goes to everyone on the list, joining even a small list can bring you dozens, if not hundreds, of pieces of e-mail every week, if the list's members are particularly chatty. Unless you are truly fascinated by the subject at hand or have an abundance of free time, you'll probably want to limit yourself to only a few selected lists.

A BRIEF INTERNET GLOSSARY

The Internet is filled with (some might think plagued by) acronyms and obscure terminology. Here are some of the key terms you'll need to know to make sense of the Net.

FTP (**File Transfer Protocol**): a protocol used to provide file transfers across a variety of types of computer systems. FTP sites are Internet sites that have files that you can download using FTP. To download these files, you need to be using software that supports FTP. (Most Web browsers do.)

Gopher: **A menu-based tool for searching public databases on the Net.**

Home page: **The page that you land on when you first access a Web site. It often contains an index and/or links to other pages of information.**

Hypertext: **A way of creating documents that allows for interactive navigation**—that is, for jumping from one place in the text to another via links within the document itself. Most electronic encyclopedias and many online help systems use hypertext—allowing users to delve into topics or go off on related tangents simply by clicking on a highlighted or specially formatted word, phrase, or picture. Web pages also use hypertext—not only for navigating within a page, but for jumping from one page to another, and from Web site to Web site.

HTML (**HyperText Markup Language**): The language in which Web pages are formatted and Web information is distributed.

HTTP (**HyperText Transfer Protocol**): The method by which documents are transferred from a Web site to your host computer (the computer you're logged into) and from the host computer to you. You'll often see this acronym at the beginning of Internet site addresses, which are known as URLs.

ISP (**Internet Service Provider**): A Net site that, for a fee, serves as a conduit for users to temporarily connect to the Net. Unless you have access to a Net site through your work, ISPs are your only access route to the Net other than the online services.

TCP/IP (**Transmission Control Protocol/Internet Protocol**): The network communications protocol used to connect diverse types of computer systems across the Internet.

Telnet: **A network program that lets you log onto and use a computer that's on the Net; in other words, operating a computer remotely via the Net.**

URL (**Uniform Resource Locator**): An Internet site address that begins with the transfer format (http:// for Web documents, Gopher:// for gopher sites, new:// for newsgroups, ftp:// for ftp sites) followed by the name of the server where the site's files are stored, the file's directory path, and its file name.

Usenet (**USEr NETwork**): A computer network, accessed through the Internet, that consists of over 10,000 newsgroups (online forums) on almost every topic imaginable.

WWW (**World Wide Web**): A system that allows for worldwide hypertext linking of multimedia documents, so that information can be linked and accessed regardless of its physical location.

UNDERSTANDING INTERNET ADDRESSES

In case you're interested, Internet addresses have three basic parts. First is the person's user name—the name the user types when logging into the computer that has his or her Internet account. Next is the host name and, in some cases, the host's domain(s). (A domain is a group of hosts, often within the same organization, such as a university or governmental agency.) The third part is the name of the host's primary domain. There are six such domains for U.S. Internet sites: com (commercial), edu (educational), gov (government), mil (military), net (network), and org (organization). Any address that doesn't end with one of these six domain names is probably located outside the U.S. To give an example, the address smith@spark.berkeley.edu refers to a person with a user name of Smith who logs into a host computer named spark, which is part of a domain named berkeley (for the University of California at Berkeley), which, in turn, is part of the domain named edu (for education). The address lisabiow@sfo.com refers to a person with a user name of lisabiow, who is logged into a host named sfo (for San Francisco Online), which is part of a domain named com (for commercial). Note that Internet e-mail addresses are different from URLs (Uniform Resource Locators): The former are used to identify a particular user on the Net, the latter to identify an Internet server—that is, a computer that makes information available to others on the Net. The URL is what you type into your Web browser program to tell it to go to and display the home page for a particular Web site.

(Don't worry. It's just as easy to get off a list as it is to get on: A single e-mail message to the list administrator should do the trick.)

Usenet newsgroups are electronic discussion groups through which people with shared interests exchange information and ideas. Usenet itself is actually a separate computer network, but most Internet hosts provide access to Usenet, so that Internet users can participate in its newsgroups. Unlike mailing lists, where every person on the list gets every piece of mail, newsgroup articles are stored on a computer called a news server. To read the articles, you need a program called a newsreader. (Many Web browsers now include newsreaders, as do the Internet access programs provided by the online services.) The newsreader shows you a list of current articles in any newsgroups you've subscribed to and you can decide which ones you actually want to read. In other words, you have far more control than you do with a mailing list: you get to scan a list of topics and choose the ones that interest you. You can also post questions and answer the questions of other subscribers.

There's no central registry of mailing lists or newsgroups, although there are a few brave souls and organizations who make some attempts to catalog them. As of this writing, you can get lists of mailing lists and newsgroups at the Web site http://www.tile.net. You can also often find lists and newsgroups using search tools. And most of the online services provide some tools for locating newsgroups as well.

SENDING BINARY FILES ON THE NET

As mentioned, in order to send a binary file via the Internet, you must *encode* the file (translate it into a special format using a program called an encoder). The person receiving the file must then decode it, using the same encoder program, before using it. At the moment, the most widely used encoding programs are WinCode and Mime, both of which are available on the Internet itself. (Use whatever search tools you have available to search for Web sites with the words WinCode or Mime in their descriptions.)

GETTING ONTO THE NET

At the moment, probably the simplest and least intimidating way to try out the Net is through an online service. All of the major online services now offer some form of Internet access, and most offer graphical interfaces, including Web browsers, as part of the deal. On most online services, the basic monthly charge covers a set number of hours on the service, including Internet access. You can either pay an extra hourly charge for any time over the specified limit (often five hours), or you can switch to a different pricing plan that includes a higher number of access hours.

Not only do the prices vary from one service to the next, the features differ as well. For example, some online services, such as AOL, let parents block specific newsgroups or pages whose names contains specific words, and to place similar restrictions on Web pages. The breadth and utility of search tools also vary from service to service. CompuServe offers up to 50 different search "engines" for sifting through information on the Web. Some of the services also offer only a single home page and perhaps a few pages of "cool" Web sites, while others provide dozens of Web pages, with information on a range of subjects and links to other Web pages and newsgroups. Because each of the services constantly offers new and improved tools and features, it's impossible to say which service's Internet access is the "best" or even to give an up-to-date account of their offerings. (As of this writing, many people currently find AOL's Internet access the best overall, but the other services are scrambling to catch up.) Computer magazines are one of the best sources for up-to-date information on the relative merits of various online services. Both *PC Magazine* and *Byte* have featured articles comparing the Internet offerings of the various online services.

One advantage of using the online services is that they do some of the work of organizing the information for you—offering tours and tutorials, and their own lists of interesting sites, mailing lists, newsgroups, and downloadable software.

If you find you use the Internet more than occasionally, you'll probably want to find an independent Internet Service Provider. This gives you the luxury of using the Internet access software of your choice. In many cases, it also wins you a small amount of storage space on the provider's server which you can use to set up your own Web site should you care to. The first step in going this route is finding an ISP with a local access number and reasonable rates. Asking friends, checking local computer magazines, and, if you have access to someone else's Net account, searching online are all good ways to track down providers. (See the upcoming section entitled "Learning More" for the URL of a site that lists ISPs.)

The next step is finding and installing the software. As recently as a year or two ago, using the Net required juggling several different programs. There are now software packages that let you access different types of sites and resources, send and receive e-mail, and comb the Net's vast resources for information on particular topics. Many popular browsers—including Netscape and the browsers supplied by the online services—are now more properly called Internet browsers than Web browsers, because they include e-mail capabilities, newreaders, tools for downloading files from FTP (File Transfer Protocol) sites, and several search engines. There are also integrated packages—such as Internet Office by CompuServe Internet Division, and Internet Chameleon by Netmanage—that offer e-mail programs, Web browsers, newsreaders, FTP clients, and various search tools in a single package. Again, this is a realm that changes from moment to moment: Probably your best source of information will be computer magazines and other denizens of the Net.

If you are accessing the Internet via an independent ISP, you'll also need software that allows you to dial up your provider and establish the TCP/IP connection that lets your computer become a part of the Net. If you have either a Mac or Windows 95, the necessary software is built into the operating system. If you have Windows 95, the process of configuring the software is a bit complex; you can save yourself a lot of headaches by buying and installing Microsoft Plus, which includes both a wizard that steps you through the process fairly painlessly and its own browser program.

NOTE *Even though your browser can do many things, you may opt to use specialized programs for some purposes. For example, many Net mavens swear by an Internet e-mail program called Eudora, which lets you perform e-mail feats you won't be able to manage with most integrated packages—including sorting your mail and addressing mail to lists of people.*

Most ISPs offer two or more different types of accounts. Many offer shell accounts, which only allow you to view text on the screen. If you want to be able to see anything other than text, however, you'll need something known as a PPP (Point to Point Protocol) account. Given the emphasis on graphics in most Web pages, a PPP account is a must if you plan to do much Web surfing. As of this writing, PPP accounts are becoming the standard and have become little more expensive than shell accounts.

SHELL VERSUS NON-SHELL ACCOUNTS

Technically, the difference between shell accounts and non-shell accounts like PPP and SLIP accounts has to do with how you are accessing the Net. When you use a shell account, you're just dialing into a computer that is part of the Net. With the non-shell accounts, your computer is actually becoming a part of the Net temporarily. The names of the account types specify the protocol used for building this bridge between your computer and the Net.

Learning More

One of the best places to learn about the Net is on the Net itself: There are dozens (if not hundreds) of Web sites full of information on the Internet, the Web, Web browsers, search tools, and interesting sites to visit. Once you either find a friend with access to the Net or get your own account, and figure out where to type in URLs, you can begin your Internet education in earnest. A few places to start are:

Exploring the Web: Learning Outcomes

http://www.gactr.uga.edu/exploring/toc.html

This page, created by the University of Georgia Center for Continuing Education, is a crash course in Internet fundamentals, including topics like what is the Web and what hardware and software you need to connect to the Internet.

Internet Tour

http://www.globalcenter.net/gcwev/tour.html

This tour of the Internet, created by Global Village, leads you through several different tasks on the Net, including checking the stock market and finding a government document. It also leads to collections of search tools and catalogs of other Net resources.

EFF Extended Guide to the Internet

http://www.eff.org/papers/eegtti/eeg_toc.html

This page, which is a joint project of the Electronic Frontier Foundation and Apple Computer project, includes a list of ISPs by state, as well as advice on using e-mail systems and tutorials on various search tools.

INDEX